High Performance Options Trading

John Wiley & Sons

Founded in 1807, John Wiley & Sons is the oldest independent publishing company in the United States. With offices in North America, Europe, Australia, and Asia, Wiley is globally committed to developing and marketing print and electronic products and services for our customers' professional and personal knowledge and understanding.

The Wiley Trading Series features books by traders who have survived the market's everchanging temperament and have prospered—some by reinventing systems, others by getting back to basics. Whether a novice trader, professional or somewhere in between, these books will provide the advice and strategies needed to prosper today and well into the future.

For a list of available titles, please visit our Web site at www.Wiley Finance.com.

High Performance Options Trading

Option Volatility
& Pricing Strategies

LEONARD YATES

WILEY

John Wiley & Sons, Inc.

Published by John Wiley & Sons, Inc., Hoboken, New Jersey.
Published simultaneously in Canada.

For general information on our other products and services, or technical support, please contact our Customer Care Department within the United States at 800-762-2974, outside the United States at 317-572-3993 or fax 317-572-4002.

Wiley also publishes its books in a variety of electronic formats. Some content that appears in print may not be available in electronic books.

For more information about Wiley products, visit our web site at www.wiley.com.

Library of Congress Cataloging-in-Publication Data:
Yates, Leonard.
   High performance options trading : option volatility & pricing strategies / Leonard Yates.
       p. cm.— (A marketplace book)
    ISBN 0-471-32365-9 (CLOTH/CD-ROM)
1.   Options (Finance) I. Title. II. Series.
   HG6024.A3Y38 2003
   332.64'5—dc21

                                                                    2003002428

Printed in the United States of America.

10 9 8 7 6 5 4 3 2 1

This book is dedicated to my loving wife, Karen.

Acknowledgments

Many thanks to Elwood Brent, Jim Graham, Tom Heffernan, and Karen Yates for their tremendous help proofreading and editing.

L. Y.

Contents

A Note From the Author

I don't remember exactly how I discovered options, only that I discovered them in early 1975 while working at IBM. I was immediately captivated by the lure of potential short-term gains and low capital requirements. I remember checking stock option prices in the *Wall Street Journal* every day. At that time, only call options were available, but that was okay; it was a bull market.

I opened an account with Rotan-Mosle with $2,000 and immediately bought short-term calls on about three different stocks. Shocked by how quickly these calls went to half their value, I was glad to sell them for even money a few days later. In the following days and weeks I traded in and out of many positions, but it wasn't long before my capital was all gone. Ironically, my original options, had I kept them, would have resulted in a gain of 10 times my initial investment. This was my first experience with how human emotions can get in the way of successful trading.

However, I was not discouraged. Even after I was out of the market, I continued to study options. I graphed option prices. I kept meticulous records to see whether any particular option strategy worked to produce regular gains. Every time I thought I was on to something, I scraped together some capital and traded again—sometimes making gains at first, but ultimately losing my capital. And so it went. Over the years, I learned by direct study of the markets and firsthand experience. This made it a *long* learning experience. I could have made things easier on myself by reading books on options and trading, but I wasn't aware of them.

When personal computers first became available, I bought one and immediately set about programming it to retrieve stock and options prices and to search through them for potential opportunities. That was the beginning of my work on options software—work that continues to this day. While my first programs were intended for my own use, in 1981 I developed a sufficiently advanced general-use program and began selling copies to the public.

This book relates all I know about options. It is a product of what I've learned over 25 years in the options business. While this book is bound to contain some information that overlaps with other options books you've read, you'll be getting my unique perspective—that of an engineer and amateur trader. I understand the mathematics behind options, and I know how it applies in practical terms. I'm not a great trader, but I've done a lot of trading, and I've experienced just about everything that can happen to the options trader.

Happily, I'm in the black for my trading career. Yet I'm not going to hype options to you. Options trading is not easy, and it's not for everyone. But it is fascinating. And I'm happy to share with you what, to my knowledge, works and what doesn't. In fact, I've tried to keep the whole book on a very practical level, because my purpose is to share with the reader everything he or she needs to know to become a successful options trader. In the latter part of the book, I explain the essential math concepts surrounding options in layman's terminology. Don't skip it. This is stuff you need to know!

Enjoy reading this book. I hope it helps you. And may you experience successful options trading in the years ahead.

Len Yates

Introduction

From high school days, I've had a head for finance and the stock market. And I can't say that there was a family member or friend who influenced me in that direction. Rather, I think it was hearing stories like KFC stock going from 3 to 60 that peaked my interest, although at that time I lacked the resources to act on my interests.

I first heard about options when I was finished with school and working as a young engineer at IBM. I was immediately intrigued by the combination of high leverage and small capital requirements needed to buy options. In those days the Chicago Board Options Exchange (CBOE), the only options exchange at that time, offered options on about 200 stocks, and they only had call options—no put options. That was okay. It was January 1976, and the market was rebounding vigorously from a nasty post-Nixon bear market.

I opened a small account at a full-service brokerage called Rotan-Mosle. (In those days they were *all* full-service brokerages.) I was assigned to one of the two brokers at the firm who were familiar with options. He tried to persuade me to start out using options for covered writing. Covered writing seemed profitable (especially the way they presented it), but that approach was too slow for my blood. I was determined to buy options and make a killing.

Personal computers weren't available yet, so there was no consulting a model to see whether options were fairly priced. You just looked at the options listed in the *Wall Street Journal* or another business daily and picked them by the seat of the pants. The temptation was great to go for the cheaper out-of-the-money options, and that's what I did. I did not understand time decay at that point. It was not until much later that I began to understand time decay and its effect on these kinds of positions.

I bought calls on several popular stocks that were going up. Immediately, the market corrected, and in just three days my calls were worth half their original value. This was a shock to my system. I was not prepared for how fast options could lose value! Nevertheless, I held on and saw these positions through to at least breakeven.

After that, I do not remember specifics; only that the market continued to rally in fits and starts, and that, despite the fact that I was buying calls, I lost all my capital in just a few weeks. This was no doubt due to jumping in and out too frequently and at the wrong times.

The next time I had some capital to trade was in 1980. PCs were just being introduced. I bought a TRS-80 III from Radio Shack. Options still held a burning attraction for me, so the first thing I wanted to do with my new PC was write some software to retrieve option prices from Dow Jones, evaluate spreads, and find unusual opportunities. I was determined to succeed this time. I wanted to prepare myself and employ a systematic approach, so I "teched up."

It's amusing to think back on what technology had to offer in those days. The early PCs offered a simple programming language called BASIC, which was easy to learn, so I started writing my first options programs in BASIC. I stored my work on an ordinary audio cassette player/recorder attached to the PC. It could take several minutes to write my program to tape or read my program into memory! Floppy drives were only available on the more expensive PCs, and they used 8-inch-diameter floppy disks that could only hold 360k bytes.

I began a subscription to the Dow Jones retrieval service, and used a 300-baud modem to connect with it. Can you imagine? That was only 30 characters per second—about twice the rate of a fast typist.

I was also moving into a more advanced option strategy at that time: horizontal debit spreads (calendar spreads). Intrigued with how that strategy made money over time, I spent several months meticulously plotting the values of calendar spreads on several different stocks. With these charts I proved to myself that the strategy worked and made steady gains over time. So that was the approach I used, with my new computer program retrieving prices and selecting spreads that were especially good values to start out with.

Unfortunately, soon after I started trading with this system, the market went into a period of above-average movement. If you're familiar with calendar spreads, you know that excessive movement is bad for them. Once again, my trading capital was gone in a few months (at least it lasted longer this time). That was when I realized that my test period had coincided with a relatively quiet period in the markets, and that is why the strategy worked on paper. It was also when I first began to realize that no particular option strategy works all of the time. Rather, each strategy has its own time and place.

However, there was more ground to cover before I was finally convinced of this. After some time off from trading, the next strategy to capture my imagination was naked writing. Again, I made a thorough study of it on paper, then gathered up some trading capital and got started. I experienced several successes at first. Then I took a sizable short position in out-of-the-money Howard Johnson call options. They were extremely overvalued, according to my model. What I did not realize was that there was a reason for those options to be expensive. In just a few days, Howard Johnson was bought out. I had to cover those options for a much higher price, with the result that my account was wiped out. Actually, my account was instantly reduced to just a few dollars—which was quite remarkable. I could easily have been hurt much worse and been forced to come up with more money. That was the last time I wrote naked calls on individual stocks.

I traded in spurts many times over the following years. Each time I funded my account and began trading, I lasted only a few months. In short, I experienced failure many times before getting to the point of having some success. The process was lengthened, I think, by my not reading many trading books nor attending any seminars. I'm not sure why I took such an independent path. I guess I just thought I could figure it out on my own.

I've done a lot of trading over the years. I've had some success with volatility-based trading, and I've had some big successes with directional trading during the bear market of 2000–2002. I've also had some spectacular roller-coaster rides that I'll never forget. One time, I funded an account with $2,000, traded it down to just $137, then recovered the account all the way up to $10,000, only to lose it all again in a series of about eight losses in a row. (That was directional trading using simple put and call purchases.)

I have experienced many home runs on individual stock options, or index options with just a day or two till expiration. I once bought 10 puts on the XMI index at 1-3/8, and sold them just four hours later for more than 11. During the bubble "pop" of spring 2000, there were many instances when I bought puts on individual tech stocks and sold them three to five days later for six to eight times my investment. Of course, I realize that the important thing is *finishing* with gains, and being able to *withdraw money from my trading account and bank it*. Nevertheless, experiences like these are thrilling and I'll never forget them.

I've always been skeptical of technical analysis methods, and I don't believe that very many of them work. For directional trading, I've relied mostly on gut feel and pattern recognition—performed by my own eyes and brain, using a plain bar chart. This has served me well in down markets, but not as well in sideways or up markets. While volatility-based trading is a little boring for my temperament, it works, and I highly recommend it to most traders.

I wrote this book for both new and experienced options traders, in hopes of shortening their road to success, and that they might benefit from my mistakes. In this book, I share *all* the best of what I know about options trading. High performance options trading has always been my goal. If it is yours as well, then please accept my advice: "study up" and "tech up" first.

CHAPTER 1

The Language of Options

In the Chicago area, where I live, many people know what options are. That is because several of the world's largest options exchanges are here, and many people either work at one of the exchanges or know someone who does.

Still, more people are probably unfamiliar with options. And so it happens that when someone asks about my line of work, the discussion invariably leads to the subject of options, and I find myself having to tell them, in the briefest terms, what options are.

After a short description, I pause, and the words that often come back to me are "Well, that sounds too complicated for me." At that point, I usually hesitate to go much further, because I don't want to make them listen to what might be, to them, an arcane subject. But what I want to say, and sometimes do come right out and say, is that options are not really that complicated. Sure, there is a terminology to learn. But I like comparing options to the game of chess. Like chess, you can learn all the rules about options in just about 20 minutes. Then you're off and running.

Admittedly, some practice is needed to become successful. Options have a number of strategies to become familiar with, but hardly as many as chess! Anyone with average intelligence can learn all about options in a short time.

Also, it's easy to set up an account and begin trading options. Almost every brokerage that allows you to trade stocks also allows you to trade stock or index options. And almost every brokerage that allows you to trade futures also allows you to trade futures-based options. Establishing an options trading account just requires a little extra paperwork, including signing a statement that you have read and understood the options prospectus and are prepared to assume the risks involved.

Options are fascinating to trade, and they have some unique qualities as a trading vehicle. There are many strategies, some involving the use of two or more options in combination, or the use of options along with a position in the underlying security or futures contract, that have extraordinary risk/reward characteristics.

However, options trading is not for everyone. While there are some conservative options trading strategies, there are some risky strategies as well, where your capital can be lost very quickly. It is up to the individual, after learning about options, to decide whether he or she has the temperament for it.

THE BASICS

Suppose you agree to sell something. And suppose you and the other party have agreed on a price and a time to complete the sale. In such a case, you have what is called, in the realm of finance, a forward contract.

However, if you agree to let someone have the privilege of buying something from you at a stated price and for a limited time, *if and when the other party decides to do so*, you have sold an *option*.

The holder of the option possesses the right, but not an obligation, to buy something at a stated price for a limited time. The party who sold the option is obligated to deliver the goods if the options holder decides to exercise his option.

The asset that would be delivered is called the *underlying asset*, or just the *underlying*. The price agreed to is called the *strike price* or *exercise price* of the option.

For example, let's say I have a piece of real estate worth $100,000. I could agree to let someone have an option to buy the property from me for, say, exactly $100,000 at any time during the next two years. The option's strike price is therefore $100,000, the underlying is the property itself, and the expiration date is two years from today.

Now, why would I enter into such an agreement? After all, if the property increases in value over the next two years, that appreciation would be lost to me because I have agreed to sell the property for $100,000. Furthermore, I am locked into owning the property, and may not sell it to anyone for the next two years—because if the option holder decides to exercise, I am obligated to deliver the property. So why should I put myself in such a constrained position?

First, for the money I receive. An option has value and won't be granted without compensation. I may need to receive, for example, $15,000 for this particular option. The $15,000 (should the option buyer agree to that amount) would be mine to keep, regardless of the outcome (whether or not the buyer decides to exercise his option). The price paid for an option is usually referred to as the *premium*.

The second reason for me to do this is that I may be unwilling, or unable, to sell the property at this time. Under those circumstances, I might be happy to at least receive $15,000 immediately, especially if I do not believe that the house is likely to appreciate more than $15,000 over the next two years.

What happens at the end of the two-year period, as we approach the expiration date of the option? If it turns out that the property appreciates less than $15,000, then I'm better off for having sold the option. If the property appreciates exactly $15,000 during the next two years, I end up with the same outcome as if I had not sold the option. And if the property appreciates more than $15,000, then I may regret having sold the option.

Why might someone want to *buy* an option? For one thing, leverage. In this example, for just $15,000, an option buyer can have control over a $100,000 asset. Without incurring the hassle of ownership, he has the *right* to own the property anytime simply by submitting an exercise notice and paying the agreed $100,000. Suppose, during the next two years, he pursues his plans for the property, and those plans don't come together the way he hoped. He now has greater flexibility in getting out because, in fact, he never got in; he never bought the property. He can simply let his option expire.

Also, the option buyer may believe that the property will appreciate more than $15,000 during the next two years. If it does, he could exercise his option and then sell the property for more than $115,000.

Another reason to buy an option, rather than the asset itself, is the limited risk. Although real estate doesn't often drop in price, if the value of this property, for whatever reason, were to fall below $100,000, the option holder is not likely to exercise. Why should he pay $100,000 for something that could be bought, on the open market, for less than $100,000? And if the value of the property were to fall to less than $85,000, the option buyer would be happy that his loss is limited to the $15,000 he paid for the option, rather than having bought the property and now seeing a loss of more than $15,000.

Does the strike price of an option have to be precisely equal to the property's current fair value? Of course not. I could have written (sold) my option at a strike price of, say $110,000, $10,000 above the current fair value. Such an option wouldn't be worth as much, however, and I probably would not get $15,000 for it. When an option's strike price is above the underlying's current market value, the option is said to be "out of the money."

(More on this later. As we will see, I might prefer selling an out-of-the-money option because it gives my asset room to appreciate.)

Does this option have to end either in exercise or by letting it expire? No, there is a third possible outcome. If the two parties are willing and can agree on a price, the option seller may buy back his option, effectively canceling it out.

Again, to open an option position the buyer (holder) pays the seller (writer) an agreed amount (premium) for the option. This premium is the writer's to keep, regardless of the outcome.

Table 1.1 summarizes the possible closing option transactions.

Note the use of a new term—*assigned*. When an option holder exercises, an option writer is assigned, meaning he is being called upon to fulfill his obligation.

LISTED OPTIONS

In the example above, an option was transacted between two individuals. Its strike price and duration were created by agreement between the two parties to meet their specific needs. Its price was also reached by negotiation. The underlying asset was a specific and unique piece of property. Options that are tailored to a specific situation, with the terms negotiated, are often called over-the-counter (OTC) options. As you can imagine, this process is cumbersome, and finding a willing counter-party usually involves a third party. That's why these types of options are done primarily by large institutions.

In contrast, individuals are more likely to trade *listed* options. These are standardized contracts traded on exchanges and available on many

TABLE 1.1 Summary of Possible Closing Option Transactions

If the Option Holder . . .	The Option Writer . . .
Exercises	Is *assigned*
Pays for the asset	Receives payment for the asset
Receives the asset	Must deliver the asset
With the option writer's agreement, sells his option back	Buys the option back, effectively canceling the position and eliminating any further obligation
Does nothing, allowing his option to expire	Gets to keep his asset, and no additional cash changes hands

stocks, indexes, bond futures, commodity futures, and currency futures. There are even options on interest rates, inflation rates, and the weather.

With listed options, you do not need to worry about the trustworthiness of the other party to the transaction. A single clearing agency, such as the Options Clearing Corporation, stands in the middle of every trade, guaranteeing the transaction to both the buyer and the seller.

If an option holder exercises his option, the clearing corporation assigns any party holding a short position on a random, arbitrary basis. An option buyer never finds out, nor does he care, who sold the option to him. An option seller never finds out, nor does he care, who bought the option from him.

Listed options have many attractive features. For one thing, several strike prices are usually available at regular price intervals. Also, several different durations (expiration dates) are usually available, following a set pattern. In stocks, for example, one set of options expires in 30 days or less, another set of options expires in approximately 31 to 60 days, another set expires in approximately 3 to 6 months, and so on, going out as far as 2 years or more.

Each listed option is standardized for the same quantity of the underlying asset. In the United States, for example, one stock option is based on 100 shares of an underlying stock, and one futures option is based on one futures contract. By standardizing options contracts, the exchanges make them appealing to large groups of investors, which results in heavy trading and a liquid market.

As the markets are constantly moving, options prices are continuously quoted and changing. Market makers at the options exchanges are always publicly posting prices at which they are willing to buy and sell each option. They stand ready to take the other side of your trade, and thus *make a market* in the options they are responsible for. This allows an option holder to sell his option(s) at any time, and an option writer may buy to close his position at any time.

In the real estate example discussed previously, it is very possible, even likely, that the option holder will exercise his option prior to expiration. In contrast, the vast majority of listed option buyers never exercise them; they simply sell them back on the open market. Many of these people are speculators who only expect to hold their option for a short time. Once the underlying makes a move in the expected direction (or perhaps a move in the wrong direction) they sell. In a sense, options are like hot potatoes being tossed around among speculators. This accounts for quite a bit of the options trading volume.

Another big source of trading volume is institutional trading. Institutions may use options to hedge large positions, or simply trade large positions for speculation.

So far we have only talked about options to *buy*. Options to buy something at a stated price for a limited time are *call* options. There is another type of option: an option to *sell* something. While these options can be a bit more difficult to conceptualize, options to sell something at a stated price for a limited time are *put* options.

NOMENCLATURE

An option is identified by stating its underlying asset, the expiration month, the strike price, and the type (call or put), usually in that order. For example,

> Motorola April 20 calls

would define an option expiring in April of this year. If the option expires more than a year from now, one might need to include a year indication of some kind, as in the following example.

> Motorola April04 20 calls

In this example, "04" means the year 2004.

Also important is the way options prices translate into dollar amounts. Most stock options have a multiplier of 100, based on the fact that one option is for 100 shares of stock. So if you were to buy one option at a price of 2.20, for example, you would pay $220. Most index options also have a multiplier of 100. Multipliers for futures-based options vary from 50 to 500 or so.

LONGS AND SHORTS

Most investors are familiar with being *long*, whether they realize it or not. When you own something, you are said to have a long position in it. When you are long in the market, it means you hope to make a profit from a rising market.

Going *short* means to sell something, without first owning it, to profit from a falling market. The concept of going short can be confusing at first. How can you sell something you don't own? In securities, going short involves borrowing the securities (usually from your broker) to sell. Later, to close the position, you buy, giving the shares back to your broker. With instruments such as futures and options, it's much easier. You're entering into an agreement to buy or sell—that's all. It is a contract with rights and obligations like any other contract. The only difference is that with futures and options, you may get out of the contract at any time by placing an order that cancels your position before the obligations come due.

However, the concepts of long and short are a bit more involved when working with options. When you buy an option, you are long the option. With a call option, you stand to benefit from the underlying going up, so you can be considered to be, in a general sense, long the underlying as well. However, when you buy a put option, you stand to benefit from the underlying going down, so you can be considered to be, in a general sense, short the underlying. Table 1.2 summarizes the four possible scenarios.

A BIT MORE TERMINOLOGY

Now just a bit more terminology, and then we can look at why options are such an interesting trading vehicle.

It is very important that the options trader be familiar with the terms and concepts. In this section, the examples refer to stock options. However, the same terms and concepts apply to all asset types.

The value of an option is comprised of two components: intrinsic value and time value. You'll never see these two components quoted separately. You'll just see the total price of the option. Nevertheless, it is important to realize that the value of an option comes from these two elements.

To draw an analogy, the value of a company can be said to consist of (a) book value plus (b) all the rest. Book value, meaning what the company is worth if one were to break it up and sell all its assets, is like an option's intrinsic value. All the rest, including good will and the potential for future earnings, is like an option's time value.

An option's intrinsic value is what you could gain by exercising the option and immediately closing your new position in the underlying. For example, say the price of IBM is 100 and you have a 95 call. If you were to exercise your option, you'd pay 95 for the stock. Then you could immediately sell the

---

TABLE 1.2 Four Possible Scenarios

Position	Exposure
Long calls	Long the underlying
Short calls	Short the underlying
Long puts	Short the underlying
Short puts	Long the underlying

stock on the market for 100, realizing a profit of 5. Thus, the intrinsic value of the option is 5.

An option is said to be *in the money* when it possesses some intrinsic value. Call options are in the money when their strike price is below the current price of the underlying (as in the preceding example). It's the reverse for put options. Puts are in the money when their strike price is above the current price of the underlying.

When an option's strike price is *equal to* (in practice, very close to) the price of the underlying, it is said to be *at the money.*

Call options are said to be *out of the money* when their strike is above the current price of the underlying. Puts are out of the money when their strike is below the current price of the underlying. (See Figure 1.1.)

Time value, the other component of an option's value, represents the possibility of the underlying moving in the option's favor (up for calls, down for puts) during the remaining life of the option. "Isn't it just as possible for the stock to move the wrong way?" one might ask. Yes it is. However, if the stock moves the wrong way, an option's value can drop, at most, to zero. On the other hand, if the stock moves the right way, the option's value can, theoretically, go up without limit. That is why options almost always have some time value. Time value represents the summation of all the possible intrinsic values the option might have, at all the different underlying prices possible on or before expiration, factoring in the probabilities of the stock reaching each of those prices.

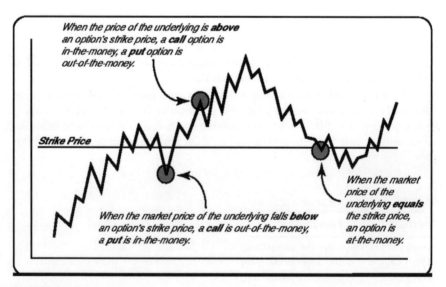

FIGURE 1.1 Strike Price

Time value can be a challenge to estimate. For that reason, options traders refer to mathematical models, implemented in computer programs, to compute the fair value of an option.

In the previous IBM example, we showed how an in-the-money option could be exercised to get into a stock position at below market price. Would it ever make sense to exercise an out-of-the-money option?

The answer is no. To exercise an out-of-the-money call would be to pay more than the current market price for a stock. To exercise an out-of-the-money put would be to sell a stock for less than the current market price of the stock. It never makes sense to exercise an out-of-the-money option.

In fact, it seldom makes sense to exercise an in-the-money option either. Why? Because you'd be throwing away its time value. Let's illustrate this by extending the IBM example. You have a 95 call and the stock is currently at 100. Your call, if it has more than a few days of life left, is probably worth something more than 5; let's say 6.5. (This would be an intrinsic value of 5 plus a time value of 1.5.)

If you exercise the option and then sell the stock, as before, you gain $500 on the stock transaction. However, you no longer have an option worth $650. Thus, you lost $150—the option's time value. It would be better to sell your option on one of the options exchanges. Not only do you recover the full value of your option this way, but it is also simpler to do just one option transaction, versus two transactions the other way.

Here is a little pop quiz to see if you have grasped the concepts we have been discussing.

1. A stock is at 60. A 65 call on this stock has a price of 1.75. Is this option in-the-money, at-the-money, or out-of-the-money? What is this option's intrinsic value? What is this option's time value?

   Answers: The option is out-of-the-money and has an intrinsic value of zero and a time value of 1.75.

2. A stock is at 70. A 60 call on this stock has a price of 11.40. Is this option in-the-money, at-the-money, or out-of-the-money? What is this option's intrinsic value? What is this option's time value?

   Answers: The option is in-the-money, has an intrinsic value of 10 and a time value of 1.40.

3. A stock is at 50. A 55 put on this stock has a price of 6.60. Is this option in-the-money, at-the-money, or out-of-the-money? What is this option's intrinsic value? What is this option's time value?

   Answers: The option is in-the-money, has an intrinsic value of 5 and a time value of 1.60.

4. A stock is at 50. A 50 call on this stock has a price of 3.20. Is this option in-the-money, at-the-money, or out-of-the-money? What is this option's intrinsic value? What is this option's time value?

   Answers: The option is at-the-money, has an intrinsic value of zero and a time value of 3.20.

One final question: In question 2 above, do you think this option could trade below 10 (its intrinsic value)?

Answer: Yes it could. Anything could happen in an open market. However, practically speaking, it would not trade for much less than 10. That is because traders are constantly watching the options markets for bargains, and snap them up in an instant. So if you were to offer this option for sale at, say, 9.8, someone would quickly buy it from you, because they know they can immediately exercise it and sell the stock, realizing a 0.20 point profit.

Even if an option's time value has dropped to zero, it is always worth its intrinsic value, and you should be able to sell it for intrinsic value, or perhaps just a bit less. Thus intrinsic value serves practically as a "floor level" for the price of an option. When an option is trading at intrinsic value, it is said to be trading *at parity*.

Previously, I pointed out that a great many options are never exercised. It does not make sense to exercise an option that has any appreciable time value; you'd be throwing away money. However, it is when an option's time value is zero or nearly zero that option holders *are* likely to exercise. Conversely, if you sell (short) an option with zero or nearly zero time value, you are apt to be assigned—and it can happen that very day.

Early assignment may or may not be a significant danger to you. It depends on the nature of the position you would be left holding. (More will be said on this in Chapter 4.)

OFFSETTING OPTION TRADES

The only way to close an option position before expiration is to do the opposite transaction in the marketplace. This applies to both puts and calls, whether long or short. When you have bought a call, the only way to rid yourself of the position is to sell the same call. Buying a put will not do it. Selling some other call on the same underlying does not do it. Such trades might reduce your risk, but they would only build (and complicate) your original position.

EXPIRATION, EXERCISE, AND ASSIGNMENT

The alternatives to closing a position with an opposite transaction are to let the option expire or to exercise it. If the option is out-of-the-money at expiration, it has no value and therefore should be allowed to expire worthless. However, if the option is in-the-money at expiration, it has value and should be exercised.

When you exercise a stock option, you pay for and receive shares of stock. This is an important point to remember. Let's say you have a long call position that gives you the right to buy 100 shares of a stock at $50. If you intend to exercise it, make sure you have enough in your account to cover the $5,000 payment you need to make! Futures and index options work differently. When you exercise futures options, you are immediately in a futures position and no cash changes hands. When you exercise index options, you simply receive the intrinsic value as a cash settlement. For example, if you have an index option that is 4.00 in-the-money at expiration, you receive $400 posted to your account. There is no delivery of anything (besides cash), and it does not create a new position in another security.

It is not always required that the option holder submit an exercise notice. Exercise is automatic for some instruments if the option is a certain amount in-the-money. It is important to understand what will happen if you do nothing with an in-the-money option at expiration. Speak with your broker if you are unsure. It never hurts to submit an exercise notice, as you would not want to let a valuable option just disappear!

AMERICAN VERSUS EUROPEAN

Options can also be classified in terms of *style*, which relates to the two ways in which they can be exercised. If an option can be exercised anytime up until expiration, it is said to be *American style*. However, many options can be exercised only on expiration day. These are said to be *European style*. Note: This is not a reference to which continent the options trade on. Both American and European style options trade in America, Europe, and on other continents.

In the United States, all stock options and more than half of the index options are American style; the remaining index options are European style. Some futures-based options are American style and others are European style.

An option buyer intending to exercise needs to know which style options he is getting. An option seller might prefer European style options, because he'd rather not be concerned about being assigned before expiration. For the options buyer who has no intention of exercising, the only difference is that American style options are a bit more valuable—and a quality options pricing model will bear this out.

QUOTATIONS

Figure 1.2 illustrates how options are quoted in two popular business newspapers. Both identify the underlying stock in boldface type and list several options per stock. For each option, they print the option's expiration month, strike, last trade price, and day's volume. Note that many more options exist than what is shown. One newspaper lists only actively traded options and the other apparently lists only the nearby options (the ones expiring the soonest).

More complete listings can be seen in trading software, as in the example in Figure 1.3. This matrix of IBM options shows the stock price, today's price change, and volume (number of shares traded), as well as the price, change, and volume for 42 of IBM's options. Even more options are available at strikes above and below those shown (and could be seen by

OPTION/STRIKE		EXP.	VOL.	LAST	VOL.	LAST
AmOnline	25	Feb	1587	2.40	...	...
27.35	25	Mar	2014	2.70	1082	0.50
27.35	27.50	Feb	1229	0.10	1568	0.35
27.35	27.50	Mar	1180	1.15	866	1.45
27.35	32.50	Apr	1577	0.50	20	5.40
AT&T	15	Mar	698	1.15	1494	0.55
15.65	17.50	Jul	5661	0.95	120	2.65
Abb L	55	May	141	3	1707	1.95
56.27	60	May	1901	0.80	4	4.60
Activisn	25	Mar	2060	3.40	5	1.35
AdvncPCS	30	Feb	805	0.45	1293	0.40
A M D	12.50	Feb	1194	2.50	...	...
Aetna	35	Apr	18	1.45	2593	3.50
Amazon	15	Feb	1622	0.10	335	1.20
A Hess	65	Mar	1365	2.40	...	...
AmIntGp	75	Mar	109	3.50	2413	1.35
77.17	80	Feb	645	0.05	6775	3.20
AmerisBrgn	65	Aug	1250	4.90	...	...
Amgen	55	Feb	2059	3	877	0.05
58.00	55	Mar	1673	4.40	1319	1.10
58.00	60	Feb	1699	0.05	489	2
58.00	60	Mar	1609	1.25	236	3.20
58.00	60	Apr	1254	2.50	44	4.30

P C	Strike Price	Vol.	Price	Vol.	Price	Vol.	Price
		Feb		Mar			
eBay					Close 60.00 Apr		
c55		616	5.20	69	6.40	20	8.10
c60		1125	0.65	822	3.20	24	5.20
c65		no tr		967	1.15	135	2.60
c70		6	0.05	68	0.35	229	1.25
c75		no tr		no tr		197	0.55
c80		no tr		no tr		465	0.30
c90		no tr		299	0.05	198	0.10
p45		no tr		183	0.30	14	0.80
p50		no tr		304	0.60	155	1.50
p55		303	0.05	327	1.50	77	2.85
p60		1228	0.50	566	3.20	76	4.80
i2 Tech					Close 6.20 Apr		
c7.50		101	0.05	240	0.35	381	0.65
AbbotLabs					Close 56.27 Apr		
c50		2	6.10	266	6.40	no tr	
c55		382	1.35	179	2	141	3
c60		no tr		116	0.15	1901	0.80
p55		55	0.10	269	0.85	1707	1.95

FIGURE 1.2 Option Quotes

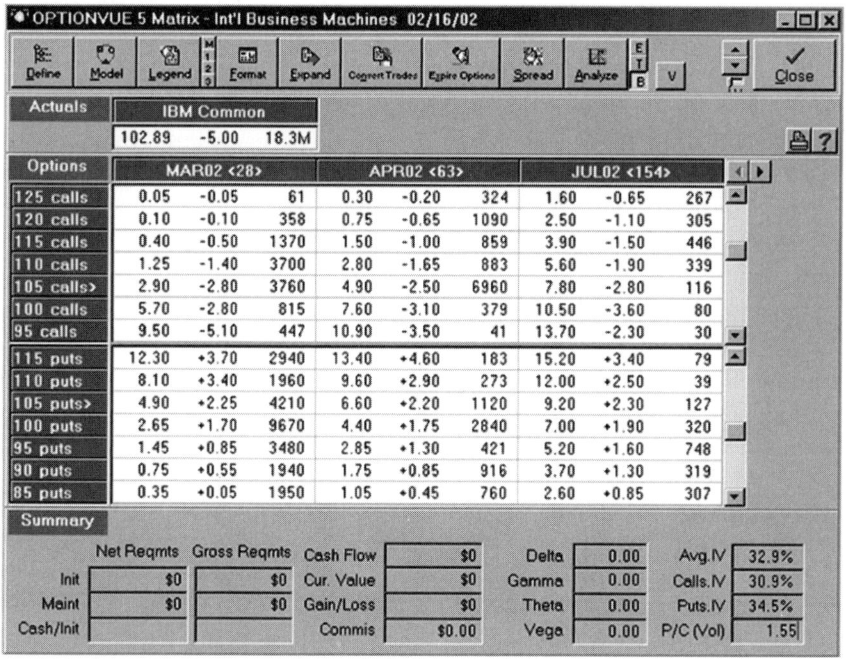

Options	MAR02 <28>			APR02 <63>			JUL02 <154>		
125 calls	0.05	-0.05	61	0.30	-0.20	324	1.60	-0.65	267
120 calls	0.10	-0.10	358	0.75	-0.65	1090	2.50	-1.10	305
115 calls	0.40	-0.50	1370	1.50	-1.00	859	3.90	-1.50	446
110 calls	1.25	-1.40	3700	2.80	-1.65	883	5.60	-1.90	339
105 calls>	2.90	-2.80	3760	4.90	-2.50	6960	7.80	-2.80	116
100 calls	5.70	-2.80	815	7.60	-3.10	379	10.50	-3.60	80
95 calls	9.50	-5.10	447	10.90	-3.50	41	13.70	-2.30	30
115 puts	12.30	+3.70	2940	13.40	+4.60	183	15.20	+3.40	79
110 puts	8.10	+3.40	1960	9.60	+2.90	273	12.00	+2.50	39
105 puts>	4.90	+2.25	4210	6.60	+2.20	1120	9.20	+2.30	127
100 puts	2.65	+1.70	9670	4.40	+1.75	2840	7.00	+1.90	320
95 puts	1.45	+0.85	3480	2.85	+1.30	421	5.20	+1.60	748
90 puts	0.75	+0.55	1940	1.75	+0.85	916	3.70	+1.30	319
85 puts	0.35	+0.05	1950	1.05	+0.45	760	2.60	+0.85	307

	Net Reqmts	Gross Reqmts						
			Cash Flow	$0	Delta	0.00	Avg.IV	32.9%
Init	$0	$0	Cur. Value	$0	Gamma	0.00	Calls.IV	30.9%
Maint	$0	$0	Gain/Loss	$0	Theta	0.00	Puts.IV	34.5%
Cash/Init			Commis	$0.00	Vega	0.00	P/C (Vol)	1.55

FIGURE 1.3 IBM as Seen on Trading Software

scrolling vertically), as well as farther out expiration dates (which could be seen by scrolling to the right).

This illustrates the rather large array of options available on many stocks and other types of financial instruments. The strike prices are shown vertically at five-dollar ("nickel") intervals. The options are separated into two sections: calls in the upper section and puts in the lower section. In each section, the row where the strike is marked with a ">" represents the closest-to-the-money strike. In the top section (calls), rows above that mark represent progressively farther out-of-the-money strikes, while rows beneath it represent progressively farther in-the-money strikes. In the bottom section (puts), the reverse is true, since strikes are listed in the same numerical order.

You might want to take a few moments to study how option prices vary by strike and by expiration. Can you see the smooth progression from expensive to cheaper options as you go from in-the-money toward out-of-the-money? Also, options expiring the soonest (called the *nearbys*) are in the left column, while farther out options flow to the right. Do you see that the farther out options (with more time remaining) are more valuable than the nearby options?

As this was a significant down day for IBM, with the stock dropping 5 points, you can see the relative amounts by which the call options dropped and the put options gained in value. Higher-priced options changed the most. However, lower-priced options probably changed by greater percentage amounts. Also note that trading volume is especially concentrated in the nearby expiration months and in those options closest to the money. Many of these options traded thousands of contracts on this day.

THE SPECIAL PROPERTIES OF OPTIONS

Options have some unique properties that make them very special as a trading vehicle. For starters, unlike stocks and futures, their performance is nonlinear. Every point a stock or futures contract moves results in the same amount gained or lost. Their performance graph is a straight line (see Figure 1.4).

In contrast, an option's performance graph curves upward, meaning that as the underlying moves in favor of the option, the option makes money faster. Yet, as the underlying moves against the option, the option loses money slower. (In Figure 1.5, focus on the dotted line, which represents *today's* performance of the option.)

The fact that the performance line curves upward like this, and that ultimately an option's value can go up without limit but can drop only to zero, is a very attractive feature for option buyers.

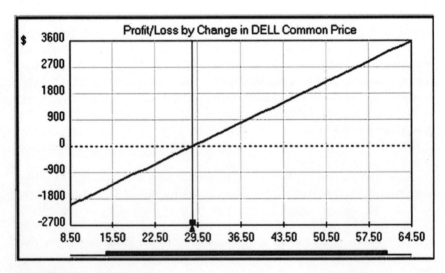

FIGURE 1.4 Straight Line

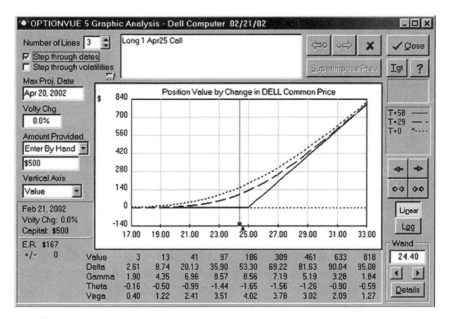

FIGURE 1.5 Curved Line

TIME

Another property of options is a pesky little thing called "time decay." With the passing of time, all other things being equal (i.e., the underlying price has not changed), an option's value falls. In Figure 1.5, the dashed line represents the theoretical value of this call option 64 days from now (halfway to expiration), while the solid line represents the theoretical value of the option at expiration. As you can see, if the stock does not move above 25 (the strike price of this option), the value of this option will fall gradually and inexorably to zero.

Many options traders are attracted to selling options (rather than buying them) in order to put this time decay property in their favor. While it is wonderful to have time working in your favor, this can convey a false sense of security. Time is precisely what gives the underlying a chance to move—potentially against the option seller's position.

So there is a trade-off. The option buyer has the nonlinear performance line of an option in his favor, but time works against him. The option seller has time in his favor, but the nonlinear performance line of the option works against him.

To limit the damage of time decay, the option buyer may determine to hold his position for only a short time. To limit the damage from an adverse price movement, the option seller may decide to use a stop order.

Time Decay

The traditional time decay curve that is frequently given in options books and literature is depicted in Figure 1.6.

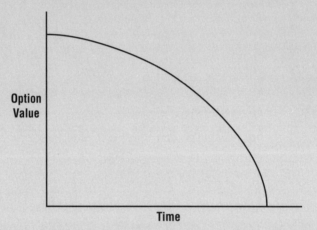

FIGURE 1.6 Traditional Time Decay Curve

It is important for the option trader to understand that this is only correct for at-the-money options. In-the-money and out-of-the-money options have different time decay curves (see Figures 1.7 and 1.8).

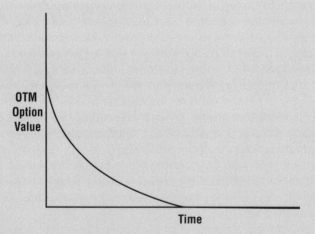

FIGURE 1.7 In-the-Money

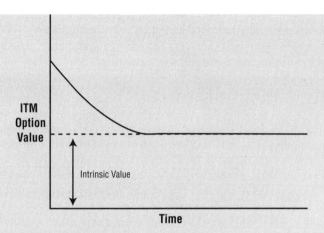

FIGURE 1.8 Out-of-the-Money

To visualize how time decay works for options at different "money" levels, consider this analogy. You have a funnel full of liquid that is slowly draining out. The center of the funnel represents at-the-money options. To the left of center are the progressively in-the-money options and to the right are the progressively out-of-the-money options (see Figure 1.9).

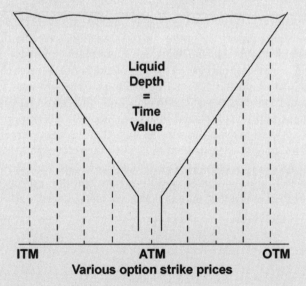

FIGURE 1.9 Funnel Analogy

(Continued)

The depth of the liquid at various places represents how much time value remains in these options. For instance, the depth of the liquid in the middle shows that the at-the-money options have the greatest time value. The deep in-the-money and far out-of-the-money options, where the liquid is shallowest, have the least time value.

Now visualize the liquid slowing draining out. As the surface level gradually drops, the deep in-the-money and far out-of-the-money options will be the first to lose all of their time value. Over time, the liquid's surface level will drop faster, because the drainage rate is constant and there is less surface area. Eventually, the at-the-money options will be the only ones with any time value, and that will be slipping away faster than ever as very little liquid remains in the funnel. At the expiration date, all of the liquid has drained, and none of the options have any time value.

In truth, at-the-money options have faster time decay (a higher *theta*) than in-the-money and out-of-the-money options, so this analogy is not entirely correct. To be more accurate, we would need to begin the analogy with the surface of the liquid somehow "heaped up" near the center, and picture the surface of the liquid gradually flattening out over time as the at-the-monies lose time value faster.

VOLATILITY

The other unique property of options is their sensitivity to volatility. Options on more volatile assets, all else being equal, are more expensive. Options on less volatile assets are cheaper. This can make a big difference. Even options on the same underlying can be twice as expensive during a period when the asset's price is perceived to be volatile than during quieter periods.

This gives options an extra dimension. Not only can options be traded based on expected price moves in the underlying (called directional trading), but they may also be traded based on expected swings in volatility levels. You would buy options when volatility is low and the options are cheap, and sell options when volatility is high and the options are expensive. This kind of trading is called volatility-based trading, and is discussed in detail in Chapter 3.

HOW OPTIONS RESPOND TO CHANGING CONDITIONS

As we have learned, options can be said to have (and move in) three dimensions: (1) price, because options respond to changes in the price of their underlying; (2) volatility, because options respond to changes in the perceived volatility of their underlying; and (3) time, because an option's value decays over time, all else being constant.

The first two dimensions are tradable, as these elements fluctuate, giving traders the opportunity to speculate on their future direction. Time is different. While a trader may put time on his side by selling options, time is not quite the same as the dimensions of price and volatility. Time only marches forward, and the effect of time decay is very gradual, accelerating somewhat for an at-the-money option approaching expiration.

One other factor that affects option prices is a change in interest rates. However, this effect is very small, and it will not be discussed in much detail in this book.

It is important to understand how changes in all these factors affect the value of options. Changes in the underlying price or interest rates cause the values of calls and puts to move in opposite directions. For instance, when the price of the underlying goes up, calls go up and puts go down. Volatility and time affect calls and puts in the same way. When the underlying becomes more volatile, both the calls and the puts go up in value. With the passing of time, both calls and puts decline in value.

How changing conditions affect option values is summarized in Table 1.3.

THE GREEKS

Options traders use several parameters, named after Greek letters, that tell them how sensitive an option is to changing conditions.

The first of these is *delta*. Delta measures how much the price of an option moves in response to a one-point increase in the price of the underlying. For example, if an option moves up 0.5 when its underlying moves

TABLE 1.3 How Changing Conditions Affect Option Values

	Call Options	Put Options
Underlying price goes up	Go up	Go down
Underlying price goes down	Go down	Go up
Volatility goes up	Go up	Go up
Volatility goes down	Go down	Go down
Time passes	Go down	Go down
Interest rates increase	Go up	Go down
Interest rates decrease	Go down	Go up

up 1.0, the option's delta is said to be 50, because you would theoretically gain $50 per option contract.

Since the values of call and put options move in opposite directions with a change in the underlying price, calls have positive deltas and puts have negative deltas. Call options have deltas ranging from 0 to 100, while put options have deltas ranging from –100 to 0.

Note that at-the-money calls typically have a delta close to 50, while at-the-money puts typically have a delta close to –50. To illustrate this, let's contrast buying 100 shares of stock versus buying one at-the-money call. If the stock goes up one point, the stockholder gains $100. However, the option holder will theoretically gain $50. So why not just buy the stock then, since it makes more money? Because the option costs much less than the stock, and gains a greater percentage. Note that buying two of these options would obtain the same delta as buying 100 shares of the stock. And typically, two (or even 10 or more) of these options cost less than 100 shares of stock.

Another greek, *vega*, measures how much the price of an option moves in response to a one-point increase in volatility. For example, if an option has a vega of 23, and volatility increases from 18% to 19%, the option's price will increase by 0.23 and its value by $23. All options have positive vega.

Theta measures how much the price of an option should drop today, due to the passage of time. For example, if an option has a theta of –5, its price should fall 0.05, and its value by $5, by the end of the day. All options have negative theta.

Rho measures how much the price of an option should change (positive for calls and negative for puts) in response to a one-point increase in interest rates. For example, if a call option should increase 0.02 when interest rates go up one point, the option's rho is said to be 2.

All the greeks are theoretical. That is, they measure how an option *should* respond to changing conditions. The same mathematical models used to calculate an option's fair value also produce the greeks as byproducts. That's important to understand. Just as an option's fair value constantly changes in response to changing inputs, the greeks also change. In fact, there is another greek—*gamma*—that's just for measuring how fast delta changes!

Sophisticated options traders use the greeks to gauge their risk, as the greeks reveal the exposures of their current position. In a way, the greeks are more valuable the more complicated the position gets. For example, market makers often hold positions (long and short) in many different options on a particular asset. By viewing the net greeks of their position (computed by adding up the greeks of each option in which they have a position, times the number of contracts they have in each option), they can determine their net risk, and make adjustments if necessary. For example, if they see that their net delta is –617, they may buy 600 shares of stock to change their net delta to –17, bringing it reasonably close to zero, or *delta-neutral*. Holding a delta-neutral position means the total position value should remain unchanged when the price of the underlying changes.

THE ROLE OF THE MARKET MAKER

Individual investors seldom trade with each other. More often, though never knowing it, they trade with market makers. Market makers must post two prices for every option: the price they are willing to buy it for (the *bid* price) and the price they are willing to sell it for (the *asked* price). Market makers are bound by agreement with the exchanges to post bid and asked prices and trade with interested buyers and sellers at these prices. By doing so, they are *making a market*.

An individual market maker is usually assigned to one or more underlying assets, and each underlying asset has one or more (typically more) market makers assigned to it. When multiple market makers are assigned to an underlying, they are in competition with each other.

While market makers must trade with interested parties at the stated bid and asked prices, they are not required to trade an unlimited number of contracts. The exchanges only require them to honor their prices for a certain number of contracts at a time. For example, most stock options would have at least 10 contracts "up" at a time. If an investor wants to trade more than 10 contracts, he will get the stated price for the first 10 contracts but may have to pay a bit more (if buying) or accept a bit less (if selling) for any additional contracts.

While 10 is a minimum requirement, many of the most heavily traded options markets have hundreds, even thousands, of contracts available at the posted bid and asked prices. Many online pricing services show how many contracts are available at the bid and the asked. For example, you may see a bid of 2.20, an asked of 2.40, and a number like 200×500. This indicates 200 contracts are available at the bid and 500 contracts are available at the asked.

Market makers are kind of like bookies, taking a small piece of the action from all participants. Consulting a computer model that computes options' fair values, they typically post a bid price just below fair value and an asked price just above fair value. If a seller comes along, offering options at a reasonable price, the market maker buys from them. If a buyer comes along, the market maker sells to them. Since the market maker's selling price is higher than his buying price, he typically makes a profit.

The problem for the market maker is that the market is seldom so convenient that a seller comes along immediately after a buyer, and vice versa. Often, a string of orders come at him on the same side. For this reason the market maker usually works to hedge his position. For example, after taking on a new long position in a call option, the market maker immediately looks for any other call options on the same underlying that he can sell at reasonable prices. He will sell an appropriate quantity of these to bring his delta back to near zero. Or he may look for any puts that he can buy on the same underlying. If no such opportunities are available, he will probably sell (short) an appropriate quantity of the underlying itself.

As you can see, the market maker is always working to manage his risk. The new long call position places the market maker in a net long (positive delta) position, exposing him to losses if the stock were to drop. Not being interested in betting on the stock's direction, he looks for a way to neutralize, or hedge, his position. Any of the trades mentioned above will accomplish that. A computer model helps the market maker figure out what the appropriate quantity would be.

VOLUME AND OPEN INTEREST

Volume is simply the number of contracts traded on a given day. Both volume and open interest are indications of the depth of a market. Neither is more important than the other. However, volume could be considered a more immediate indication of liquidity.

Open interest is the total number of contracts outstanding. To illustrate, say a new standard option contract becomes available. At first, its open interest is zero. Suppose you put in a buy order and I put in a sell order (both of us to open new positions). We make the trade. Now, open interest is one, because there is one contract open—you have the option to buy (presuming it's a call) and I have the obligation to supply, if called upon, the underlying.

Now suppose more buyers and sellers come in, each side opening new positions, just as we did. This will make open interest go higher as new contracts are opened.

However, if someone with a long position comes in with an order to sell, and gets matched up with someone with a short position who is buying to close, open interest will go down after they trade because contracts are being canceled out.

If someone who is closing his or her position gets matched up with someone who is opening a position, open interest remains unchanged. To help picture this, suppose you and I are the only parties who have a position in an option. You're long one contract and I'm short one. Therefore open interest is one. What if you sold your contract to an interested third party? Now, you're out of the position, the third party is long one contract, and I'm short one contract. Open interest is still one.

A high open interest simply says that a large number of contracts have traded during the life of the option, and that there is a potential for these open contracts to translate into more volume as traders unwind their positions. (Note the word *potential*, because traders do not *have* to unwind their positions if they don't want to; they may hold until expiration and then exercise.)

If there is a large open interest in the nearby, at-the-money options, and it is the final day of trading for the nearby options, I have often seen the underlying stock price be driven toward the at-the-money option during the course of the day. This is one of the few instances when you can observe the tail (the options) wagging the dog (the stock).

For example, say GM stock is trading at 26 and there is a large open interest in the 25 calls, as well as the 25 puts. Today is the final day of trading for these options. Here is what happens. With the stock at 26, the calls have one point of intrinsic value. Holders of the calls, knowing that they must make a decision today, put in sell orders because they are interested in redeeming any value before it is too late. When the market maker absorbs the sell orders, he also sells stock to balance his position, thus transferring downward pressure onto the stock. If enough call option holders sell, the stock may be driven all the way down to 25, at which point it is no longer worthwhile for remaining call holders to sell.

Meanwhile, put option holders have been watching the stock, hoping it will drop below 25 sometime during the day so they can sell for some worthwhile amount. If it does, the put holders will begin selling. In fact, the farther the stock goes below 25, the more put selling is probably going to be triggered. As put holders sell, it has the opposite effect to that of calls. As the market maker absorbs the sell orders, he also buys stock to balance his position, thus transferring upward pressure onto the stock. If enough put holders sell, the stock may be driven back up to 25, at which point it is no longer worthwhile for remaining put holders to sell. Thus the stock is pushed up toward 25 by put selling every time the stock dips below 25, and downward toward 25 by call selling every time it tries to go above 25.

It is not unusual to observe many stocks "locking in" on the price of the nearest strike price on an option's final trading day. Is there any way to take advantage of this? I don't believe there is. The idea of selling a straddle (selling both calls and puts) on or just prior to the final day comes to mind, but this is likely to backfire on you (by the stock making a significant move instead of staying quiet) just often enough to cancel out your profits in the long run. The one way I *have* used this knowledge to my benefit is when I'm one of those call or put holders who is hoping to recover even just a small amount before it is too late. As I look for the right time to sell, I keep in mind that there are many other traders in competition with me, and that I'd better take a decent price when I see it, without delay.

CHAPTER 2

Option Strategies

H aving covered basic options terminology and some of the mechanics, we've now laid a foundation for a discussion of options strategies. *Strategy* might sound like an overall approach to trading the market, but in options parlance, it simply means a kind of position (e.g., short calls or long puts). We will begin by discussing single-option strategies, and then move on to more complex strategies that involve multiple options.

You may recall there are four single-option strategies:

Long call
Short call
Long put
Short put

When you consider that each of these strategies could be used to complement a position in the underlying, you now have eight single-option strategies. Before listing all eight, there are two more terms you need to know: *covered* and *naked*.

When an option writer already has a position in the underlying asset that will fulfill his obligation if the option is exercised, he is said to have a covered position. For example, when an investor is short a call option and also owns the underlying that could be delivered in the event of assignment, his short call option position is said to be covered. Otherwise, with no stock to deliver, a call option position is said to be naked.

Likewise, when an investor is short a put option, and he is in a short position in the underlying, his short put option is said to be covered. Otherwise his short put option position is said to be naked.

Thus the eight single-option strategies are as follows:

Long call
Short covered call
Short naked call
Long call with short stock
Long put
Short covered put
Short naked put
Long put with long stock

We'll now go over each of these strategies in detail, including how each performs and when you would want to use it. Along the way, we'll introduce the concept of *margin requirements*. While these examples refer to stock options, the concepts apply just as well to options on every kind of underlying asset.

LONG CALL

We first discussed this strategy in the real estate example in Chapter 1. The buyer of the option on the property had a *long call* position.

When a call option on stock is purchased, the call option holder controls the stock without actually possessing it, and does so for a fraction of the cost. Therefore the long call is a *leveraged* position in comparison to owning the stock itself. If the stock's price goes up just a few percentage points, it is safe to say that its call options will increase by a greater percentage. Some may even double in value.

Other important characteristics of this strategy are its *limited risk* and *unlimited potential*. An option buyer can lose only the amount paid for the option—nothing more. At the same time, the profit potential is theoretically unlimited. A call option's value rises without limit as the price of the underlying goes up.

The qualities of leverage, limited risk, and unlimited potential make call option buying attractive for speculators looking for a quick move to the upside. I say quick because, remember, the option buyer's enemy is time decay. Each day, the option loses some of its value. For this reason, call buying works best when the speculator is working in a short time frame, expecting a move to happen within a few days at the most.

The performance graph for the long call illustrates this strategy's limited risk and unlimited potential (see Figure 2.1). The three lines illustrate how time decay affects the position. The dotted line represents the long call's theoretical performance as of today, while the solid line represents the performance at expiration (the final day of trading), and the dashed line represents the performance midway between today and expiration.

SHORT COVERED CALL

This strategy is also known as a *covered write* or *buy write*. In the real estate example in Chapter 1, the option seller also owned the property, so he had a short covered call position. When a stock owner sells a call against his stock position, he becomes a covered call writer, giving up control over his stock for a limited time in return for income from the sale of the option. This income is his to keep no matter what happens later.

While the speculative call buyer usually holds his position for a short period of time, the covered call writer often expects to hold his position to expiration. If the option is out-of-the-money at that time, it expires worthless. If the option is in-the-money at expiration, the investor may decide to buy the option to close the position and keep his stock or he can do nothing and see his asset *called away*. Some

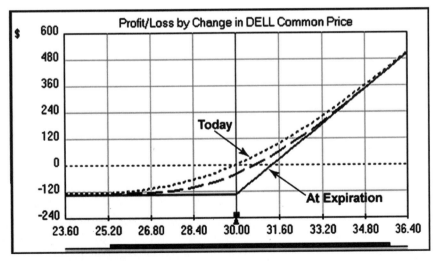

FIGURE 2.1 Long Call

investors keep their stock and repeatedly sell more covered calls after each expiration, thus continually adding to their income. A real plus is that covered writers make money during periods when their stock holdings are going nowhere. The income they can generate can be impressive: Upwards of 40 percent annual returns are typical. Remember, however, such returns are possible only if the stock goes up or remains at around the same price.

Covered writing is a conservative strategy. The sale of call options against stock holdings reduces the overall variance of returns, thus reducing risk in the traditional sense.

The need for a risk-reduction tool is why options were created in the first place, not for speculation. Still, speculators are an important part of the equation. Speculators assume the risk that portfolio managers would like to off-load. Thus, options are an essential mechanism for risk transfer—from those who don't want it (hedgers) to those who do (speculators).

While covered writing is attractive because of the extra income it generates, it does have a shortcoming. The covered writer has the same downside risk as he did just owning the stock. At the same time, his upside potential is limited.

The short covered call performance graph illustrates this strategy's downside risk and limited potential (see Figure 2.2).

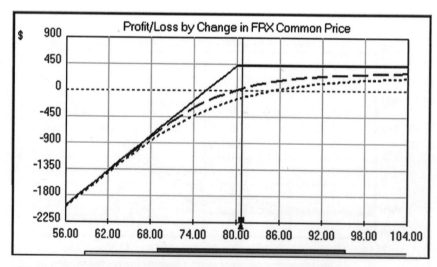

FIGURE 2.2 Short Covered Call

SHORT NAKED CALL

The naked call seller is interested in the same thing as the covered call seller—income. The difference is that the naked option seller does not own the underlying. If assigned, he has to buy shares on the open market to deliver. Of course, he has to pay the current market price, whatever it is.

The primary difference between being short a naked option and being short a covered option is that without the stock to complement the short call option, there is nothing to limit the position's risk if the stock goes up.

Selling a naked call gives you precisely the opposite performance characteristics from buying a call: unlimited risk and limited potential. The most an option seller can gain is the amount he was initially paid for the option—no more. At the same time, he has theoretically unlimited risk, as the call option's value goes up with the price of the stock. As losses mount, a point will be reached where you need to buy back the option to close the position (or be assigned and have to buy stock to deliver, resulting in almost the same monetary outcome).

Still, some investors are attracted to the prospect of earning time decay dollars, and the position costs less to put on than a covered write. In fact, your account is credited immediately after the sale of the option. So what stops traders from putting on large positions—as large as they want? They can't, because brokerage firms require investors to keep money in their account to cover potential losses. This cash reserve is called the *margin requirement*. (Actually, *margin requirement* is old terminology. The new term, *performance requirement*, is closer to the mark, but the old term still lives on.)

There is a standard formula for computing the requirement for naked short options. Without going into detail, the amount required is roughly 5 to 20 times the credit received from the sale of the option(s). For example, if you sell an option and receive a $1,000 credit, you can count on having to put up anywhere from $5,000 to $20,000 collateral to support the position.

Naked option writers rely on stops to help them control the theoretically unlimited risk. That works well, provided the underlying trades continuously; that is, its price never jumps dramatically. As many investors have seen, however, a stock can sometimes close the day at one price and open the next day at a very different price. This kind of risk cannot be controlled using stops. To limit this exposure, some traders stick to writing index options, since indexes don't have price jumps the way individual stocks do.

The performance graph for the short naked call illustrates this strategy's unlimited risk and limited potential (see Figure 2.3). As you can see, it makes money as long as the underlying price does not go up.

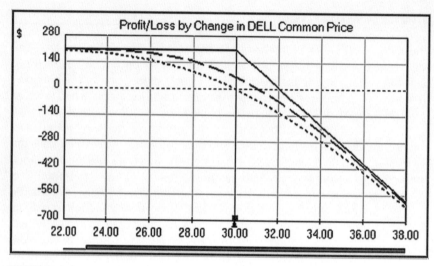

FIGURE 2.3 Short Naked Call

LONG CALL WITH SHORT STOCK

This is a rare strategy that is seldom used or even discussed. Traders with a short position in a stock can buy calls to protect their short stock position from an adverse price move (to the upside). Then they can participate in the expected down move without worrying about the stock jumping in the wrong direction. However, it costs money to buy those calls—money that subtracts from the profit the investor expects to make. And if the investor wants continued protection after the calls expire, he'll need to buy more.

The performance graph for the long call with short stock illustrates this strategy's limited risk and unlimited potential (see Figure 2.4).

LONG PUT

The put option buyer gains the right to sell stock without actually possessing it, and does so for a fraction of the cost of shorting the stock itself. Buying a put is a highly leveraged bearish position. If the stock price goes down just a few percentage points, its put options will increase by a greater percentage. Some may even double in value.

Like the long call, the long put has the characteristics of limited risk and unlimited potential. An option buyer can lose the amount paid for the

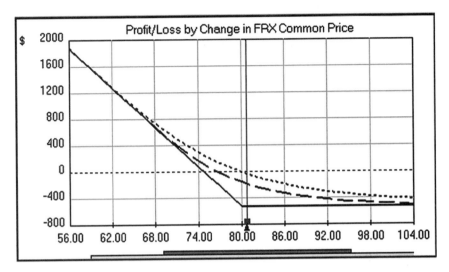

FIGURE 2.4 Long Call with Short Stock

option, and nothing more. At the same time, the profit potential is theoretically unlimited. A put option's value rises without limit as the price of the underlying goes down. (Well, it's not *absolutely* unlimited, as the furthest the put could increase in value is if the stock goes to zero.)

As with buying calls, the qualities of leverage, limited risk, and unlimited potential make put option buying attractive for speculators looking for a quick move to the downside. Again, the option buyer's enemy is time decay, so put buying works best when the speculator is looking for a move to happen fairly quickly.

The performance graph for the long put illustrates this strategy's limited risk and unlimited potential (see Figure 2.5).

SHORT COVERED PUT

This strategy is so seldom used or discussed that the term *covered write* is universally understood to mean buying stock and selling calls. But shorting stock and selling a put is technically also a covered write. The covered put writer gives up control over his short stock position for a limited time in return for income from the sale of the put.

Much as a long stock holder sells call options for extra income when he feels the stock price may be stalled, the short stock holder can sell puts for extra income when he feels the stock may not fall immediately.

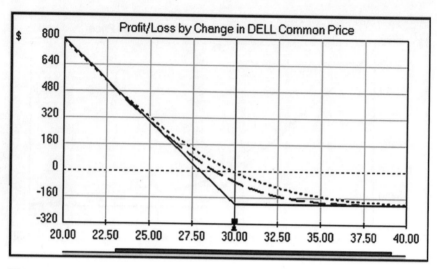

FIGURE 2.5   Long Put

The performance graph of this strategy is a mirror image (in terms of stock price direction) of the traditional covered write (see Figure 2.6).

SHORT NAKED PUT

The naked put seller is interested in income. With this strategy, the investor is expecting the underlying stock to remain at the same price or go up, thus allowing his short put to expire worthless. If the stock drops, he's likely to be assigned, and instantly be long shares of the underlying stock. The price he'll pay for the shares, of course, is the strike price of the puts. So this investor often shorts out-of-the-money puts at a strike price where he would consider the stock purchase a bargain.

Selling a naked put confers precisely the opposite performance characteristics as buying a put: unlimited risk and limited potential. (Again, not *absolutely* unlimited risk, as the furthest your short put can be driven into the money is if the stock goes to zero.)

Still, investors are attracted to the prospects of earning time decay dollars in a bullish to neutral position. As with selling naked calls, your account is credited for the initial sale of the option and your brokerage requires collateral to cover the position.

Naked put writers rely on stops to help them control the risk from a downward move in the stock if they are not interested in owning shares of

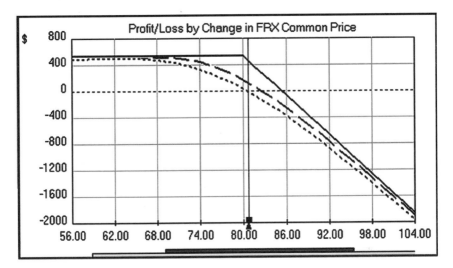

FIGURE 2.6 Short Covered Put

the underlying. That works fine as long as the stock trades continuously. But since a stock can sometimes close at one price and open the next day at a very different price, this kind of risk cannot be completely controlled using stops.

The performance graph for the short naked put illustrates this strategy's unlimited risk, limited potential, and shows that it makes money as long as the stock price does not go down (see Figure 2.7).

LONG PUT WITH LONG STOCK

This strategy, often called a *married put* or *protective put*, is considered the most effective way of hedging long stock positions, as it absolutely limits the downside risk. The only other way of hedging long stock positions using options is to sell covered calls, but this only brings in a finite amount of cash, and therefore only compensates for the stock dropping a certain amount. With puts, stocks may drop indefinitely, and those puts will keep on increasing to compensate.

Fund managers, unwilling to sell their stock (often for tax reasons), sometimes buy puts to see their positions through what they think might be a rough period. However, note that it costs money to buy those puts, and that subtracts from a fund's overall returns. And if the fund manager wants continued protection after the puts expire, he'll need to buy more.

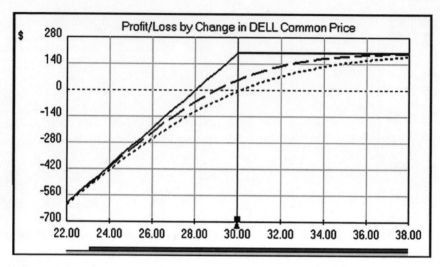

FIGURE 2.7 Short Naked Put

The performance graph for long put with long stock illustrates this strategy's limited risk and unlimited potential (see Figure 2.8).

I have often touted the buying of protective puts during bear markets, especially the great bear market that began in 2000. It's a shame how many investors passively watched their stock portfolios shrink in value when they could have been more active. Using puts, they could have protected their capital. We'll visit this topic again in Chapter 5.

EQUIVALENT STRATEGIES

The performance curve for all options is one basic shape—flat to the out-of-the-money side and sloping 45 degrees to the in-the-money-side. There is only one basic shape, and only four ways of showing it—flipped top to bottom and/or flipped left to right. The performance curve of a long put is the same as that of a long call, only mirror-imaged left to right. The performance curve of a short option position is the same as that of a long option position, only mirror-imaged top to bottom.

While discussing the eight basic options strategies, if it seemed like you saw each performance graph twice, in fact, you did. The performance curve of a stock position is a straight line at 45 degrees. So when a complementary stock position is added to an option position, the stock's 45-degree line combines with the option's line to rock the line in

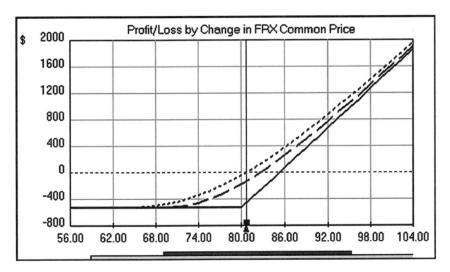

FIGURE 2.8 Long Put with Long Stock

such a way that the flat-line portion becomes a 45-degree portion, and the 45-degree portion becomes a flat line.

Therefore, each of the four single-option strategies not involving stock has a counterpart with an identical performance curve that *does* involve stock. For example, the long call and long put long stock strategies have identical curves. Table 2.1 summarizes the equivalent strategies.

How does one decide whether to use a single-option strategy or its counterpart involving the stock? Well, certainly, if one is in an existing stock position he wants to keep, the correct approach would be to add the appropriate option to the position. But what if the investor is constructing a new position from scratch?

A position involving the stock requires more capital and involves more transactions—two to get in and two to get out. Also, shorting stock has its limitations (the up-tick rule and how many shares are available to borrow). Therefore, the single-option strategy is often preferable, because it usually accomplishes the same objective and requires less capital.

TABLE 2.1 Strategies

Single-Option Strategy	Equivalent Multi-Option Strategy
Long call	Long put long stock
Short naked put	Short covered call
Short naked call	Short covered put
Long put	Long call short stock

It is possible to visually add together the performance graphs of two sim-ple positions to arrive at the performance graph of a combined position. This process is intuitive. For example, when you add the performance graph of long stock (ramping upward to the right) to that of short stock (ramping downward to the right), the result is a flat horizontal line. This is the correct result, because a long stock position and a short stock position cancel each other out (presuming the same number of shares, of course). (See Figures 2.9 to 2.11.)

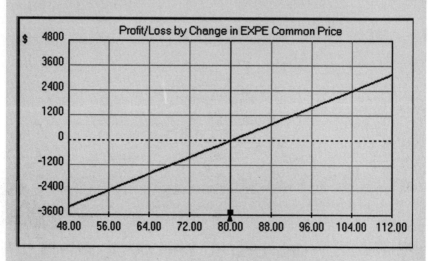

FIGURE 2.9 Long Stock

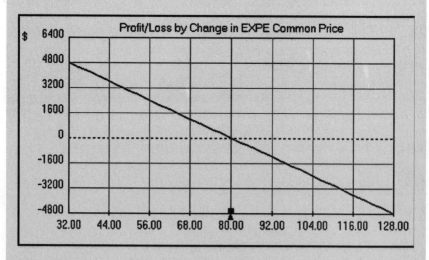

FIGURE 2.10 Short Stock

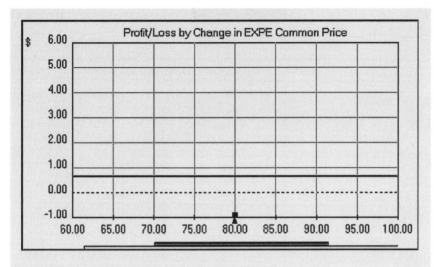

FIGURE 2.11 Combined

When an option is involved, there are two line segments to think about, one to either side of the *inflection point*—the point where the option's performance line suddenly changes slope. For instance, consider adding the performance graph of a short call to that of long stock. (See Figures 2.12 and 2.13.) Left of the inflection point, the option's performance is a flat, horizontal line. When added to the stock's down-sloping line (to the left) in that same section of the graph, the result is still a down-sloping line (to the left), because adding a flat, horizontal line to any other line does nothing to change the shape of the other line. (See Figure 2.14.)

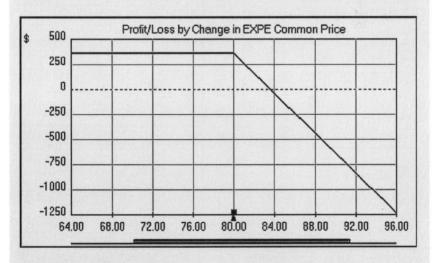

FIGURE 2.12 Short Call

(Continued)

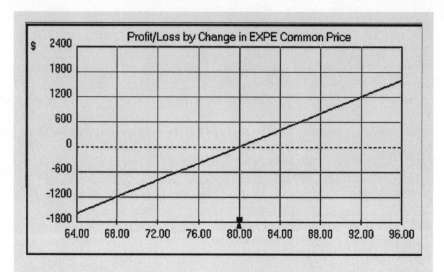

FIGURE 2.13 Long Stock

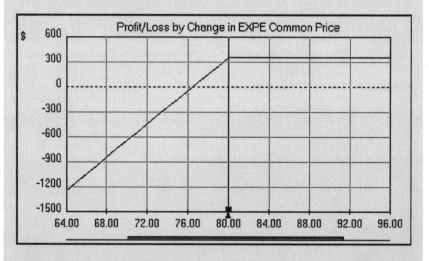

FIGURE 2.14 Combined

Right of the inflection point, the downward slope of the option's performance line cancels out the upward slope of the long stock's performance line, with the result that the combined position's performance is a flat horizontal line in that section.

COMBINATIONAL STRATEGIES

Having discussed single-option strategies, it's time to begin introducing the multi-option strategies. However, rather than marching on in the same style, we're going to introduce the multi-option strategies in a less formal manner over the next several chapters. The single-option strategies were covered in a formal manner for the express purpose of planting the shape of each single-option performance curve firmly in your mind. When we start putting two or more options together, you'll see their combined performance curves form new and interesting shapes.

Combinational strategies involve taking positions in two or more different options and, possibly, in the underlying as well. Each strategy is a unique tool. Like combining hydrogen and oxygen to form a unique substance (water), putting options together in various combinations results in some amazingly unique risk/reward profiles.

For example, the sale of a naked at-the-money option is a very risky strategy, and the purchase of an out-of-the-money option has a poor probability of success. However, combining these trades (using two options that are of the same type and in the same expiration month) forms a *credit spread*—one of the safest and most successful strategies there is. (See Figure 2.15 for an example put credit spread's performance graph.)

Another example is the *long straddle*. Buy an at-the-money call or put and the chances are good that you will lose all your money (stops notwithstanding). However, buy both a call and a put at the same strike price and

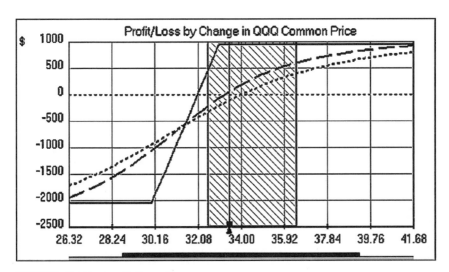

FIGURE 2.15 Credit Spread

expiration month, and the possibility of losing all your money is practically nil (the underlying would have to finish precisely on the strike price). (See Figure 2.16.)

A straddle is a nifty (and popular) strategy to use when you expect a stock to make a big price move to the upside or to the downside—you just don't know which.

Note that no strategy automatically makes money. New options traders often imagine there is a magical combination that will produce positive returns over the long term. There is not. Since each (fairly valued) option has a net zero expected return, no matter how many of them you put together, you will still have a net zero expected return.

Any combination of fairly valued options is a fairly valued combination. By definition, fair value means neither the buyer nor the seller has an advantage. So, to make money, either your model must reveal that the options are mispriced (which happens pretty often), or you have a directional prediction that comes true. Note that your directional prediction might be complicated—for example, "The stock will either break out strongly to the upside or drift lower." By the way, the best strategy for this kind of prediction would be a call *backspread*. We'll discuss backspreads in detail later on.

Since no particular strategy is suitable for every opportunity, the trader needs to be able to apply the most appropriate strategy in any given situation. This requires familiarity with all the various strategies and how they perform. Tables and diagrams that show which option strategies are

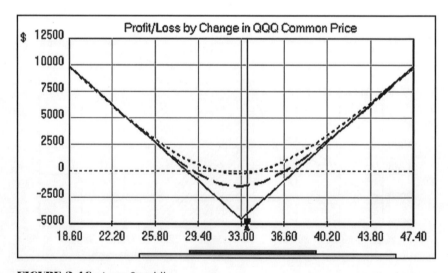

FIGURE 2.16 Long Straddle

bullish, bearish, aggressive, moderate, or neutral are somewhat useful, but often fail to account for *all three* primary considerations: price direction, time frame, and volatility. A feel for how the various strategies perform is best gained through experience, and may be accelerated by the use of software that can simulate the performance of any strategy in all three of these dimensions.

When I stated that options are mispriced fairly often, I was referring not to the idea that one individual option is mispriced, but to the concept that *all* the options of a given asset are sometimes too expensive or too cheap. It is rare that an individual option is mispriced, and when it happens it is usually such a short-lived event that you would never catch it.

However, it is easy to find situations when all the options of an asset are collectively expensive or cheap. Buying cheap options and/or selling expensive options is called *volatility trading*, and we cover this reliable approach in the next chapter. In fact, before we say anything further about strategies, let's talk about volatility . . .

CHAPTER 3

Volatility

When trading a security or a futures contract, you have one overriding concern: its price. However, options are more like a 3-D chess game, with the three dimensions being price (of the underlying), time, and volatility. Of these, volatility is probably the most misunderstood and neglected dimension, and often the last thing a novice trader learns about.

An options trader needs to understand volatility and appreciate its effects to be successful. Option prices are highly sensitive to the perceived volatility of their underlying. The savvy options trader is aware of current volatility levels and adapts his trading accordingly, buying options when they are cheap, and finding ways to sell options when they are expensive. This gives him an advantage over traders who do not understand volatility. How much of an advantage? Sometimes an enormous one.

For example, Figure 3.1 shows a six-year history of volatility for Eastman Kodak. The two lines represent two different measures of volatility. We'll be discussing these soon, but for now, notice how high the dashed line is currently. It is at 48%—practically matching an all-time high for the six-year period. This means options are more expensive now than they have been in the past.

Just to give you an idea, the near-term, ATM (at-the-money) Kodak call option is priced at 2.0 right now, compared with a more normal 1.25. You could say that option buyers are facing a stiff theoretical disadvantage here! So rather than buying options, you would prefer to use a strategy that involves selling these options.

For instance, say you're bullish on Kodak. Rather than buying calls,

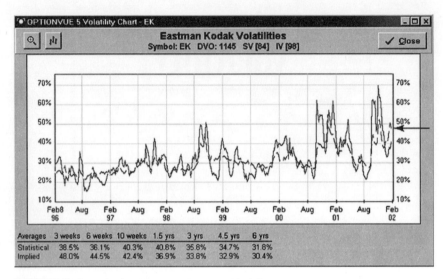

FIGURE 3.1   Volatility History—Eastman Kodak

you might consider selling naked puts, or using a vertical credit spread in puts. We'll be discussing vertical spreads in the next chapter, but for now, let's just say that a vertical credit spread makes you a net seller. Or, if you're *conservatively* bullish, you might consider a covered write. All of these approaches allow you to sell options as you construct a bullish position.

Bottom line: Pay attention to what's happening with volatility. Each time you analyze an asset, check whether today's volatility reading is higher or lower than usual. If it is higher than usual, you may sell options with greater confidence. If it is lower than usual, you can feel free to buy options, knowing that you're getting a bargain. Current volatility readings are available in any good options analysis software. The options trader who ignores volatility trades foolishly.

VOLATILITY TRADING—BUYING AND SELLING VOLATILITY

Many sophisticated options traders go beyond just keeping an eye on volatility, choosing to focus on volatility as the main aspect of their trading. How do they do this, and why?

The essence of volatility-based trading, or V-trading for short, is buying options when they are cheap and selling options when they are dear. The reason it's called volatility-based trading comes from the way we measure cheapness or dearness—using a parameter called *implied volatility*, or IV for short. Soon we'll say exactly what IV is, but for the moment, it will suffice to say that high IV is synonymous with expensive options and low IV is synonymous with cheap options.

Actually, there are two ways of judging the cheapness or dearness of options. The first is simply by comparing current IV with past levels of IV on the same underlying asset. The second is by comparing current implied volatility with the volatility of the underlying itself. Both approaches are important and come into play in all V-trading decisions. The most attractive opportunities are when options are cheap or dear by *both* measures.

The V-trader typically uses puts and calls in combination, selecting the most appropriate strikes, durations, and quantities to construct a position that is said to be *delta-neutral*. A delta-neutral position has nearly zero exposure to small price changes in the underlying. Sometimes the trader has a directional opinion and deliberately biases his position in favor of the expected underlying trend. However, more often the V-trader is focused on making money just from volatility and is not interested in trying to make money from underlying price changes.

Once a position is on, it may need adjusting at times to reestablish the appropriate delta. These adjustments can be costly in terms of transaction costs and should be minimized, but not to the point where you expose yourself to too much delta risk.

Once volatility returns to a more normal, average level, the position can be closed. If not many adjustments were required in the meantime, the trader should see a profit.

Since options are so sensitive to volatility, trading options on the basis of volatility can be lucrative. Occasionally, options become *way* too expensive or *way* too cheap. In these situations the V-trader has a *considerable* edge.

The options trader can always count on volatility returning to normal levels after going to an extreme. This principle is called the *mean reversion tendency of volatility*, and it is the foundation of volatility-based trading. That volatilities "mean revert" is well established in academic writings.[1] You can also see it for yourself by looking at a few historical volatility charts. You will notice that when volatility goes to an extreme level, it always comes back to normal. Sometimes it doesn't happen right away. It may take anywhere from days to months, but sooner or later it always comes back.

---

[1]Michael Dueker, "Mean Reversion in Stock Market Volatility," 1994; H. Schaller, "A Panel Data Test for Mean Reversion Using Randomization," 1993 (http://econpapers. hhs.se/paper/carcarecp/93-04.htm); T. Bollerslev, "Long-term Equity Anticipation Securities and Stock Market Volatility Dynamics," 1996 (http://econpapers.hhs.se/ paper/fthtinber/96-33.htm); Galen Burghardt and Morton Lane, "How to Tell if Options Are Cheap," 1990.

Implied volatilities seem to change from week to week, if not day to day. V-traders find profit opportunities in this.

TOOLS OF THE V-TRADE

As was mentioned earlier, we measure how expensive or cheap options are using a parameter called *implied volatility*, or IV for short. The term *implied volatility* comes from the fact that options imply the volatility of their underlying, just by their price. A computer model starts with the actual market price of an option, and measures IV by working the option fair value model backward, solving for volatility (normally an input) as if it were the unknown. (Actually, the fair value model cannot be worked backward. It has to be worked forward repeatedly through a series of intelligent guesses until the volatility is found that makes fair value equal to the actual market price of the option.)

Again, high IV is synonymous with expensive options; low IV is synonymous with cheap options. It can be useful to plot an asset's IV over a period of years to see the extent of its highs and lows, as well as what constitutes a normal, or average, level.

We measure how much the price of an asset bounces around using a parameter called *statistical volatility*, or SV for short. There are several different computer models for measuring SV. All of them seek to quantify the extent, or magnitude, of the asset's price swings on a percentage basis, and use varying periods of the asset's recent price history (for example, 10, 20, or 30 days). SV can also be plotted, so that the investor can see the periods of relative price activity and inactivity over time.

Much of the options trading community refers to this as historical volatility, but we at OptionVue Systems prefer to call it statistical volatility, reserving the word *historical* for when we are referring to the history of both IV and SV.

Regardless of the length of the sample period, when we compute SV, we always normalize the number to represent a one-year, single standard deviation price move of the underlying asset. IV is normalized in the same way. Thus IV and SV are directly comparable, and it is very useful to see them plotted together.

It is customary to state volatility levels as percentages. Don't let this confuse you. Volatility is just a number. For example, if the number resulting from calculating SV or IV is 0.27, you would commonly see it expressed as 27%.

What does this number relate to in the real world? Truthfully, volatility does not relate to anything tangible. It is just a number, and it only relates to other volatility numbers. However, I'll give you something to hang your hat on that is *roughly* correct. Note that volatility is the percentage standard deviation of price changes. Therefore, as an example, when a stock is 100 and its volatility is 27%, this would indicate that in the coming year this stock's price should be in a range from 73 ($100 \times (1 - 0.27)$) to 136 ($100/(1 - 0.27)$) roughly 68% of the time. (From statistics, a standard deviation encompasses 68% of the data samples.)

SELLING HIGH VOLATILITY

When the options of a particular asset are more expensive than usual, it is sometimes justified by unusually high volatility in the underlying. While it may be a decent opportunity to sell options in this case, it is even more advantageous to sell options when the extra IV is *not* accompanied by extra SV. One example of this kind of situation was the gold/silver index (XAU) in October 2002 (see Figure 3.2). IV (represented by the dashed line) was at a relatively high level, but these high IV levels were not supported, or justified, by a correspondingly high SV.

Clearly, the advantage is with the trader who sells this high volatility, and that means selling options. Generally, any position in which you are short more options than you are long is also short volatility. The purest way to sell volatility is to sell a *naked strangle*, which involves selling out-of-the-money calls and out-of-the-money puts. Some traders also like to buy farther out-of-the-money calls and puts at the same time for protection (thus creating credit

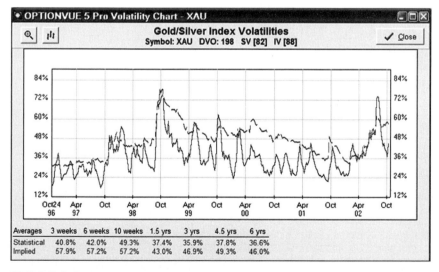

Averages	3 weeks	6 weeks	10 weeks	1.5 yrs	3 yrs	4.5 yrs	6 yrs
Statistical	40.8%	42.0%	49.3%	37.4%	35.9%	37.8%	36.6%
Implied	57.9%	57.2%	57.2%	43.0%	46.9%	49.3%	46.0%

FIGURE 3.2 IV and SV Levels—Gold/Silver Index

spreads), but this considerably weakens the position's vega, or sensitivity to volatility. We want a substantial vega, so that when IV eventually comes down, our position makes money. See Figure 3.3 for the matrix of XAU options, including a naked strangle constructed by selling 5 calls and 7 puts. For each option, the figure shows the price, IV, and potential trade.

We are using an unequal number of calls and puts because no puts could be found that were the same price as the calls. After locating some puts that were of a somewhat lower price than the calls, we determined, with the help of the software, that 7 of the puts would appropriately balance out the position in 5 calls, to give us a delta-neutral position to start with. See Figure 3.4 for the graphic analysis of this short strangle position.

We constructed this position using options expiring in 71 days. You can see from the three time lines that this position develops a profit over time. If held all the way to expiration, both options expire worthless (your best outcome) if the index is between 55 and 70. As you are receiving approximately 6 points of credit for selling the strangle, the two breakeven points for this strategy are at roughly 6 points below 55, or 49, and at 6 points above 70, or 76. More precise breakeven values can be seen in the lower left area of the figure.

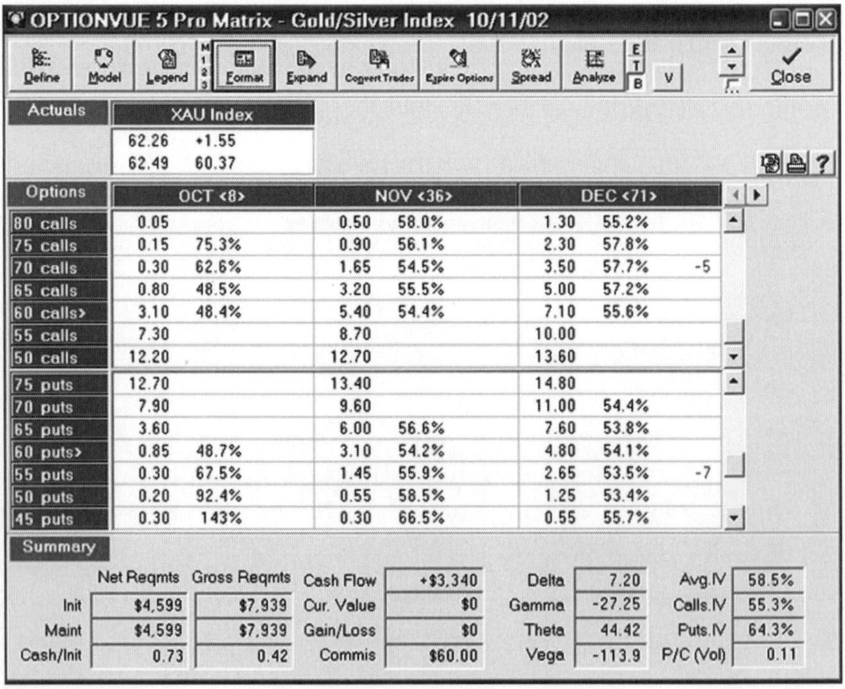
OPTIONVUE 5 Pro Matrix - Gold/Silver Index 10/11/02

Define | Model | Legend | Format | Expand | Convert Trades | Expire Options | Spread | Analyze | V | Close

Actuals	XAU Index	
	62.26	+1.55
	62.49	60.37

Options	OCT <8>		NOV <36>		DEC <71>		
80 calls	0.05		0.50	58.0%	1.30	55.2%	
75 calls	0.15	75.3%	0.90	56.1%	2.30	57.8%	
70 calls	0.30	62.6%	1.65	54.5%	3.50	57.7%	-5
65 calls	0.80	48.5%	3.20	55.5%	5.00	57.2%	
60 calls>	3.10	48.4%	5.40	54.4%	7.10	55.6%	
55 calls	7.30		8.70		10.00		
50 calls	12.20		12.70		13.60		
75 puts	12.70		13.40		14.80		
70 puts	7.90		9.60		11.00	54.4%	
65 puts	3.60		6.00	56.6%	7.60	53.8%	
60 puts>	0.85	48.7%	3.10	54.2%	4.80	54.1%	
55 puts	0.30	67.5%	1.45	55.9%	2.65	53.5%	-7
50 puts	0.20	92.4%	0.55	58.5%	1.25	53.4%	
45 puts	0.30	143%	0.30	66.5%	0.55	55.7%	

Summary

	Net Reqmts	Gross Reqmts						
			Cash Flow	+$3,340	Delta	7.20	Avg.IV	58.5%
Init	$4,599	$7,939	Cur. Value	$0	Gamma	-27.25	Calls.IV	55.3%
Maint	$4,599	$7,939	Gain/Loss	$0	Theta	44.42	Puts.IV	64.3%
Cash/Init	0.73	0.42	Commis	$60.00	Vega	-113.9	P/C (Vol)	0.11

FIGURE 3.3 Matrix of Options—Gold/Silver Index

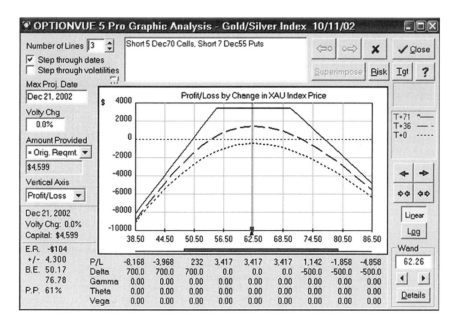

FIGURE 3.4 Short Strangle Position—Graphic Analysis

The strangle need not be held all the way to expiration, however. While the position benefits from time decay, it benefits even faster from a drop in IV levels, should that happen. If we projected a not-too-unreasonable 10 percentage point drop in IV, from the current 57% down to 47% (this projection is made subjectively by the trader, as he views the historical volatility chart), we see that this position may be closed out at the halfway point (36 days from now) for a significant profit—as much as $2,100 on a $4,600 investment. (See Figure 3.5.)

Whether held to expiration or closed early, this position has a significant edge from inception because we are selling overvalued calls and puts.

Out-of-the-money options are preferable in a strangle trade because it gives the underlying some room to wander and increases the likelihood of realizing a profit. Generally, the farther out-of-the-money you go, the lower your returns, but the greater the probability of achieving those returns. By giving the underlying room to move, the trader minimizes his chances of having to make costly adjustments.

One other strategy for selling volatility (but which cannot apply to index options, unfortunately) is covered writing, which involves buying stock, or futures contracts, and selling calls. However, covered writing is not delta-neutral and, since it usually involves the ownership of a portfolio of stocks, it is in a camp by itself. There are many mutual funds and indi-

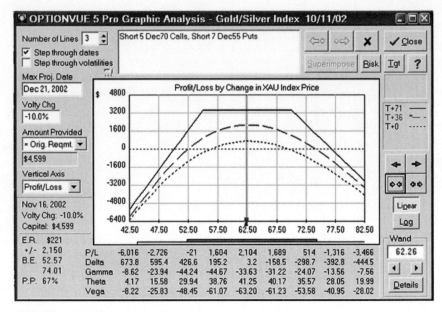

FIGURE 3.5 Effects of 10 Percent Drop in IV

vidually managed covered writing programs. Managers of these funds do well to pay attention to IV levels in timing the sale of their calls.

When selling volatility, it is best to use the longest-term options available, provided they have decent liquidity. Longer-term options have higher vega and will respond best when IV comes down. Longer-term options have the additional advantage of having a lower gamma. As noted in Chapter 1, gamma measures how fast delta changes with price changes in the underlying. By using lower gamma options, it takes a bigger price change in the underlying to imbalance your position.

BUYING LOW VOLATILITY

Low volatility situations can be just as lucrative. I have heard arguments against buying options because time decay is against you. Time decay is a funny concept. Do you remember using "imaginary numbers" in math class to deal with the square roots of negative numbers? Time decay (measured as theta) is kind of like that. It's an imaginary number. It says that if the underlying asset's price holds perfectly still, the option will decay at a certain rate. But what underlying asset price holds still? None, obviously. In fact, time is what gives the asset its freedom to move!

I may have a short volatility position, and let's say it has a theta of 100. This means I'm making $100 dollars per day from time decay. Should I feel gratified to see this? Not really. It's a false gratification, because today's movement in the underlying could easily take away $100 or more.

There is nothing wrong with buying options. When an option is fairly valued, by definition there is no advantage to the buyer or the seller. If you buy a fairly valued option, you have not taken on an implicitly disadvantaged position. Why? Because, despite the option's time decay, the underlying is in constant motion.

The situation in orange juice options in the spring of 2002 is a good example of extremely low volatility (see Figure 3.6). Current IV was approximately 15%, way below normal levels and the lowest it had been in five years. Computer simulations showed that when orange juice's IV returned to a more normal 24 to 32%, the long-dated orange juice options would approximately double in price. In this situation the recommended strategy would be to buy calls and puts in a straddle or strangle purchase.

A straddle, remember, is a popular strategy formed by buying both calls and puts on the same underlying, at the same strike and in the same expiration month. A strangle is like a straddle, except that it allows the calls and puts to have different strike prices. In Figure 3.7, we have entered a prospective straddle in the long-dated orange juice options.

Once again using an unequal number of puts and calls in order to con-

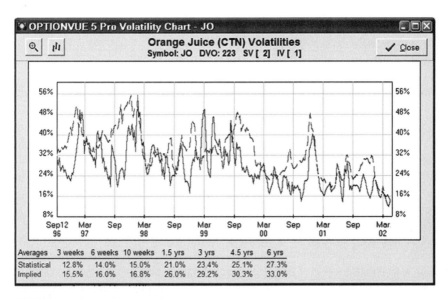

FIGURE 3.6 Low Volatility

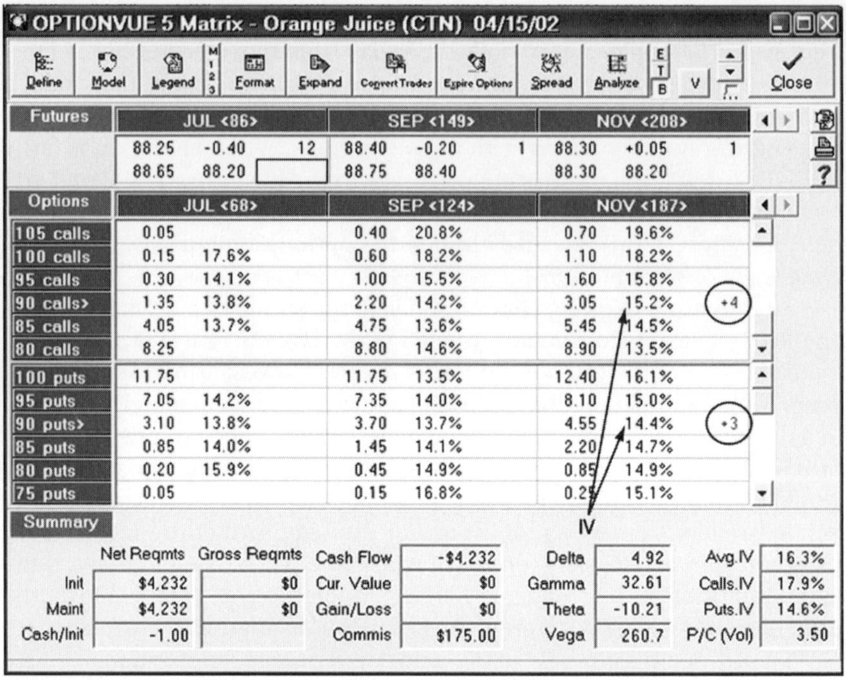

FIGURE 3.7 Example of Straddle

struct a delta-neutral position, the position costs $4,200 to put on. The average IV of the options we're buying is 14.8%—making the options a veritable bargain by recent standards.

Figure 3.8 shows the graphic analysis of this position, with the midterm line highlighted—the line representing the theoretical profit/loss of the position halfway to expiration (94 days from now). Thus, the numbers along the bottom and in the lower left area reflect this midterm scenario. From looking at the historical volatility chart, we felt it reasonable to expect IV to go up 10 percentage points by this time frame. Therefore we entered a +10 in the Volty Chg field, and the analysis reflects this projected increase. While there is no guarantee that IV will go up 10 percentage points, if it does, the model shows that our investment has a 94% probability of profit, making it truly an excellent trade!

When buying options, it makes sense to buy near-the-money. That way, a sharp move in the underlying has a better chance of helping the position. When that happens, not only does IV normally receive a boost, driving up the value of both sides, but the move may also drive one of the sides deep in-the-money and give you a gain just from price movement.

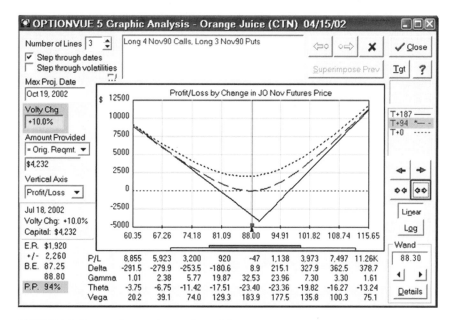

FIGURE 3.8 Graphic Analysis of Straddle

Of course, this price movement might not happen right away, but use of the longer-term options should help allow plenty of time. When buying volatility, just as when selling volatility, my advice is to use the longest-dated options you can find that give you decent liquidity. The reason is the same: high vega. The long-dated options, with their higher vega, will respond the best when IV increases.

It is notable that long volatility positions have a completely different feel than short volatility positions. Short volatility positions usually gratify the holder with steady, almost daily, gains, but can suddenly lose money if the underlying makes a sharp move. Long volatility positions can dribble away value day by day for many weeks, then suddenly gain very quickly. Despite their opposite psychological feels, a mix of both types of positions belongs in the V-trader's portfolio.

Deciding when to close a long volatility position can be a challenge. If a move in the underlying has caused your position to show a gain, it has probably imbalanced your position. One leg is now stronger than the other, and the dominant leg is more sensitive to changes in the underlying. The first thing to consider is whether volatility has returned to normal levels. If it has, you should consider closing the position. If it has not, you might consider continuing with an adjusted (rebalanced) position.

There are many ways to adjust the position. A small adjustment can be made by simply buying or selling one or more contracts of the same options you already have in the existing position. A larger adjustment can be made by closing one leg and reopening it at a new strike. Or sometimes it's better to simply close your position and open a completely new one. If you do this, you may want to consider changing expiration months as well, to give yourself more time.

There is no science about deciding which kind of adjustment is best in any particular circumstance. The correct adjustment to make is the one that leaves you completely comfortable with the new position going forward.

DELTA-NEUTRAL TRADING—IN A NUTSHELL

The type of V-trading we've been discussing so far is called delta-neutral trading. It is the main type of V-trading. To recap, you begin by opening a long straddle (or strangle) in an asset whose implied volatility is low (i.e., cheap options), or a short straddle (or strangle) in an asset whose implied volatility is high (i.e., expensive options). (Please note that the latter would be naked writing, and for this, the investor would need to thoroughly understand the risks.) In the absence of any directional bias with regard to the underlying, you would open this position "delta-neutral" by selecting the appropriate strikes and quantities of each leg in such a way as to create a position that, theoretically, gains or loses nothing with a small change in the price of the underlying.

Note that options analysis software is needed for modeling and what-iffing positions this way. It would be next to impossible to do delta-neutral trading without it.

Over time, the underlying price naturally moves away from the starting place, throwing your original position out of balance. A small amount of delta should probably be tolerated, because the transaction costs associated with keeping the position perfectly delta-neutral would eat away at profits. However, when delta moves an uncomfortable distance from zero, the trader needs to consider making an adjustment.

Note that in the case of being *long* a straddle, technical traders might want to leave an imbalanced position alone if they feel that the strong leg of the straddle (and therefore delta as well) favors a new trend in the underlying. On the other hand, pure volatility traders will want to adjust.

Your position may be closed when implied volatility returns to normal levels, as judged by viewing a historical volatility chart. If not too many adjustments were necessary during the life of the position, you should normally be able to post a profit.

To find good candidates for delta-neutral trading, you need some kind of system for screening and finding assets whose implied volatility is extremely low or high right now. Some options-oriented web sites provide this kind of service for a reasonable fee. It can also be found in the software and services that OptionVue Systems provides.

SEASONAL PATTERNS IN THE GRAINS

In general, V-traders buy cheap options and sell expensive options, as opportunities arise, hoping that IV soon returns to average levels and they can realize a profit. It's an extra bonus when the cycles of nature come into play and lend an element of predictability to the timing.

Not many assets exhibit a seasonal pattern. However, a strong and regular seasonal pattern exists in the grains that can be exploited. In the dead of winter, corn and soybean prices, for example, are usually stable and their options are cheap. With the onset of spring, IV begins to rise. It continues to rise throughout the spring, reaching a peak sometime during the summer when uncertainty surrounding crop yields is at maximum, and when the slightest change in the weather forecast sends tremors through the markets. Then, beginning in late summer or early fall, IV comes tumbling back down again. The magnitude of the cycle is significant, with summer IV levels often double those of winter. Figures 3.9 and 3.10 show six-year historical volatility charts for corn and soybeans.

The cycle can be played both ways. Let's discuss buying low IV in the wintertime first. From examining the charts, it would seem that IV usually begins ramping up in February, suggesting that February might be the best time for buying a straddle. However, are we sure it should be a straddle? Note that rising IV has usually been accompanied by rising prices in recent years, suggesting that we might consider just buying calls.

Consider soybeans for a moment. From the charts, I notice that whenever the cycle begins with soybean prices being near their multiyear floor level of around 440, it turns out you would have been better off just buying calls. Otherwise, it was safer to buy both calls and puts, as soybean prices were just as likely to fall as rise if their starting point was above, say, 480. Note that once, in the summer of 1999, soybeans' IV spike coincided with a price collapse. In corn, it would seem that the best approach is always to buy a straddle, as a floor price is harder to discern in that commodity.

Both corn and soybeans are amazingly regular, at least in recent years, in the level to which IV goes in the summer. When you see IV go above 30% (the same for both, remarkably), you can sell your long position and get ready to play the downside of the cycle. Before we look at the downside of

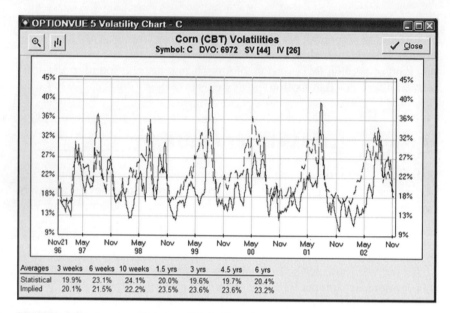

FIGURE 3.9 Seasonal Pattern of Volatility—Corn

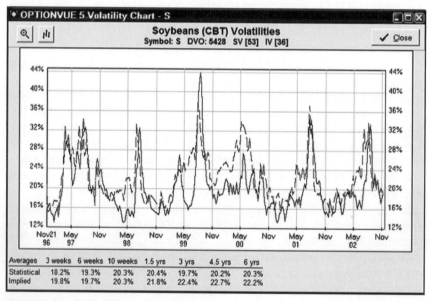

FIGURE 3.10 Seasonal Pattern of Volatility—Soybeans

the cycle, however, why don't we take a look at how well the upside strategy would have paid off recently?

Table 3.1 shows what could have been achieved in the spring/summer of 2001 and 2002 using this strategy. All four trades were initiated in mid-February. Since soybean prices were near 440 in mid-February both times, we simulated buying calls instead of straddles. In this study, the timing of the exits was admittedly optimized with the benefit of hindsight, so actual results may not be as good (unless you're one of those people who can sense the perfect time to exit). The results nevertheless illustrate the potential of this strategy.

Note the use of September options. This is recommended because it allows time in case the peak arrives late in the season. Also note that the options bought were at-the-money or very nearly at-the-money. That is conservative. You could just as well consider using out-of-the-money options (especially on the call side), shooting for better returns, because with the arrival of summer one usually sees a radical skew in grain options, giving the out-of-the-monies an amazing boost. (We haven't discussed the concept of skew yet, but we will shortly.)

Now let's turn our attention to the downside of the cycle. Shortly after closing your long straddle (or just calls, if that's all you bought), it is time to consider selling the high IV. This is best done by selling naked strangles. I wouldn't use credit spreads (in both calls and puts) because, although it limits your risk, it also limits your potential. I prefer to manage risk by keeping a close watch on the position and possibly rolling out one of the legs if it goes in-the-money.

Table 3.2 shows what could have been achieved in the summers of 2001 and 2002 by selling naked strangles in corn and soybeans. The results are shown in dollar terms this time because, with naked options positions, it is important to consider margin requirements. Contrary to the principle espoused earlier of using long-term options, we felt compelled to use the

TABLE 3.1 Upside Strategy

Commodity	Strategy	Description	Date Opened	Opening Price	Date Closed	Closing Price	Price Change
Corn	Buy straddle	Sep 240	2/16/01	37.5	6/25/01	49	+11.5
Corn	Buy straddle	Sep 230	2/15/02	32	8/14/02	43.5	+11.5
Soybeans	Buy call	Sep 480	2/16/01	23.75	7/17/01	56.5	+32.75
Soybeans	Buy call	Sep 480	2/15/02	19	8/14/02	112	+93.0

TABLE 3.2 Downside Strategy

	Date Opened	Credit	Gross Reqmt.	Net Reqmt.	Date Closed	Gain/Loss
Corn Sell 10 Sep 250 Calls Sell 10 Sep 210 Puts	07/17/01	$5,875	$8,800	$2,950	08/24/01	$5,875
Corn Sell 10 Sep 260 Calls Sell 10 Sep 230 Puts	07/26/02	$4,500	$7,950	$3,450	08/13/02	$190
Closed above and rolled into Sell 10 Sep 280 Calls Sell 10 Sep 260 Puts	08/13/02	$1,500	$6,600	$5,100	08/23/02	$1,500
Soybeans Sell 10 Sep 520 Calls Sell 10 Sep 470 Puts	08/03/01	$5,200	$11,900	$6,700	08/24/01	$5,200
Soybeans Sell 10 Sep 590 Calls Sell 10 Sep 530 Puts	08/02/02	$9,250	$14,770	$5,500	08/23/02	$9,250

nearby options because they were the only ones showing an IV of 30%+. The farther-out options had so much lower IVs—for example, 22% to 24%—that they weren't worth selling. One of the corn strangles, and both of the soybean strangles, could be held all the way to expiration without adjustment, expiring worthless, so our gains in those trades were precisely equal to the initial credits received. The corn strangle of 2002 ran into trouble, however, when corn prices rose above the strike price of the initial calls. So the initial strangle was closed for a small gain and a new, balanced strangle was opened the same day. The new strangle expired worthless in just 11 days. These tables include a conservative commissions estimate of $25 per contract.

From Tables 3.1 and 3.2, you can see that trading the seasonal corn and soybean cycle could have been very profitable the last two years. While not guaranteed to be profitable every year (and certainly a longer-period study would be helpful), from this you can begin to see why trading the annual cycles in corn and soybeans is one of my favorite strategies.

OTHER COMMODITIES

While not as regular as the grains, orange juice has a seasonal pattern as well, with IV often reaching its highest levels in late December. (See Figure 3.11.) Perhaps more important would be the observation that orange

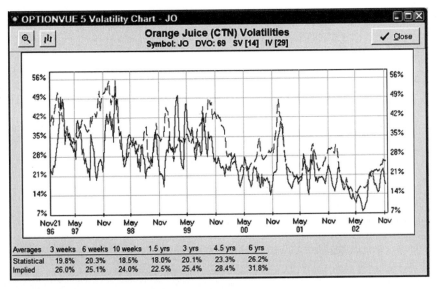

FIGURE 3.11 Seasonal Volatility of Orange Juice

juice's IV fluctuates a lot. After falling to a low extreme, it's not very long before IV goes back up, and after reaching a high extreme, you can usually count on IV coming back down before long. For the V-trader, this is a desirable trait.

Another good asset for V-trading, with frequent IV fluctuations and a good base IV level of about 30%, is crude oil. (See Figure 3.12.)

Also worth mentioning is natural gas, which often peaks in the winter but can also shoot up at other times during the year. Buying IV every time it falls to the apparent floor level of 40% looks like a decent ploy. However, be careful about selling high IV in this asset, as it sometimes spikes to *extremely* high levels. I once knew a trader who was ruined when, after he had taken naked short options positions in natural gas, volatility pushed relentlessly higher and he was forced to liquidate at the worst price levels. (See Figure 3.13.)

VOLATILITY SKEW—WHAT IS IT AND HOW CAN I USE IT?

Traders say that volatilities are *skewed* when the options of a given asset trade at increasing or decreasing levels of implied volatility as you move through the strikes.

I'll illustrate using a situation that existed in the gold market at the time

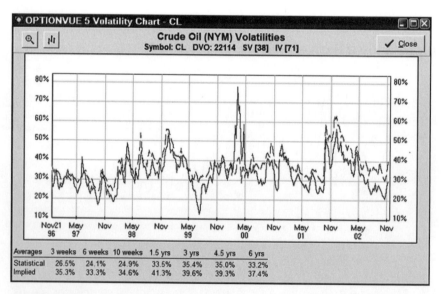

FIGURE 3.12 Seasonal Volatility of Crude Oil

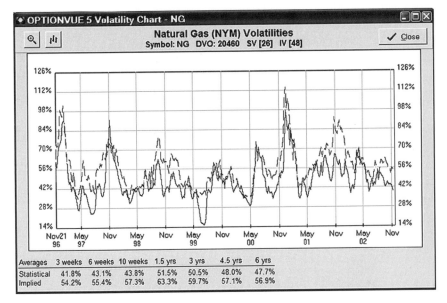

FIGURE 3.13　Seasonal Volatility of Natural Gas

of this writing. (The most significant skew situations seem to happen in the commodities. However, skews also happen in securities and index options, and the principles discussed here apply in those markets just as well.)

The gold situation described here was an outstanding opportunity. It shows what can be done using the dimension of volatility—*a dimension only options can provide.*

The price of gold had jumped 9 percent in a few days, fueled by Japanese investors worried about their country's economic woes. Checking the gold option volatilities, I noticed that there was a large *skew* at the time, with out-of-the-money calls trading at much higher IVs than at-the-money calls. Figure 3.14 shows the price and IV of each option. You can clearly see how the IVs go higher the farther out-of-the-money you go in the calls.

When the skew is this pronounced, it represents an opportunity to construct a position with favorable odds of success. Figure 3.14 portrays an example of a fairly aggressive position that takes advantage of this skew. The position involves selling 10 far out-of-the-money calls (with an IV of 30.3%) and buying one at-the-money call (with an IV of 18.8%) to hedge. The position costs $3,500 to put on. Note that only one of the short calls is covered; the remaining nine are naked. If gold moves higher, more collateral may be required.

The single long option almost overcomes the negative delta of the 10

OPTIONVUE 5 Matrix - Gold (CEC) 02/08/02

Toolbar: Define | Model | Legend | Format | Expand | Convert Trades | Expire Options | Spread | Analyze | B | V | Close

Futures

	MAR <21>		APR <52>			JUN <115>		
	303.90	-1.80	304.40	+3.80	574	304.90	+3.70	2
	305.70	303.90	307.30	302.70		307.80	303.50	

Options

	APR <29>		JUN <92>			AUG <155>	
370 calls	1.10	44.8%	3.00	32.2%		.....	
360 calls	1.40	42.3%	3.50	30.3%	-10	5.00	26.2%
350 calls	1.70	38.8%	4.30	28.8%		5.70	24.6%
340 calls	2.50	37.1%	5.70	28.0%		6.30	22.5%
330 calls	3.00	32.4%	7.00	26.2%		7.90	21.3%
320 calls	4.70	30.6%	8.90	24.5%		10.20	20.4%
310 calls	7.00	27.6%	10.50	21.0%		13.20	19.4%
300 calls>	11.00	25.5%	14.00	18.8%	+1	17.30	18.6%
290 calls	16.30	20.5%	20.30	19.2%		23.50	19.1%
310 puts	12.60	27.7%	15.50	20.9%		17.80	19.3%
300 puts>	6.60	25.4%	9.10	18.8%		12.00	18.5%
290 puts	2.00	20.9%	5.50	19.3%		8.40	19.3%

Summary

	Net Reqmts	Gross Reqmts						
			Cash Flow	+$1,605	Delta	-17.64	Avg.IV	24.1%
Init	$3,514	$5,119	Cur. Value	$0	Gamma	-0.59	Calls.IV	26.0%
Maint	$2,731	$4,336	Gain/Loss	$0	Theta	54.08	Puts.IV	20.2%
Cash/Init	0.46	0.31	Commis	$275.00	Vega	-274.3	P/C (Vol)	1.21

FIGURE 3.14 Skew in the Gold Market

short options, giving us a nearly zero net delta. This is important because it gives us breathing room in case gold moves further to the upside. The one thing that could ruin this position is gold moving *much* higher, and it is important that we be able to respond to such a move by controlling our risk. There is room for gold to move up some without requiring any action, but beyond a certain point we might need to trim our short option position or add more long options.

Figure 3.15 shows the theoretical performance of this amazing position. It is profitable across a wide range of underlying prices. If gold goes nowhere or down, we make $1,600. We make even more if gold moves up modestly. Losses will occur only if gold goes above 370 by expiration.

The software has estimated that the chance of gold going above 370 would be only 1% (referring to the 99% probability of profit [P.P.] in the lower left corner). Still, I would not be that optimistic. The program's projection is based on recent volatility readings, but years of experience in commodities tells me there might be a 5% chance of gold going above 370, and mentally I'm going to be prepared for the possibility of gold doing that. It's better to be conservative.

Opportunities to sell expensive out-of-the-money call options come along fairly often in the commodities markets. In fact, a similar opportu-

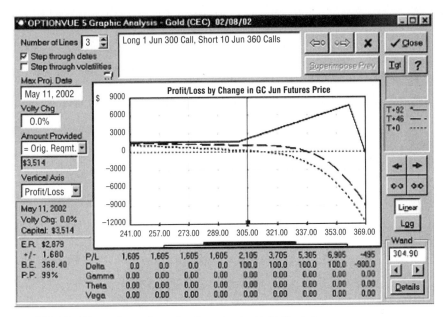

FIGURE 3.15 Profiting from the Skew in the Gold Market

nity also existed in silver at the time of this writing. While some skew always seems to be present in the precious metals options, the skew is often more pronounced just after a minor shock wave moves through. At such a time, speculative fever flares up and tends to inflate all of the call option prices, especially the cheaper, far out-of-the-monies. For example, with the recent jump in the price of gold, advisers are popping up and calling for further action to the upside. I don't know about you, but I'd rather fade them.

Other commodities, such as coffee and orange juice, exhibit tremendous skewing in their call options each year as the potential frost season approaches. I would caution against being too aggressive in shorting naked calls in those markets, however. Once every few years a serious frost *does* hit, and the commodity may jump a high percentage overnight. However, small, conservative positions in these commodities can be rewarding.

The gold market might feel more comfortable for positions like this, because one would think that worldwide supplies should keep a better lid on price. And gold usually provides more opportunities for this kind of trade. It seems like several events per year come along affecting the precious metals markets.

SOME WORDS OF WARNING ABOUT NAKED WRITING

I have seen traders who regularly use naked writing post regular gains for
months and even years on end, and then suddenly and spectacularly blow
out. It happens at times when the market goes to an extreme that no one
has ever seen before. (Of course, it probably *has* happened before; there is
nothing new under the sun. People just don't remember it.)

This doesn't have to happen to you. If you use naked writing, have a
prearranged plan on how you will hedge or reduce your position at certain stages.

In the gold example above, why do you suppose the out-of-the-money
calls jump so dramatically every time there is an event that moves the
price of gold just 10%? For starters, it is because other traders, somewhat
panicked, are getting out of the very kind of position you are considering
getting into. They are covering their short calls, driving the prices up.

You were smart, of course, to have waited for the opportunity to sell at
better prices. But what happens if gold surges higher still? Are you going
to be the one who panics to cover his naked calls at even higher prices? Or
are you going to find a way to reduce your exposure in stages and allow
yourself to stay with the position?

If you decide to stay with your position, plan ahead at each stage what
you'll do if the market moves even further against you. Smart naked writers guard against allowing that one "unthinkable" event to blow them out
of the water.

THE RELATIONSHIP BETWEEN VOLATILITY AND PRICE

Since volatility is measured using *percentage* price variations, higher-
priced assets don't exhibit higher volatilities just because of their higher
price. Therefore, one would think that volatility and price would bear no
correlation. However, it so happens that with most assets, volatility and
price *do* exhibit some degree of correlation. In stocks, the correlation is a
negative one; volatility increases as stock prices decline, and volatility declines as stock prices increase.

The reason volatility increases as stocks decline is presumably because falling stock prices mean deteriorating business conditions,
which translates into higher risk and greater uncertainty. This leads to
greater daily price fluctuations (on a percentage basis) and, thus,
greater volatility.

On the other hand, as stock prices climb, this implies improving
business conditions and greater stability. In that climate, stocks exhibit

smaller daily price fluctuations (on a percentage basis)—in other words, lower volatility.

Would logic dictate that the converse be true? Does a period of low volatility presage a drop in stock prices? While it would be false logic to assume the converse is true, it turns out from historical observation that this is often the case. Does extremely high volatility mark the bottom of a bear market? Again, very often it does.

In Figure 3.16, the solid line represents statistical volatility (how much the price of the Nasdaq-100 shares (QQQ) has bounced around recently). The dashed line represents implied volatility (how much underlying volatility is implied by current option price levels). Also superimposed is a price chart. Notice how often volatility peaks corresponded with market bottoms, and volatility bottoms corresponded with market tops.

So what does this mean to the options trader? How can we profit from this information?

For one thing, volatility can be used as a confirming indicator. When volatility is high, for example, you know that the bottom is probably near. When volatility is low, one should be on guard for a potential breakdown. Also, the low volatility at market tops should make us lean toward buying options at those times, and the high volatility at market bottoms should make us want to sell options then.

When volatility is low, we can watch for signs of a breakdown and go

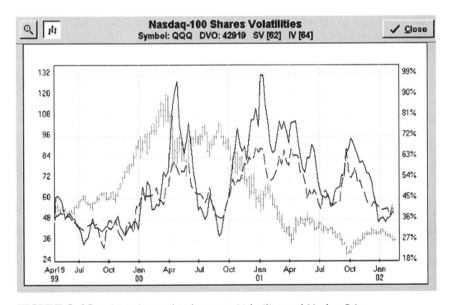

FIGURE 3.16 The Relationship between Volatility and Market Price

short by buying puts. One of the most reliable signals of a breakdown is when the market begins to fall off the right shoulder of a head-and-shoulders formation. If a sell-off actually develops, the originally cheap options will expand from the double barreled effect of falling prices and increasing volatility.

To get more of a bang from a possible volatility increase, one could buy farther out options, as farther out options expand more when volatility increases. The downside is that the farther out options cost more money and respond more slowly to falling prices. However, they are a lower risk position compared with the "fast lane" nearby options. It is important for the trader to take appropriate risks according to his own goals and temperament.

Once prices are falling and the options are expensive, if a trader still wanted to buy puts in anticipation of a further price drop, he could switch to buying nearby options that are deep in-the-money to avoid paying extra for the inflated time premiums. Even when IVs are running high, the deep in-the-money nearbys typically hold very little time premium.

When volatility is high and the options are expensive, but the trader feels that prices are showing signs of bottoming, conditions would suggest going long by selling naked puts. If a rally materializes, the options will quickly lose value from both rising prices and falling volatility.

However, selling naked puts in a down-trending market that you believe is about to reverse is rather like standing on the road in front of oncoming traffic and shouting "Stop!" It might work, but it's kind of scary. To reduce risk (and stress!) to acceptable levels, one could simply take a small position, but that won't make as much money when you're right. Luckily, with options there are several other strategies you could use that allow you to limit the risk to an acceptable level.

One approach would be to use a credit spread in puts. While a credit spread does not respond to declining volatility as well, it does make money in a rising market and limits your risk. Or a vertical debit spread in calls might make sense. Much of the high volatility is neutralized because you're selling an expensive option at the same time that you're buying an expensive option.

If you own, or would like to own, some shares of individual stocks at reduced prices, an approach to consider is the covered combo. With a covered combo, you buy (or already have) shares of the stock. You then sell both calls and naked out-of-the-money puts (1 contract of each for every 100 shares you own). Selling all these expensive options *really* places the odds in your favor. However, note that the short calls place a cap on your stock price appreciation. We'll discuss covered combos in more detail in a later chapter.

In practice, I have found that buying puts at the start of a breakdown is far more rewarding than selling options (naked or covered) at a suspected bottom. Long puts expand in value dramatically during a market sell-off. At a suspected bottom, sometimes I feel more comfortable just buying a few of my favorite stocks. If I feel strongly about my timing, I might even load up with extra shares on margin for a short time. Despite what they say about the risks of buying stock on margin, that can be a less risky approach than some of the options strategies at that juncture.

CHAPTER 4

The Option Trader's Arsenal

O ptions are enormously flexible in the ways you can use them, not only to speculate, but also to hedge or even simulate a portfolio. Through combinational strategies, you can construct a position that closely fits your goals, price predictions, time frame, and the current volatility environment. With options, it is possible to construct a position with almost any kind of performance curve.

It is important for the trader not to fall in love with any particular strategy. The trader must be flexible and take advantage of the opportunities that the market brings. This means using different strategies in different situations.

There are more than 20 different option strategies. Of these, around 18 are of interest to the individual trader, including all the single and dual option strategies, plus one triple option strategy. We'll limit our discussion to these. Other strategies, including some involving four options, are used primarily by market makers and are not practical for the individual trader.

BUYING NEARBY OPTIONS— THE SWING TRADER'S PERFECT TOOL

Years ago, the conventional wisdom was to sell options, placing time decay on your side. In recent years, pundits have made a case for buying options. Lawrence McMillan, the icon of options, in the April 27, 2000, issue of *The Options Strategist*, wrote about how often stocks make second and third standard deviation moves—more often than they should, based on the assumption that stocks follow a lognormal probability distribution. This favors option buying. And it's interesting to note that McMillan's only managed fund, at the time of this writing, is chartered to do straddle buying.

Nassim Taleb, in the September 2000 issue of *Stocks & Commodities*, wrote how his fund invests constantly in both puts and calls, tolerating the drain of time decay while waiting for the big strike. Nassim loves the nonlinear performance curve of an option. And the only way to put this quality of an option in your favor is to be long the option.

An option is a beautiful thing. Buy one. When you're correct about the direction of the market, gains are unlimited. When wrong, losses are limited. No other instrument gives you a better chance of hitting a home run.

Sure, time decay works against your position while the underlying goes nowhere, or takes an excursion in the wrong direction first, but this is an acceptable cost if the option is reasonably priced; that is, when implied volatility is at normal or below normal levels. There is nothing wrong with buying a reasonably priced option.

Prior to expiration, an option's profit/loss profile is a gentle curve, bending the most in the middle, and flattening in either direction—kind of like a bent steel bar. On one end the curve straightens out into a 45-degree angle. This is when the option is deep in the money. In the other direction the curve flattens out into a zero-degree angle. This is when the option is far out-of-the-money. See Figure 4.1 for the familiar profile of a call option purchase.

An at-the-money option is at its maximum inflection point. From there, as the underlying moves in the desired direction, your position makes money faster and faster. For example, the first point that the underlying moves in your direction, the option gains perhaps 0.5 point. The next point the underlying moves in your direction, the option gains perhaps 0.55 point. And so on until, when the option is deep in the money, it moves point for point with the underlying.

On the other hand, if the underlying moves against you, your position loses money slower and slower as the curve flattens out. This is the beauty of the nonlinear performance curve of an option.

Which Option to Buy?

The question of which option to buy is a good one, because options with different strike prices and duration will respond in widely varying degrees to price movements of the underlying and other conditions.

An out-of-the-money option has higher leverage. So if the underlying makes a swift, sizable, and immediate move in your favor, an out-of-the-

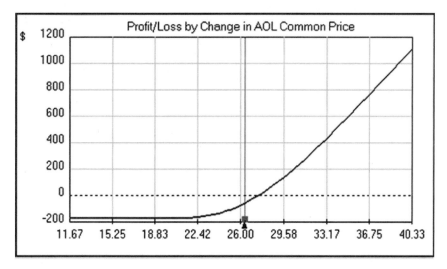

FIGURE 4.1 Call Option Purchase

money option does the best job of multiplying your money. However, if this move does not quickly materialize, the out-of-the-money option's performance will probably disappoint you.

At-the-money and in-the-money options move better with the underlying because their delta is greater. The delta of an at-the-money option is typically around 50—meaning that a one-point move in the underlying translates into a half-point move for the option. In-the-money options have deltas approaching 100—moving almost point-for-point with their underlying.

While in-the-money options best track their underlying, they are more expensive, lowering your leverage. They can also be less liquid, increasing your transaction costs. On the positive side, in-the-money options have a lower time premium component, so their time decay is slower. So you might be more comfortable using an in-the-money option when you want to allow several days or even weeks for the underlying to move.

Often the best balance of leverage, cost, and liquidity can be found in using just-in-the-money options. That happens to be my personal favorite for positions I plan on holding for one to five days.

As for duration, a good rule of thumb is to buy an option with at least twice the remaining life as the maximum length of time you plan on holding the position, although this requirement can be relaxed for deep in-the-money options where time decay is not a significant factor.

Sometimes an option does not respond predictably to a price change

in the underlying. What trader has not experienced the frustration of seeing his stock move several points and his option move very little?

While this can happen because the trader has bought an option that is
too far out-of-the-money, it is more likely due to a drop in implied volatility—something that can happen at any time but very often happens when a
stock is advancing.

Usually, when a stock advances it exhibits less and less volatility (as
measured by percentage daily price swings). Professional options traders
know this, and they gradually lower the volatilities they use in their options pricing models as the price of the stock goes up. This works against
call prices as the stock goes up, with the result that your call options gain
less than you expected, sometimes.

In contrast, as stock prices fall, implied volatilities increase and this
helps put buyers. This cause-effect relationship between stock prices and
implied volatilities is called *constant elasticity of volatility* (or CEV for
short). To draw an analogy with distance running, CEV is like having the
wind at your back if you're a put buyer, but like having the wind in your
face if you're a call buyer.

What Is a Bullish Trader to Do?

To counter the CEV effect, you can lean toward using more in-the-money
options. Deeper in-the-money options have a lower time premium, so a
volatility reduction hurts less. Another thing to consider is simply buying
the stock. Remember, the stock has zero time premium, and great liquidity! Of course, this gives you less leverage, even if buying the stock on margin, but it's worth considering.

Finally, in addition to buying just-in-the-money calls, you can also
sell out-of-the-money calls, entering into a vertical debit spread. This
lowers your cost, and volatility risk is effectively canceled out with the
addition of the short leg. However, a spread behaves differently from a
simple purchase. Reaping the full benefit from a spread requires having
the anticipated exit date coincide with the expiration date of the options.
For example, if the nearby expiration is 14 days away and your expected
holding time is also 14 days, a spread using the nearbys might be perfect.
But if the nearby expiration is 21 days away and your expected holding
time is 5 days, the spread might not fit so well; the simple call purchase
might be better.

A good options analysis program will usually show that a simple option purchase makes more money than a spread or any other option strategy, albeit with greater variance, when projecting a holding period of 1 to
10 days, even when the model includes the CEV effect. Beyond 10 days,
the software begins to favor spreads.

Finally, good discipline dictates that the trader set objectives and stops. These should be decided and written down the moment the position is opened. If the underlying moves in the desired direction, these should be reevaluated and adjusted upward at intervals. I have no advice on how to set objectives and stops, nor when to adjust them—only that you *should* set them and *obey* them. Traders must settle on a system that works for them.

DEBIT SPREADS—THE CALM APPROACH

Most traders are first attracted to options for high-leverage directional trading. Directional trading is where the trader believes he knows which way a stock, index, or future is going and opens an option position to take advantage of the expected move. More often than not, the new options trader starts out simply buying calls or puts. However, buying calls and puts is high-octane trading.

Traders, especially beginning options traders, should consider the benefits of spreads. A spread is constructed by buying an option and selling another option of the same type (call or put) on the same underlying. Usually the two options are of the same expiration month. Such a spread is said to be a *vertical spread* because the options differ only by strike, and in a matrix of options you typically picture the strikes running vertically.

When the option bought is more expensive than the option sold, the spread is said to be a *debit spread* because its opening results in a net debit to your trading account. When the option sold is more expensive than the option bought, the spread is a *credit spread*. We'll say more about credit spreads later. For now, let's just talk about debit spreads.

How Does a Debit Spread Work, and Why Use It?

When you buy a debit spread, you are essentially buying the difference, or spread, between the two options prices. You are expecting that, with the right market move, the price difference, or spread, will widen, resulting in a profit. A trader who buys a debit spread in calls expects the underlying to go up in price. As the underlying goes up, both legs (options) of his spread will increase in price, but the higher-priced leg will increase faster, thus widening the spread.

Conversely, a trader buys a debit spread in puts when he expects the underlying to go down in price. As the underlying goes down, both legs of the spread will increase in price, but the higher-priced leg will increase faster, thus widening the spread.

One reason a spread is attractive relative to a simple purchase is the size of position you can afford to own. For example, say the following two call options are available (with the same expiration month):

Strike	Price
110	3.30
115	1.50

With $3,000 you could afford to buy only 9 of the 110s. However, with the same money you could afford to enter 15 units of a debit spread between these two options, as the spread (difference) is currently 1.80.

As with buying an option, you can only lose the amount paid for a spread and no more. However, unlike buying an option, where the value of your position could theoretically increase without limit, the value of a spread can increase only to the difference in the strikes. For instance, continuing with the same example, the difference between the strikes is 5. If we buy a spread now for 1.8, the value of the spread could go either to 0 (losing the 1.8 paid because both options ended out-of-the-money), to 5 (a profit of 3.2 because both options ended in-the-money), or to any price in between (with the 110 option in-the-money and the 115 option out-of-the-money).

Figure 4.2 shows the performance of a vertical debit spread using calls (often called a bull call spread), compared to a simple call purchase with the same amount of capital. The shaded area represents our expectation that the price of IBM stock, currently 108, will increase to somewhere between 110 and 115. The dashed lines represent the theoretical performance of each strategy as of today. Clearly, the simple call purchase will outperform the spread if IBM goes up *today*.

The solid lines represent the theoretical performance of each strategy at expiration, 44 days from now. You can see that within the price range we expect, the spread outperforms the simple call purchase. The downside is the same for both trades (i.e., you could lose the amount paid). However, if you are wrong and the price increases substantially, your profit with the spread is capped, while your profit with the simple call purchase increases without limit.

Psychological Factors

A spread behaves very differently than a simple purchase, so traders must decide whether spreads are appropriate for their psyche. The price of a spread changes very gradually as the price of the underlying moves. Thus it is more sedate, requiring less attention. Again, a spread has minimum

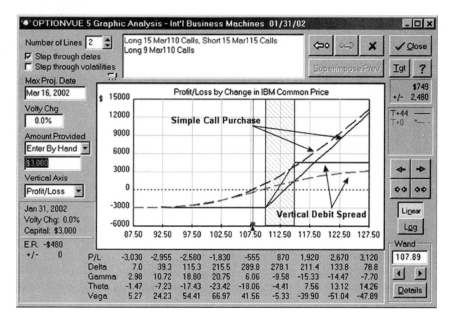

FIGURE 4.2 Bull Call Spread

and maximum outcomes. Thus, much like a casino bet, you either win or lose. The angst of picking an exit point, so critical with simple option buying, is abated.

Simple option buying requires great discipline. A simple call or put position is like raw energy. It responds dramatically to every move in the underlying. Therefore the trader must bring his own discipline into play—using objectives, stops, and perhaps trailing stops.

In contrast, spreads allow the trader more time to make an exit decision. Spreads may even be held all the way to expiration without concern for rapid time decay. In fact, if the underlying has made the move you expected, your spread, now in-the-money, *makes* money with the passage of time.

In times of exceptional volatility, when options are more expensive, the option buyer is at a disadvantage. However, the spread trader gets to neutralize this effect by selling an overpriced option at the same time he is buying an overpriced option.

One caveat with spreads is that if the underlying quickly makes the move you expected, you may be disappointed to see that your spread has not gained much, and that achieving its full potential requires holding the spread to the final day of its life. Not only could this be too boring for your trading psyche, but it also risks giving the underlying time to slip back.

Also note that since spread trading involves trading more option contracts with the same capital, it incurs greater commission charges.

Bottom line: For directional trading, the trader needs to use a strategy that best matches his or her trading psyche. A lot depends on how involved you want to be, or can afford to be, in watching the markets. Your trades should be interesting but not anxiety producing. If you find that buying calls and puts causes you too much emotional stress, you may need to consider switching to milder, more casual spread trading. Successful traders are unemotional, unstressed traders.

STRATEGIES FOR TRENDING MARKETS

A lot of money can be made by simply riding a trend. Not only is going with the trend wise, but buying and holding a position for weeks is less stressful than day trading or swing trading.

New options traders are often surprised to learn that it is possible to make greater returns with less risk using combinational strategies such as vertical debit spreads, horizontal debit spreads, backspreads, and synthetics. These strategies use two or more different options on the same underlying to create unique risk/reward profiles that single option positions cannot provide. Again, spreads are slower acting than single option positions. You don't have to watch them as closely. And a single countertrend day won't be as likely to scare you into exiting your position prematurely.

As you have learned, a *vertical spread* is constructed by buying one option and selling another option of the same type (call or put) in the same expiration month. When the option bought is more expensive than the option sold, the spread is said to be a debit spread because its opening results in a net debit to your trading account.

A *horizontal spread* (also known as a *calendar spread*) is constructed by buying one option and selling another option of the same type (call or put) with the same strike price but in different expiration months. The spread is called horizontal because the options differ only by month, and in a matrix of options you usually picture the months running horizontally.

As shown in Figure 4.3, using the S&P 100 Index (OEX) and a moderately bullish target (represented by the shaded area), I had the Option-Vue 5 options analysis software pick the best trade using each strategy. Clearly the best vertical debit spread and the best horizontal debit spread (tent-shaped line) beat the best simple call purchase within the target area. All three strategies can potentially lose 100 percent of the

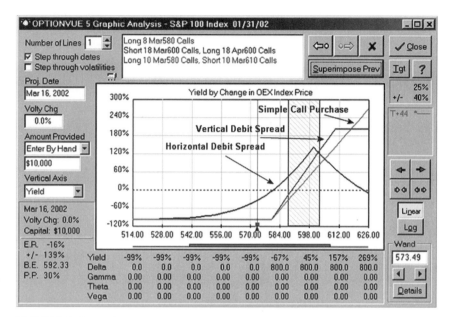

FIGURE 4.3 Performance Graph of Vertical and Horizontal Debit Spreads

investment if your forecast is wrong and the OEX declines. However, notice that the horizontal debit spread won't lose 100 percent until the OEX drops pretty far.

With the vertical debit spread, both the long and short legs have the same expiration date. However, it is important to understand that the horizontal spread does not realize its full potential until the expiration day of the short leg. So if the market makes its anticipated move quickly, some patience will be required as you wait for the spread to mature. Whenever this happens, you are likely to think to yourself, "I wish I had simply bought calls." But remember, a simple call purchase is a fast-moving position, requiring careful attention, discipline, and sometimes nerves of steel. You should remind yourself of this and ask yourself if that is what you really want.

Usually, vertical and horizontal debit spreads are the best strategies for trending markets. If your forecast is for a moderate move over the next several weeks, these strategies pay better and are less volatile than simple option purchases.

Two other strategies for trending markets—although with unique characteristics—are *backspreads* and *synthetics*. We'll discuss those soon.

Now let's look at how to use the horizontal spread in a sideways market.

THE HORIZONTAL SPREAD—A GOOD STRATEGY IN A SIDEWAYS MARKET

This section illustrates one of the big advantages of options. There are times, often weeks or months, when a stock or the market trades in a range. There is no way to make money (other than day trading small swings) being long or short the stock. However, you can profitably trade this type of market with options.

The horizontal debit spread is a neutral strategy when constructed using at-the-money options. As such, it is a good strategy to use in a choppy, sideways market. When you can catch the nearby options trading at a higher IV than the farther out options, you can put on a horizontal debit spread at a considerable advantage.

A horizontal debit spread is constructed by selling a nearby option and simultaneously buying a farther out option of the same type and strike price. The performance graph for a horizontal debit spread is a broad, tent-shaped curve, peaking over the strike price (of both options). (See Figure 4.4.)

Since your best outcome is when the underlying finishes right on the strike price, it is possible to be somewhat bullish or bearish by selecting a strike price slightly away from the current price of the underlying. For ex-

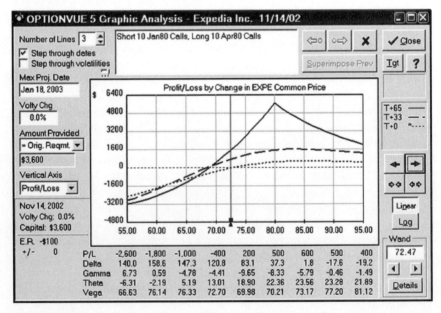

FIGURE 4.4 Performance Graph of Horizontal Debit Spread

ample, with the stock trading at 72, if you are bullish, you might select 80 or 85 for the strike price.

If you are bullish it is probably best to use calls, and if bearish, puts, in order to steer clear of shorting in-the-money options. The problem with shorting in-the-money options is the possibility of early assignment (assuming we're talking about American-style options, which may be exercised at any time by their holder).

Early assignment is more likely when short in-the-money options have very little remaining time value. Depending on the situation, early assignment could be either an important risk or just a nuisance. If early assignment happens with stock puts, you will suddenly be long stock, which, together with your remaining long puts, has almost the same risk/reward profile in the short run as you had before. So there is no urgency to respond. However, if early assignment happens with cash-based index puts, your short leg is suddenly gone (in a cash transaction), leaving you with the long leg by itself, which is highly exposed to market movement.

It is not difficult to find situations where the nearby options are trading at a higher volatility level than the farther out options. A sharp little sell-off often causes this.

At the time of this writing, the nearby options in McDermott (MDR) were trading at an IV (implied volatility) 30+ percentage points higher than the farther out options. For example, the March puts were at 138% while the May puts were at 100%. This begs the trader to use a horizontal debit spread—buying the Mays and selling the Marches. Again, a horizontal debit spread may be done at a higher strike price to create a bullish position, or at a lower strike price to create a bearish position. With McDermott stock at 12.40, the strike of choice for the slightly bearish trader would be 10.0. See Figure 4.5 for a profit diagram of a 20-lot horizontal spread using the 10.0 puts.

Thanks in part to the extra "kicker" from selling expensive nearby options, this $700 trade has an amazingly broad profit zone. At the peak (with the underlying at 10 in just 39 days), this trade should produce nearly a $3,000 profit. Notice that the dotted line—representing today's theoretical performance—lies entirely beneath the zero line. The reason this trade shows a loss right out of the starting gate is because of transaction costs.

Services exist that allow you to search for good opportunities to use horizontal debit spreads. Just to illustrate how many opportunities can be available, at the time of this writing more than 20 stocks come up under a search where the IVs of the nearbys and next month's options differed by 30 percentage points or more. These included Handspring (HAND), Elan (ELN), Metris (MXT), and ImClone (IMCL).

While a big IV differential gives a substantial theoretical advantage

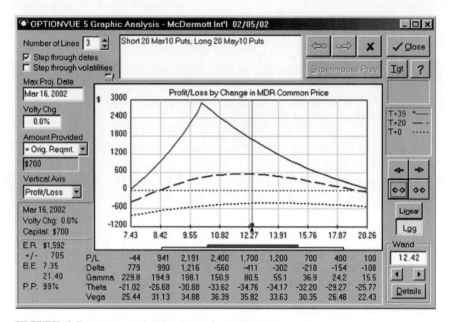

FIGURE 4.5 Horizontal Debit Spread—McDermott

to the horizontal debit spreader, it is important to realize that the differential might be there for a good reason. One reason could be that the stock is in the midst of a big move and no one knows where the stock price might settle.

Another reason could be anticipated news. The trader needs to be aware if there might be any pending announcement that could move the stock dramatically one way or the other. Expected news *is* sometimes the cause of price abnormalities in the options. Once the news comes out, if the stock moves up or down a significant amount, this tends to hurt a horizontal debit spread. However, the horizontal debit spread is sometimes worth doing *despite* the awareness of pending news, as oftentimes the stock does not move as much as people expected.

Placing Spread Orders with Your Broker

A spread order is when you enter an order to trade both legs of a spread simultaneously. As an example, let's use the following two options:

Strike	Price
110	3.30
115	1.50

A debit spread order could be given to your broker as follows: "I'm entering a spread order. Buy 15 of the IBM April 110 calls and sell 15 of the IBM April 115 calls at 1.80 debit." A spread order gets sent to the floor on a single ticket, and you will be filled in both legs simultaneously, or not at all. If filled, they will report back to you the prices at which each option traded. It doesn't make any difference what those prices are as long as they differ by 1.80 or less.

Spread orders are the safest way to open and close spread positions. The other way to do it is by placing two independent orders. This is called *legging*.

Legging can be dangerous. After getting one leg on, the market might move adversely, causing you to get a worse price for the second leg—with the result that you end up paying (debit spread) or receiving (credit spread) a worse net amount than you wanted. However, if the second order can be put through *quickly* after the first one, especially in a calm market, the risk can be managed. Legging is kind of like stepping into a small boat. You don't want to spend much time with one foot in the boat and the other foot on the dock!

The risk of legging is manageable if the trader has a direct access brokerage, where the trader is allowed to see the bid and asked prices on a particular option at all the exchanges where that option is traded, and direct his order to the exchange of his choice. The ability to route an order to the floor of one's own choosing is relatively new for the public, and is nothing short of revolutionary. Those using direct access brokerages have a "leg up," so to speak, on legging. By directing each order to the exchange with the best price, traders can often leg into or out of a spread at a very favorable net price. Or, they may decide to work the first leg by directing a limit order to the exchange where the best bid and asked are available, at a price in between the bid and the asked. Once filled, they quickly complete the spread by hitting the best bid or offer they can find for the other leg.

Novice spread traders are sometimes tempted to deliberately delay the second order in a bet that the market will move favorably in between times and they will get into or out of their spread at a bargain. This can be foolish. The trader is bound to get burned at some point. One should question whether one's purpose is high stakes gambling or sensible trading. If the trader is interested in using spreads, one would assume that his stated goal is sensible trading. Therefore the brief stints of gambling are probably outside his stated goals!

It takes extra capital to do legging. For example, if the trader has only $2,100 in free capital and wants to put on a $2,000 spread, he'll have to use a spread order. That is because the first leg he tries to put on, no matter which side he wants to put on first, will probably cost more than $2,100 and the order will be rejected.

Unfortunately, unless a spread order is entered at a net price that allows for hitting the bid of one option and the ask of the other, it won't be filled, in my experience. I don't know why this is, but if you try to keep back even as little as a tenth of a point, they tend to ignore your order. For example, consider the following two options:

Strike	Bid Price	Ask Price
110	3.30	3.50
115	1.50	1.60

Entering a debit spread order, you would need to pay 3.50 to buy the 110s, and you would be able to sell the 115s for 1.50. Thus a spread order placed at "net debit of 2.00" should be filled. However, if you place the spread order at a "net debit of 1.90," they won't fill you, in my experience.

This may be changing. I have heard from more than a couple of traders that spread orders are being executed favorably these days at the ISE.

CREDIT SPREADS—SAY "DON'T GO THERE"

A vertical credit spread is constructed by buying one option and selling another option of the same type (call or put) in the same expiration month, where the option sold is more expensive than the option bought, resulting in a net credit to your trading account.

In contrast to a debit spread, where you simply pay the difference, with a credit spread there is a margin requirement based on the difference in the strike prices. For example, consider the following two put options:

Strike Price	Price of Option
30	3
35	5

Buying the 35s and selling the 30s would form a debit spread, and you would pay the difference (2, or $200 per unit). However, if you were to buy the 30s and sell the 35s, that would form a credit spread. You would receive the difference (2, or $200 per unit), and would be required to put up the difference between the strike prices (5, or $500 per unit). Note that the $200 you receive counts toward offsetting the margin requirement, so that the net amount you have to provide in your brokerage account is just $300 per unit. Figure 4.6 shows the risk graph for an example 10-lot credit spread in these puts.

As long as the stock price is above $35 on expiration date, both options will expire worthless and you will get to keep the $2,000 credit. If you

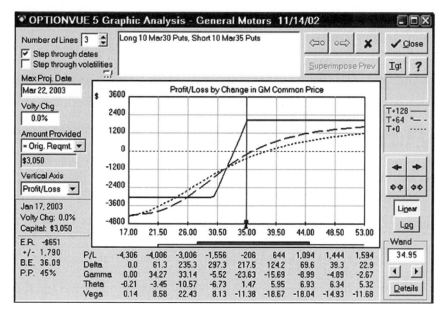

FIGURE 4.6 Credit Spread Performance—GM

are wrong, and the stock price instead decreases substantially, your maximum loss is capped at $3,000—the difference between the strike prices of the two options ($5,000) and the $2,000 credit you received.

Now you can see why a brokerage holds margin in your account for this kind of trade. They want to be certain that you have the funds to settle if the trade goes against you. By requiring margin, the $5,000 needed for the worst possible outcome is already in your account.

Note that when you place a credit spread, your price expectation is completely opposite that for a debit spread. In the call debit spread, you want the underlying to go up. This would widen the spread, allowing you to sell it later for a profit. In the call credit spread, you want the underlying to go down. This would narrow the spread, allowing you to close it later for a profit.

If this seems a difficult concept to grasp, perhaps this will help: You can think of opening a debit spread as going long the spread and opening a credit spread as going short the spread. Just as when you go long a stock, when you go long a spread you hope its value increases. And just as when you short a stock, when you short a spread you hope its value decreases (so that you can buy it back later at a lower price).

Debit and credit spreads can be formed using puts as well, with their performance curves mirror-imaging those of call debit and credit spreads. Table 4.1 summarizes these spreads.

Practically, there is little difference between the way debit spreads and credit spreads perform. Both have upper and lower boundaries to their potential values. Their value can go to a minimum of zero or to a maximum of the difference in strike prices. Neither is there much difference in what they cost, nor any practical difference in how you trade them. So when would one want to use a credit spread instead of a debit spread?

There is one distinction, and it is a subtle one. Depending on the strikes chosen, the credit spread is more often used when you have a conviction of what the underlying will *not* do (i.e., will not penetrate a support or resistance level). In contrast, the debit spread is used more often when you have a conviction of what the underlying *will* do (i.e., will continue its trend).

When there is a support level you feel the underlying will not penetrate, you would typically select a put credit spread where the short option is at or just below the support level. Likewise, when there is a resistance level you feel the underlying will not penetrate, you might typically select a call credit spread where the short option is at or just above the resistance level.

Sometimes the use of credit spreads is motivated more by the desire to sell options while avoiding naked writing. When a trader wants to sell out-of-the-money options to collect time premium (perhaps selling both out-of-the-money calls and out-of-the-money puts), he often buys farther out-of-the-money options at the same time in order to cover his short options and avoid using naked writing (either because of the open-ended risk of naked writing or because of its high margin requirements). This creates credit spreads. Just as if he used naked options, the investor is expecting that the underlying will not go as far as the strike price of the short options. If he is successful, the short options, as well as the farther out-of-the-money long options, will expire worthless. Naturally, his proceeds are less for having bought the farther out-of-the-money options for protection.

TABLE 4.1   Debit and Credit Spreads

Call debit spread	Bullish
Call credit spread	Bearish
Put debit spread	Bearish
Put credit spread	Bullish

CONDORS—TWO-WINGED CREATURES

I wrote in Chapter 2 that credit spreads are one of the safest and most successful strategies available. Building on the concepts just discussed, I'd like to present what is likely the most popular way of using credits spreads: a four-legged position called a condor. A condor consists of an out-of-the-money credit spread in calls and an out-of-the-money credit spread in puts. Initially, you try to receive approximately the same credit for each side and create a balanced, or delta-neutral, position.

Traders who prefer to have time decay on their side are attracted to condors. Many condor traders have positions on continually, sometimes in more than one expiration month. Day by day, as the market chops its way sideways (which it does more than half the time), they watch their equity build as the credit spreads decay. When the market moves, they adjust their positions to make them delta-neutral again.

Since a condor consists of credit spreads, its risk is absolutely limited. Even if the market opened with a gap up or down 1,000 points, you wouldn't be ruined. And you're always going to win on one side. For instance, say you received a 2-point credit for the call spread, and the same credit for the put spread. Each spread has a 10-point strike difference. If the market takes a severe dive, the put credit spread will go to its maximum value of 10, generating an 8-point loss. However, you win on the call side, with the 2-point credit, so your net loss is only 6.

To trade condors, you need an index or high-priced stock with high-liquidity options and many strikes to work with. A lot of strikes are needed, at relatively small intervals, in order to give you the flexibility needed for putting credit spreads on just the right distance away from the money. Also, indexes are preferred over individual stocks because indexes don't have anywhere near as much of a tendency to jump.

It is important to open the credit spreads far enough away from the money so that they have a decent probability of expiring worthless. The farther away from the money you can go, the greater the probability of the spreads expiring worthless without having to make any costly adjustments. However, the farther away options have lower premiums. In fact, beyond a certain point, those premiums fall off rapidly. Thus you are sometimes pushed into using closer-to-the-money strikes than you really want to.

For an example, let's look at building a prospective condor in the OEX options. The OEX was at 463 at the time of this writing, and more than seven out-of-the-money strikes were available in both the calls and the puts. Figure 4.7 shows the matrix. Remember, the ">" marks on the left indicate the at-the-money strikes—one among the calls and one among the

OPTIONVUE 5 Matrix - S&P 100 Index 11/15/02											
Define	Model	Legend	Format	Expand	Current Trades	Expire Options	Spread	Analyze	V		Close

Actuals	OEX Index	
	464.08	+2.94
	464.23	456.09

Options	DEC <36>				MAR <127>			
510 calls	1.25	1.60	22.6%		10.20	10.30	24.2%	
500 calls	2.50	2.65	22.7%	+10	12.60	13.90	24.6%	
490 calls	4.60	4.70	23.6%	-10	.....	.....		
480 calls	7.60	7.80	24.4%		20.10	22.10	26.1%	
475 calls	9.60	9.80	25.0%		.....	.....		
470 calls	12.00	12.50	26.0%		.....	.....		
460 calls>	17.10	17.30	26.5%		30.20	32.10	27.4%	
450 calls	23.30	24.80	28.5%		.....	.....		
475 puts	20.70	22.20	26.1%		.....	.....		
470 puts	18.20	19.20	26.3%		.....	.....		
460 puts>	13.50	14.00	26.9%		26.60	28.60	26.9%	
450 puts	10.00	10.50	28.3%		.....	.....		
440 puts	7.20	7.70	29.5%		19.20	20.50	28.4%	
430 puts	5.40	5.80	31.3%	-10	.....	.....		
420 puts	3.90	4.10	32.6%	+10	13.40	14.70	30.0%	
410 puts	2.70	3.00	33.9%		.....	.....		

Summary	Net Reqmts	Gross Reqmts						
	Net Reqmts	Gross Reqmts	Cash Flow	+$3,150	Delta	-40.10	Avg.IV	27.4%
Init	$16,850	$20,000	Cur. Value	$0	Gamma	-3.73	Calls.IV	25.7%
Maint	$16,850	$20,000	Gain/Loss	$0	Theta	64.83	Puts.IV	29.4%
Cash/Init	0.19	0.16	Commis	$200.00	Vega	-171.5	P/C (Vol)	0.92

FIGURE 4.7 Condor on OEX Matrix

puts. Out-of-the-money strikes in the calls lie above that mark, and the out-of-the-money strikes in the puts lie beneath that mark.

To get some idea of how far away from the money to go, the first thing a trader might want to do is get some idea how far the OEX could move within a given time frame. The OptionVue 5 software comes with a probability calculator that can be used for this purpose. Inputting the current price, volatility, and a time frame equal to the remaining life in the second month options (the nearbys were expiring in less than a week, so we're looking to the second month this time), we find that a first standard deviation move for the OEX could take it down to 426 or up to 495. In other words, there is a 68% chance of the OEX being between these two prices at the end of the projected time frame. We'd like to go even farther away from the money if possible, to get a better chance of success without adjustment. (See Figure 4.8.)

However, referring again to Figure 4.7, we find that only at one standard deviation are the option premiums still worth doing. Any further

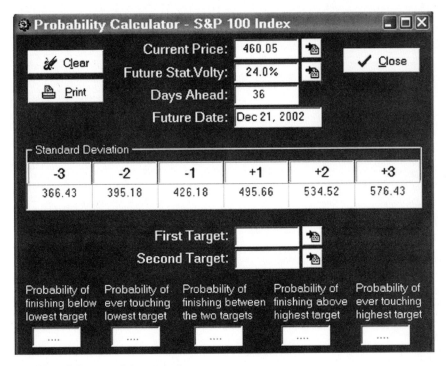

FIGURE 4.8 Probability Calculator

away and the premiums are too low to be worth selling. So, as is often the case, we are practically constrained to doing a one standard deviation condor. Figure 4.9 provides the graphic analysis of the condor that was entered in the matrix of Figure 4.7.

The lines of progression show how this position develops profitability over time. Projected all the way to expiration, the analysis shows that this position has a 66% probability of success. If necessary, adjustments can, and usually do, increase the probability of success of the actual trade, but they also reduce its yield.

Note that condors are only practical if your commissions are very low. That is because you'll be trading a lot of options, especially when you consider the occasional adjustments.

Condor traders are risk-averse traders. Besides having absolutely limited risk, a condor is also a very slow-acting position. Even a relatively big one-day market move affects the condor very little, because one wing of the condor benefits while the other is hurt. Be careful, though, if your position includes a close-to-the-money credit spread in the final days before expiration. If you are short a close-to-the-money option in the final week,

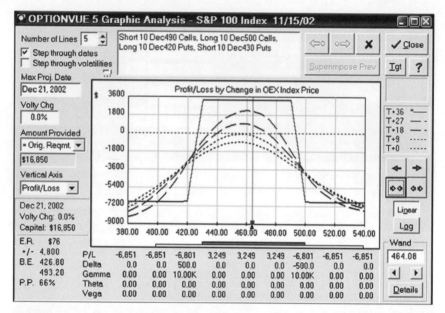

FIGURE 4.9 Graphic Analysis of Condor

you might want to consider closing that position early to avoid the possibility of being hurt by it.

So for the trader who enjoys actively managing a position in several options and seeing his account value grow almost daily, who doesn't feel he can predict the direction of the market or doesn't want to try, the limited-risk, slow-moving condor might be just the thing.

THE BACKSPREAD—A DIRECTIONAL STRATEGY THAT COSTS NOTHING IF YOU ARE WRONG

I'm a great believer in using the right tool for the job. The backspread is an amazing little strategy when you expect a potentially big price move, but at the same time you realize that there is a chance you could be wrong and no move whatsoever develops. One example when it would be appropriate to use a backspread might be when a drug company is approaching a deadline for FDA approval of a new product. Another good time to use a backspread is when bottom fishing near what you think is the end of a market sell-off.

A backspread is constructed by shorting a near-the-money option and buying a larger quantity of options of the same type (calls or puts) at a farther out-of-the-money strike. A 2×1 ratio is most common. Normally you try to select the options in such a way that the options you're shorting bring in a sufficient credit to cover the cost of the options you're buying, resulting in a net cash flow of nearly zero.

Since in a backspread you are net long options, the profit potential is unlimited. At the same time, the sale of a smaller number of more expensive options effectively pays for the options purchased, with the result that if both legs of the backspread expire worthless, it costs you nothing. The short leg of the backspread also effectively eliminates time decay as a worry.

If all that sounds too good to be true, I'll tell you what the catch is. There is a price zone where the backspread loses money. It occurs when the underlying moves in the desired direction by only a small amount.

Let's illustrate using a call backspread in Sun Microsystems (SUNW) options (see Figure 4.10). Caught in the recession of 2001, Sun stock dropped way down. However, many expect a recovery; we just can't be sure when. If you go along with this, a call backspread might be a perfect way to play it. (Note that backspreads can be constructed in puts just as well as in calls. Put backspreads behave in a mirror-image fashion to call backspreads.)

This particular 2×1 backspread costs $2,250 to put on. (The cost of a

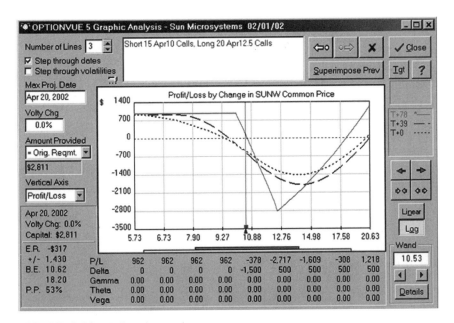

FIGURE 4.10 Call Backspread

backspread arises from the collateral requirement for a 1 × 1 credit spread plus the cost of the extra calls purchased.) Note that this position loses money when Sun is in a range from 10.25 to 14.79—the "dead zone." However, it is very difficult to lose *all* your money, as Sun would have to finish at precisely 12.50 (the long leg's strike price) on expiration day. Contrast this with simple option buying—where it is very easy to lose all your money!

Big profits can be made if Sun moves above 15. Below 10, you gain $263 no matter how far Sun may fall.

Noteworthy is the outstanding risk/reward characteristic of the T+39 line (the dashed line), representing the halfway point in the life of this position. If the expected rally happens within this time frame, you're golden. If not, you may consider closing the position at this time for just a small loss.

A Variation

By fiddling with the ratio of calls bought to calls sold, it's possible to construct a backspread that produces a sizable credit when you put it on. Figure 4.11 illustrates a position that probably should be considered bearish, as it makes money from the current price on down. However, notice that

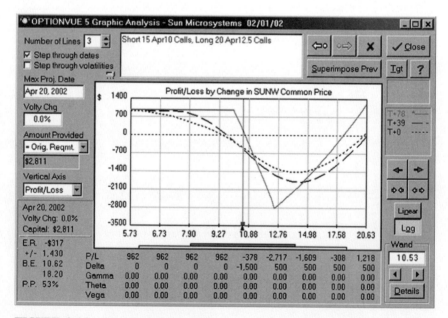

FIGURE 4.11 A Bearish Backspread

the loss zone is wider than in the previous example. And to the upside, only a move above 18.20 would make the trade profitable. It was constructed by selling 15 at-the-moneys and buying 20 out-of-the-moneys. This $2,800 investment makes $960 if the market goes down; not bad, but not great either.

Note that, compared to the original backspread, we took this position halfway to being a vertical credit spread. If you're truly bearish and don't care about the upside potential of this stock, perhaps you should go all the way and make it into a vertical credit spread.

Gold Bug

Let's look at a real-life example of where the backspread was the perfect strategy to use. At the time of this writing, gold plateaued for a few days after having jumped 20 points on Japanese buying in the wake of an important change in bank policy. Refer to the price chart in Figure 4.12. Can you see a pattern here?

Each time gold jumps to a higher level, it falls all the way back down. Gold just doesn't seem to want to *drift* lower. If you assume that this pattern should repeat itself, you would have to say that if gold begins to drop, it will fall at least 15 to 20 points. In other words, it is not likely that gold would fall just 5 points or so and stay there. We should

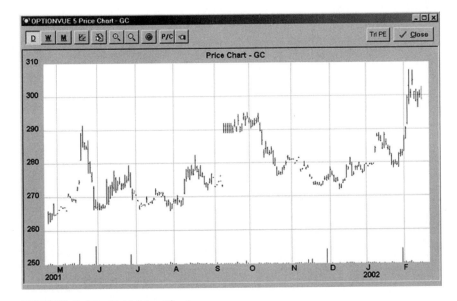

FIGURE 4.12 Gold Price Chart

also be prepared for gold to move higher; it probably won't, but we don't want to be hurt if it does.

Now, one way to play this would be to place a stop order to buy puts if gold falls below, say, 295. However, we might be filled at a high price if gold gaps down. Or if gold dropped enough to hit our stop, then went back up, we'd be looking at a loss.

It might be better to construct an appropriate backspread and put our position on right away. Figure 4.13 shows an example of a 2 × 1 put backspread that would work well here.

From the performance graph in Figure 4.14, you can see that this position makes money fast after gold falls below 290. Or, if gold moves higher, it still makes a small profit. Costing less than $1,200 to put on, the spread makes a $2,600 profit if gold falls to 280. The only way you can lose money is if gold settles into a range between 290 and 305 and stays there, which we believe is unlikely. Simply a beautiful, tailor-fit strategy!

COVERED WRITING—ENHANCING YOUR RETURNS

Many investors use covered writing to enhance returns from their long stock portfolios. Actually, it is debatable whether covered writing truly en-

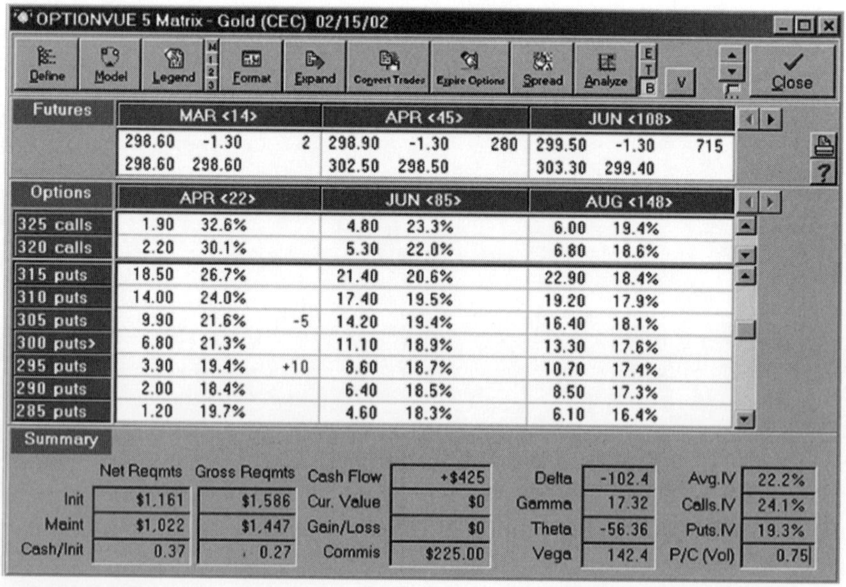

FIGURE 4.13 A Put Backspread

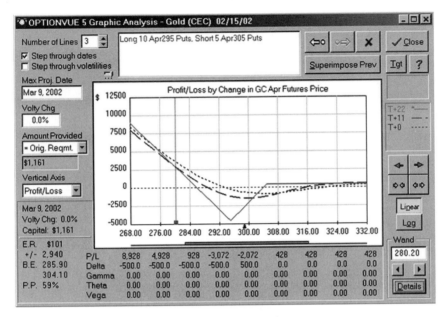

FIGURE 4.14 Graphic Analysis of Put Backspread

hances returns overall. Admittedly, stocks move in a sideways, slightly upward or slightly downward pattern much of the time, and in those times covered writers benefit greatly from the additional income generated by the sale of call options.

A covered write is the sale of a call option *against*, or *covered by*, a long position in the underlying. When you sell calls against your stocks, you are giving someone the option of buying your stock from you anytime during the life of the option for a stated price—the strike price of the option. In return for giving up all possible gains above the strike price, you receive cash for the options you sold.

When someone tells me they don't trade options because options are too risky, I usually cite the covered write as an example of using options to *reduce* risk. And it's true. The sale of covered calls reduces the risk of a stock portfolio in the sense that returns are less variable. In theoretical terms, you have reduced your portfolio's *variance*, and therefore you have reduced its *risk*.

However, the covered writer's short calls do little to protect him against losses as the market falls. This is the only knock on covered writing—that it takes away the upside and leaves you with the same downside risk as a regular stockholder.

Still, some investors manage to keep some of their upside potential through careful management of their positions. How? By rolling. After a stock moves up, they repurchase the short calls (at a loss) and sell new calls at a higher strike. This allows them to stay in an uptrending stock so that capital gains (from the sale of the stock) are deferred. Losses from repurchasing the short options can be claimed immediately.

The other smart thing covered writers do is time the sale of options when options are expensive. As we discussed earlier, option prices fluctuate between periods when they are cheap or dear. If you focus on selling when options are expensive, it can make a big difference! Historical volatility charts help you know when a stock's options are cheap or dear (see Figure 4.15).

At the time of this writing, Halliburton's options were expensive. An analysis shows an excellent potential return of 13 percent in 67 days from selling at-the-money calls. (See Figure 4.16.)

Again, that's only if the stock behaves well. Back when I was first learning about options, my broker introduced me to covered writing by handing me a copy of a handwritten sheet. On this sheet were the details of a proposed trade involving the purchase of 1,000 shares of a relatively low-priced stock on margin and the sale of 10 call options against it. The figures, which only included "return if stock called away" and "return if stock unchanged," were compelling. (I think the return if stock called away was more than 50 percent in two months.) However, it was a trap. I don't know if brokers are still handing out proposals like this today, but to

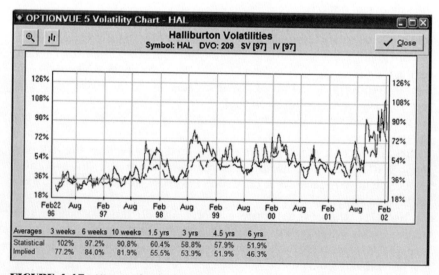

FIGURE 4.15 Historical Volatility Chart

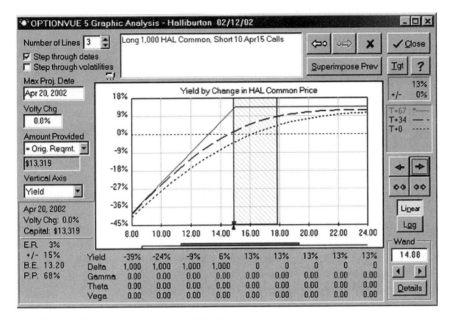

FIGURE 4.16 Halliburton's Volatility History

be more disclosing, they should also show what happens if your stock drops a certain amount, say, one standard deviation. With the stock being bought on margin, I'm sure it would have been a significant negative result! (By the way, I did not go for the proposed trade, because I was more interested in speculative option buying at that time, and probably lost my money faster as a result!)

LEAPS—AN ALTERNATIVE TO STOCK

LEAPS are an attractive alternative to stock ownership. Not only do they often have a more favorable risk/reward profile than the stock, inexpensive LEAPS are easy to find and thus come with an inherent edge.

LEAPS stands for Long-term Equity Anticipation Securities. Practically, LEAPS are just long-term options—longer term than the standard listed options. The only thing special about them is that the exchanges consider them securities and allow brokerages to lend you up to 25 percent of their value. Not all brokerages honor this, however. Note that if you have a long LEAPS position that covers a short position in any of the other options on the same underlying security, you no longer get to margin the long LEAPS.

LEAPS are available with expirations one to three years out on hundreds of the most popular stocks and many indexes. When LEAPS have only nine months of life remaining, they convert into standard listed options (and no longer have any loan value).

Valuation

One interesting thing about LEAPS is that they often trade at lower volatility levels than the nearby options on the same stock. In other words, LEAPS trade at prices implying that their underlying won't be as volatile. Thus LEAPS are, in a very real sense, cheaper than the nearby options.

There is no theoretical basis for this that I'm aware of. Some may argue that more volatility is usually expected near-term than far-term, and I know that to be true from time to time. But why should it be true on a consistent basis? Note that all volatility numbers, no matter how short the time frame, are normalized to a one-year time frame. Thus they should be directly comparable. So, theoretically, a stock's near-term volatility should be no different than its long-term volatility, barring any pending news or unusual market activity.

Not only are LEAPS valued at lower volatility levels than the nearby options, many LEAPS also trade at lower volatility levels than the statistical volatility of their underlying. (Remember, statistical volatility measures how much the price of an asset bounces around.)

Charles Schwab (SCH) was a good example of this. At the time of this writing, Schwab had January 2004 LEAPS (715 days to expiration) that were trading at a 46% volatility level. In contrast, Schwab stock's volatility had been running in a range of between 60% and 80% over the last several years. Thus the prices of these LEAPS did not fully reflect the volatility of their underlying. Unless you have some reason to believe that this stock will quiet down at some point, Schwab's LEAPS were undervalued.

Figure 4.17 shows how an at-the-money Schwab call LEAP would perform relative to an appropriate number of shares of the underlying. In the illustration, the two lines going highest to the right belong to the LEAP. The dashed line represents the performance of the LEAP in today's time frame; the corresponding solid line represents the performance of the LEAP at expiration—two years from now. The final (solid) line represents the performance of the stock position. Note that we scaled the horizontal axis logarithmically this time—thus the stock's line has a gentle bend. Sometimes it can be better to use a logarithmic scale, especially when projecting far into the future, because it appropriately brings higher stock prices into the picture.

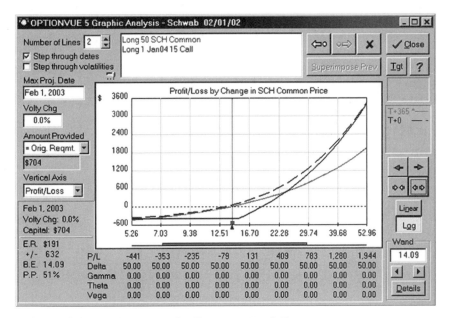

FIGURE 4.17 Performance of Call LEAP vs. Stock Shares

The appropriate number of shares to use for a direct comparison is determined by using the delta of the option. The delta of this option was 50, meaning that when the underlying moves one point, the option theoretically moves half a point. Therefore a comparable position in the underlying would be 50 shares. That way if the underlying moves up one full point, we would gain $50 from the LEAP, or an equal $50 from the 50-share stock position.

That the two different positions have the same delta can be confirmed in the illustration. Note that the vertical wand marks the current price of the stock. At that point the LEAP's current (T+0) (dashed) line and the stock's (solid) line have identical slopes.

Risk/Reward

Notice that the LEAP has better characteristics to the upside, outperforming the stock by an ever greater margin the higher the stock price goes. To the downside, the LEAP is also better below a certain point. Although both a stock and a LEAP can go to zero, in this example the shares of stock cost twice as much as the single LEAP (presuming you pay cash for the stock); thus the stock can lose more money.

In other words, the LEAP has better risk/reward characteristics because of its nonlinear performance. Just as with any call option, there is no limit to the upside, while the most you can lose is the investment.

Where the LEAP underperforms the stock is if the stock is still near its current price level two years from now. If that happens, the LEAP will gradually decay in value until it is nearly worthless. But who would expect the stock to be at the same price two years from now?

One caveat: If your stock is bought out, valuations in the LEAPS will collapse. Sure, your LEAP may be helped by a jump in the stock price, but at the same time almost all of the time value will come out of it, and you may end up worse off than if you simply owned the shares. This shouldn't be a worry, however, if you are selecting companies that are unlikely to become takeover candidates.

THE SYNTHETIC—ANOTHER ALTERNATIVE TO STOCK

Did you know there is an option strategy—involving just two options—that behaves exactly like a position in the underlying? It's called a synthetic, because you're "synthesizing" a position in the underlying.

A synthetic is constructed by buying a call and selling a put of the same strike and duration (to simulate being long the underlying), or buying a put and selling a call of the same strike and duration (to simulate being short the underlying).

Since a synthetic performs exactly the same as being long or short the underlying, the question naturally arises: Why would you do a position with two transactions when you can do it with one? Well, the fact is that the capital requirements for a synthetic can be a lot less than going long or short the stock, even when using maximum margin (50 percent) on the stock.

For example, to purchase 100 shares of Johnson & Johnson (JNJ) at a price of 58 would cost $5,800 cash, or $2,900 collateral on 50 percent margin. To buy an at-the-money synthetic would cost a net $30 cash, plus $960 collateral, for a total of $990. Not only is this a considerable difference in collateral, but the cash flow difference means that with the synthetic you get to keep your cash (all but $30 of it) and use it to earn interest.

You're probably thinking there must be a catch. Is the synthetic riskier? Actually, since the synthetic delivers exactly the same performance as a position in the underlying itself, there is no additional risk in using a synthetic.

There are just two minor catches. One is the fact that with a synthetic, you miss out on any dividend income. The other is the possibility of early assignment if the short leg goes deep in the money. Early assignment is especially likely with a short, deep in-the-money put. If this happens, you will suddenly be long the stock (instead of short a put) plus long a call option. Since the long call option is far out of the money at this point, it is low priced and has very little delta. So you are essentially just long stock, which is the same in its performance as the original synthetic. Thus you are not exposed to any sudden risk and there is no urgency to respond immediately in some way following assignment. Also, the cash flows of the assignment itself do not create a loss for you (nor a gain). The only difference is that your collateral requirement jumps up, as you now own the stock.

Figure 4.18 shows a synthetic long as compared to a long stock position. The two lines are very close together. The line for the long stock position runs just above the line for the synthetic because of dividends.

Another advantage of synthetics is that you can use them with assets where there is no tradable underlying, such as indexes.

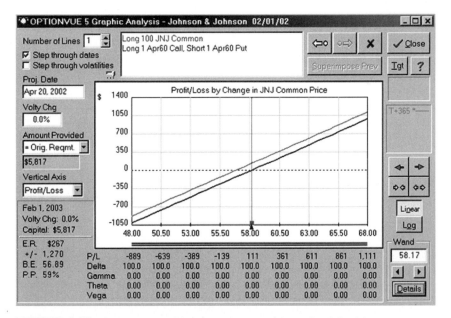

FIGURE 4.18 Comparison of Synthetic Long and Long Stock Positions

THE BUTTERFLY SPREAD—WHEN YOU HAVE A NARROW TARGET RANGE

There is a strategy involving three options that performs well when you expect the underlying to stay right where it is. It's called, very colorfully, a butterfly spread.

A butterfly is constructed using three options of the same type and of the same expiration. You sell two at-the-money options, buy one option at a higher strike, and buy one option at a lower strike. The strikes don't have to be adjacent, but the strikes of the long options need to be equal intervals away from the short options. See Figure 4.19 for an example of a butterfly spread in OEX calls.

In this instance we're using nonadjacent strikes. That's okay, just as long as the "wings" are equidistant from the center position. Also note that a butterfly is essentially a debit spread (in this case, the 540–560 spread) plus a credit spread (in this case, the 560–580 spread). The performance chart for a butterfly looks like an A-frame (see Figure 4.20).

You can see that this trade performs well only if the underlying remains in a narrow band, and does not mature until right at expiration. No-

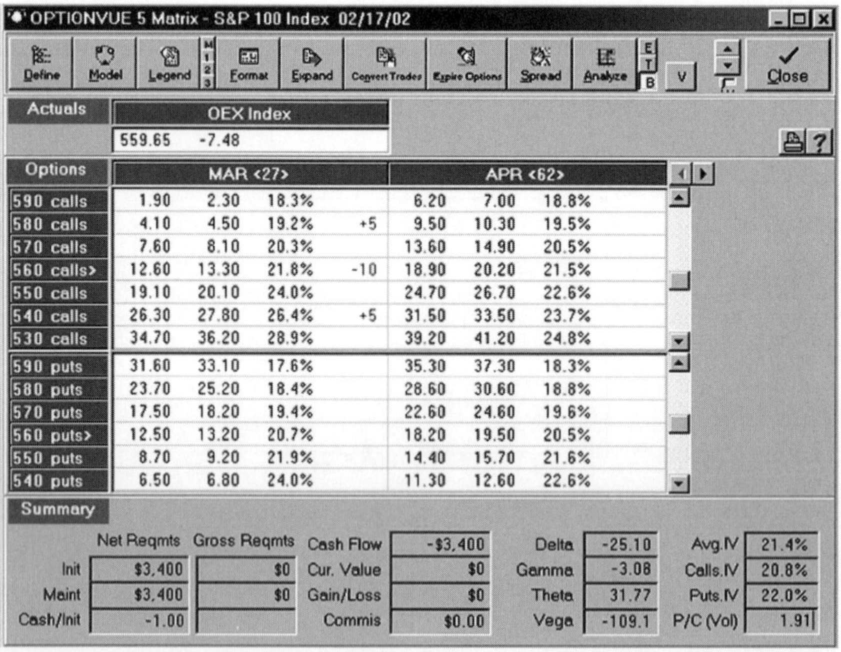

Options	MAR <27>				APR <62>		
590 calls	1.90	2.30	18.3%		6.20	7.00	18.8%
580 calls	4.10	4.50	19.2%	+5	9.50	10.30	19.5%
570 calls	7.60	8.10	20.3%		13.60	14.90	20.5%
560 calls>	12.60	13.30	21.8%	-10	18.90	20.20	21.5%
550 calls	19.10	20.10	24.0%		24.70	26.70	22.6%
540 calls	26.30	27.80	26.4%	+5	31.50	33.50	23.7%
530 calls	34.70	36.20	28.9%		39.20	41.20	24.8%
590 puts	31.60	33.10	17.6%		35.30	37.30	18.3%
580 puts	23.70	25.20	18.4%		28.60	30.60	18.8%
570 puts	17.50	18.20	19.4%		22.60	24.60	19.6%
560 puts>	12.50	13.20	20.7%		18.20	19.50	20.5%
550 puts	8.70	9.20	21.9%		14.40	15.70	21.6%
540 puts	6.50	6.80	24.0%		11.30	12.60	22.6%

Summary

	Net Reqmts	Gross Reqmts						
			Cash Flow	-$3,400	Delta	-25.10	Avg.IV	21.4%
Init	$3,400	$0	Cur. Value	$0	Gamma	-3.08	Calls.IV	20.8%
Maint	$3,400	$0	Gain/Loss	$0	Theta	31.77	Puts.IV	22.0%
Cash/Init	-1.00		Commis	$0.00	Vega	-109.1	P/C (Vol)	1.91

FIGURE 4.19 Butterfly Spread in OEX Calls

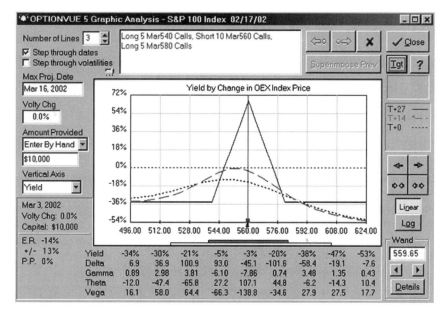

FIGURE 4.20 A-Frame Performance Chart for Butterfly Spread

tice that the preexpiration lines slope down to the right. That is because the software was including the effects of slippage and commissions. All three options would be driven in-the-money if the underlying moved higher, thus causing slippage and commissions to take a larger toll.

As with any option strategy, you can "short" a butterfly as well as "long" it. And, as with any option strategy, this would flip the performance graph top to bottom, making it a position that wins if the underlying does anything *but* stay right where it is.

Personally, I don't care for butterfly spreads. The transaction costs are high, and the performance graph usually reveals unappealing risk/return characteristics.

USING THE RIGHT OPTION STRATEGY

We have covered many different option strategies with many different performance graphs. How does the individual trader select the best strategy?

In short, the individual trader must choose the strategy that matches his or her own trading goals and psychology, based on knowledge of how each strategy performs.

Each strategy has its own unique risk/reward characteristics. Say you're trying to pick the right strategy to play an expected rally. The first strategy that comes to mind is the simple call purchase.

However, the simple call purchase is a position that responds dramatically to every move in the underlying. And once the underlying has moved your way to a certain extent, the call option, now more expensive, gains or loses even more money with every move in its underlying. In other words, its delta, or sensitivity to the underlying, has increased.

This is where trouble can arise. Increased stress on the trader, now trying to pick an appropriate selling point, may contribute to a bad decision. For example, a sudden (but not great) drop in the underlying can lower the price of the option and cause the trader remorse that he did not sell earlier. Now he must decide whether to sell and lock in whatever gain he has before the stock drops any further. On the other hand, a sudden rise in the stock can easily double the value of the call option, possibly leading the trader to feel euphoric and smug, emotions just as dangerous to successful trading as anxiety!

It takes a strong, disciplined trader to profit from simple call purchases consistently. The trader must understand the kind of position he is using and be disciplined—using an objective, a stop, and perhaps a trailing stop.

For the more conservative trader, less aggressive positions can be found among the various types of spreads. Spreads allow the trader more time to make an exit decision. You can even hold a spread all the way to expiration without concern over rapid time decay.

A computer simulation can help in selecting the best spread to use. Consider the price chart for Forest Labs (symbol: FRX) and a reasonably bullish price projection to the May expiration date (see Figure 4.21). The X1 line represents the upcoming March expiration, while the X2 line represents the upcoming May expiration. The rectangle in the upper right corner represents our projection, or target, in terms of a price range and a date range.

In Figure 4.22 we have analyzed and superimposed the performance of four different strategies. For the same money in each case ($5,000), we looked at (1) a simple call purchase; (2) a vertical debit spread in calls; (3) a vertical credit spread in puts; and (4) a 2 × 1 ratio spread in calls. Each position was singled out as having the best expected return in its strategy class, based on our projection for the underlying.

Each position has a different profile. The vertical debit spread in calls has the best overall expected return within the target zone (depicted with shading). However, that won't always be the case. Under different conditions, with a different target or time frame or a different volatility environment, another strategy might perform better. You never know until you run a simulation.

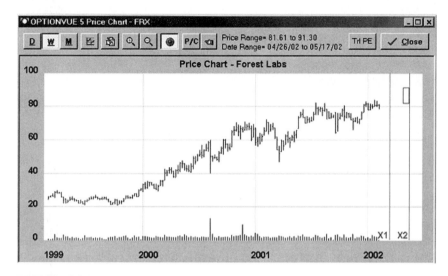

FIGURE 4.21   Price Projection

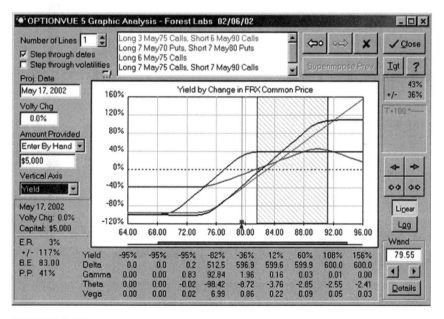

FIGURE 4.22   Four Strategies

The next best strategy, purely from the standpoint of expected returns, is the simple call purchase. However, the put credit spread's expected return is just a bit less than that, and when you consider that the performance of this strategy is flat within the target zone and better than the simple call purchase at lower stock prices, I think you'd have to agree that it beats the simple call purchase handily. (This is where it helps to have a picture in front of you!)

The flattest, most sedate line belongs to the ratio spread. This strategy performs better than the others if the trader is wrong and no rally materializes. Thus the ratio spread is the most conservative strategy this time.

By the way, all four of these strategies perform better than simply buying shares of the underlying stock—much better.

So you're trying to pick the right strategy? Select the strategy that will perform the best based on your expectations for the underlying, and at the same time will match your trading temperament. Don't pick an aggressive strategy like a call purchase just because it looks like you could make a little more profit. As I mentioned before, successful traders are unemotional, unstressed traders.

CHAPTER 5

Special Situations

From time to time, special situations occur that warp the standard options model. These include takeover deals, other restructuring plans, and even just pending news sometimes. The investor must be careful not to quickly jump on an apparent bargain. Look before you leap, because discrepancies are often there for a good reason.

PLAYING TAKEOVERS

An enormous amount of options activity accompanies takeovers and takeover rumors, and they can be a gold mine of opportunity. Yet you must be careful.

One way to play takeovers is to bet on the price. If you want to play it to the upside (as the target company's stock often *does* go much higher after the initial news or rumor), you can pick a call to purchase, or open a vertical debit spread in calls or a vertical credit spread in puts.

Or you can use some good analysis tools and do some volatility-based trading. This approach can be very safe and lucrative. Returns are more predictable, as you do not have to guess the direction of the underlying security.

Volatility-based trading does, however, require some finesse. Playing a takeover is like flying your plane through a storm. The figures can lie to you. What seems like a profit opportunity might not be. You have to be careful how you interpret the numbers.

At one time, RJ Reynolds (RJR) was awaiting a Nabisco shareholder vote about its being acquired. In anticipation of this vote, Nabisco's nearby options were inflated to higher premiums than its farther out options. For example, the October calls were trading at an IV of 37%, while the December calls were trading at only about 18%. A similar differential existed in the puts.

This automatically suggested opening a horizontal debit spread, selling the more expensive nearby options and buying the cheaper, farther out options. However, before rushing in, the trader must stop and ask himself why the options are being priced this way. Let's search for some logic that would possibly explain what you are seeing.

In Nabisco, traders were probably giving the nearby options higher premiums because, if something was going to happen with Nabisco, it was going to happen very soon or not at all. The expected near-term price volatility in Nabisco translated into a higher IV for the October options than for the December options.

Horizontal debit spreads have the life squeezed out of them when the price of the underlying moves much higher or much lower. Therefore, if you were to take a horizontal debit spread in Nabisco, you would be accepting the seemingly favorable odds (and apparent bargain) to bet on Nabisco staying about the same price, against the many traders who were accepting worse odds to bet on Nabisco taking a big jump. Were the horizontal debit spreads such a bargain after all? Perhaps not.

Big differences between put and call implied volatilities can also occur. In a previous RJR takeover situation several years prior, there was to be a large dividend payout. As you know, a dividend causes the stock price to drop the day the stock goes "ex-dividend." In this case, the dividend was to be so large that all the puts seemed extraordinarily overpriced and all the calls were "flat." Naively selling the expensive puts might have been ruinous. Good options analysis software will take the effect of dividend payments into account. Finding out about such a dividend, you would enter it into your options pricing model. As soon as you did, the calls and puts would seem to be more normally priced.

In a more recent takeover scenario, Weyerhaeuser was bidding for Willamette. During the period of time when Willamette was weighing the offer and exploring alternatives, the out-of-the-money puts were trading at high implied volatilities (see Figure 5.1). Thus they were attractive for short selling. However, one needs to question why these puts were so expensive. Even before reading the news, one could guess that many people thought there might be a good chance that the stock price would drop sharply.

A few days later, Willamette rejected Weyerhaeuser's offer and Willamette's stock plunged to 44. Anyone who had sold puts just before

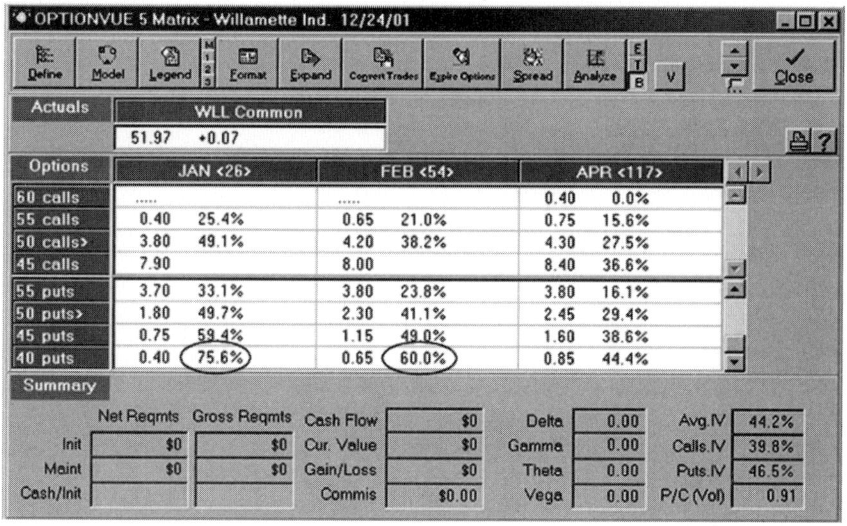

FIGURE 5.1 Expensive Willamette Puts During Weyerhaeuser Bid

this would have been sorry. However, at that point the out-of-the-money puts were still trading at high implied volatilities. Viewing the price chart at that point, one might have decided that now was a good entry point for a short put position based on the opinion that the stock price was now at an apparent support level. Also, Willamette was still in play and could be acquired at any time.

In fact, it would have been a good decision because on January 22, Willamette and Weyerhaeuser reached a definitive agreement. Willamette's stock jumped to 55 and locked in at that level (see the price chart in Figure 5.2).

Takeovers can be profitable for the option trader, but you must be shrewd. If you see something strange, try to figure out why. Read everything about the situation. Dig into the arithmetic of the deal and learn of any ratios that may apply. Then, once you're sure, act fast! Option trading opportunities in takeovers can come and go quickly.

LETTING THE OPTIONS MARKET TIP YOU OFF ON TAKEOVERS

Insider trading is illegal, but reading the telltale signs in the options market and taking a position is not! News often leaks out prior to an official takeover announcement, and people try to quietly buy call options in the

FIGURE 5.2 Willamette Stock Jumped when Agreement Was Reached with Weyerhaeuser

target company. Their activity can lead to unusually high volume and inflated premiums in the call options, and this can tip you off to a potentially big move.

Scanning services are available that can alert you to unusual call option activity. For example, on December 11, 2001, OptionVue System's OpScan service alerted subscribers to exceptional activity in Willamette calls. Call option volume was soaring that day (see Figure 5.3).

Look at the first spike in the lower chart—representing call option volume. Two days after that spike, the stock jumped several points, and four days later it moved several more points on the official announcement. Clearly, insiders knew something was coming, and they took long call options positions in advance of the announcement.

Not every takeover is preceded by unusual options activity. And not every spike in call options trading volume is followed by an event that makes the stock jump. And sometimes, even after a takeover announcement, the target stock doesn't move at all.

However, tradable opportunities come along often enough to make this a really intriguing pursuit. Once an alert has come up, how does one evaluate the situation and decide what kind of position should be taken?

After an alert, one needs to evaluate the activity and see if it bears the

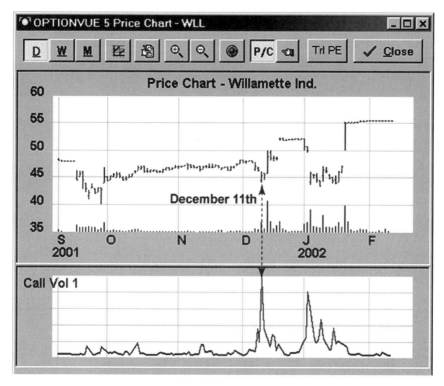

FIGURE 5.3 Call Option Activity on Willamette before Announcement of Weyerhaeuser Bid

imprint of pre-takeover buying interest. It's important to look for inflated prices. Also look for higher than usual volume, especially in the nearby out-of-the-monies, but also spread out among several of the available call options. The best way to check for inflated prices is to look for a jump in current implied volatility (IV) as compared with recent historical IV.

If IV is not higher, or if the unusually high volume is concentrated in just one or two of the call options, then there might be nothing special about this instance. It might just be that a big institutional order has been filled. In the case of Willamette on December 11, 2001, average call IV was 41.5% versus 26.7% the week before, and volume was heavy in several different call options. So far, so good!

Curiously, more volume was seen in the second expiration than in the nearby expiration. Perhaps this was because the buyers knew the deal would probably take more than a couple of weeks to consummate, and the Decembers wouldn't allow enough time. (See Figure 5.4.)

Clearly, this example fits the pattern of pre-takeover activity that we

| OPTIONVUE 5 Matrix - Willamette Ind. 12/11/01 | | | | | | | | | | | | | | |

Actuals — WLL Common
45.25 -1.15

Options	DEC <11>			JAN <39>			APR <130>		
50 calls	0.15	43.1%	300	0.85	40.6%	4300	1.70	31.5%	2440
45 calls>	1.45	42.7%	1490	2.75	44.0%	8560	3.90	34.4%	1580
40 calls	5.60			6.60		750	7.20	40.1%	4450
35 calls	10.50			10.60			11.40		
55 puts	10.20			9.80			10.10		
50 puts	5.00			5.60		30	6.30	30.9%	
45 puts>	1.20	42.3%	1860	2.45	44.3%	4600	3.50	34.4%	570
40 puts	0.10		20	1.20	57.2%	5480	2.05	41.2%	278

Summary

	Net Reqmts	Gross Reqmts	Cash Flow	$0	Delta	0.00	Avg.IV	42.6%
Init	$0	$0	Cur. Value	$0	Gamma	0.00	Calls.IV	41.5%
Maint	$0	$0	Gain/Loss	$0	Theta	0.00	Puts.IV	44.1%
Cash/Init			Commis	$0.00	Vega	0.00	P/C (Vol)	0.56

FIGURE 5.4   Higher Volume in Second Expiration—Willamette, December 2001

are looking for. A bullish position could be taken, either through buying calls, selling naked puts, buying a call debit spread, or some other bullish strategy. A simulation and graphic analysis could help you decide. A simple call purchase often turns out to be best, despite the extra expense. Taking our cue from others, we might avoid using the nearbys.

As you can see from the price chart, a bullish position would have been profitable, as the stock moved from 45 on December 11 to 52 on December 19, at which point it would have been wise to sell.

It is natural to wonder how often qualified alerts come along, and what percentage of those alerts lead to profitable trades. Jim Graham, a member of the OptionVue Research staff, did a study on this and published the results on the web site (www.optionvue.com) in October 2001.

In that study, Jim analyzed the candidates that came up during one brief period from September 25 through October 3, 2001. Twenty-two candidates come up during that period. Of these, Jim eliminated eight that did not pass his minimum price and increasing open interest filters. I'll explain these filters, because you may want to use them. He ruled out stocks priced below 7.5, based on personal preference and his usually disappointing experiences with lower-priced stocks. This eliminated two stocks. The second filter, which Jim considers very important, is that the call open interest needs to be increasing over the previous two days. To Jim, this indicates that investors are buying calls. This filter eliminated six stocks.

To the 14 qualifying candidates, Jim applied further checks, as discussed previously. He looked at the matrix of each stock and how the options volume was distributed. What he found was that all 14 stocks had lots of activity, spread across several call options. He also checked the news to make sure there had not already been a big announcement that might account for the unusual activity. None were eliminated by this rule.

So there were still 14 candidates. Here is what happened to these stocks in the ensuing days. On Friday, October 12, 16 days after the first alerts and 13 days after the last alerts, 10 had increased in price, while 4 had decreased in price. The stocks (with percentage change) that increased were ADVS (+22.1 percent), RE (+25.5), NETA (+42.5), MYG (+16.3), NWS (+9.49), AH (+16.4), SMTF (+32.3), RATL (46.4), MCDT (+47.8), and CVTX (+7). The four that decreased were CMX (–4 percent), DME (-7), CVC (-7.8), and GD (–.2). Of the candidates that increased in price, many did so by a substantial percentage, while the percentage drop for the other four was not as large.

These are indeed impressive results. However, with all due respect to Jim, by coincidence I think he may have hit an unusually good patch. My gut feeling is that the success rate, longer-term, is more like 50 percent—or perhaps even as low as 30 percent. A longer-term study is needed to determine this. Still, the approach is a good one—and an exciting one—with quick, exhilarating payoffs. When a trade does not work out, you are not in it very long, either.

A less than 50 percent success rate should not discourage you. Much like the way the venture capitalist operates, where one or two home runs can pay for several duds, your really big profits will come from the occasional trades where you get three, four, and five times or more from your initial investment. One thing to watch out for is the dry spells, sometimes lasting months, when there is no merger activity—such as the bear market we were in at the time of this writing.

Please read Jim's excellent article, "Trading Unusual Call Activity," on the OptionVue web site, to learn more about Jim's simple and consistent trading rules, as he offers some important tips on selecting the best option strategy, limiting losses, and running with winners.

COVERED WRITING WITH CONVERTIBLE SECURITIES

Often overlooked in the investment arena are convertible securities. Convertible securities are corporate bonds or preferred stock with a conversion privilege. That is, they may be converted into common stock at a prescribed ratio.

As Value Line (my favorite source of information about convertible securities) is apt to point out, convertible securities offer an attractive alternative to the common stock. First, they are higher quality securities than the common. Holders of convertible bonds and convertible preferreds have a claim on assets before stockholders in the event of financial distress. Second, the conversion privilege causes the convertible security to participate with the common in upside moves. On the other hand, if the common falls, the convertible security's fall is cushioned by its increasing yield, to the point where its investment value as a simple bond or preferred stock takes over. Many convertibles have a significant yield advantage over the common stock—sometimes yielding up to 10 percent or more.

That convertibles have more upside potential than downside risk is what makes them unique. Much like a long call option, the performance profile of almost every convertible security curves upward to the right. And since the conversion privilege is perpetual, convertible securities do not experience time decay the way call options do.

Long-term investing in top-rated convertible securities can bring about an enviable track record. Value Line, for example, boasts a 19 percent compounded annual return over the past 30 years on its convertible security recommendations. We are going to look at how the returns from these securities might be enhanced further through the sale of covered calls.

The standard covered write—where calls are sold against common stock positions—is a widely used investment strategy. Less well known is the fact that selling call options against convertible securities is also classified as a covered write. Carefully selected covered writes using convertible securities can produce some extremely interesting, high return/low risk investments.

Let's look at a couple of these now.

Millennium Pharmaceuticals (MLNM)

Millennium has a convertible bond. Statistics for this bond, as well as Millennium common, are given in Table 5.1. The projected price and interest earnings performance for the bond is shown in Figure 5.5. Note that the solid line represents the performance for the bond one year out, while the dashed line represents one half year out.

With its upward curvature, this investment looks very attractive. However, is there anything we can do, using options, to lift the left side and perhaps the center?

Let's say we'd be willing to give up some of the terrific potential gains of the right side to do it. What about selling covered calls? With a conversion ratio of 23.768, one needs to buy 5 bonds in order to write one covered call option, or 9 bonds in order to write two covered call options. We'll round up to 10 bonds.

TABLE 5.1	Millennium Pharmaceuticals

Convertible Bond	**Common Stock**
Issue 5.5s2007	Price 23
Price 89	Volatility 58%
Conversion Ratio 23.768	52 Week High 55.80
Current Yield 6.2%	52 Week Low 16.53
Intrst. Pymt. Dates 3-15, 9-15	Dividend nil

**Projected % Change in Cv. Bond vs. the Common
when the Common Is 23.05 and the Bond Is 89.37**

Common	+50%	+25%	−25%	−50%
Cv Bond	+17%	+8%	−8%	−14%

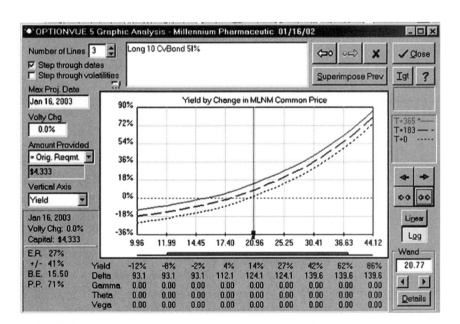

FIGURE 5.5   Millennium Pharmaceuticals' Projected Performance

The calls we're electing to sell are the just-out-of-the money Jan03 25 calls. The performance graph of the combined position is shown in Figure 5.6.

The effect of adding the calls is to lift the left side and the center, but push down the right side. The right side actually slopes down now. Why is that? Considering that the performance graph for a traditional covered write (based on the common) is flat to the right, and since we are looking

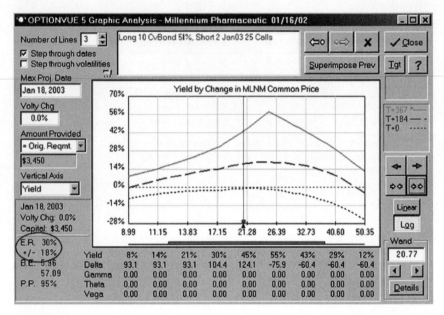

FIGURE 5.6 Combined Position—Millennium Pharmaceuticals

at a fully covered (no naked options) write here, shouldn't this investment also be flat to the right?

Not necessarily. The key lies in how the convertible moves with the common. If it moves very slowly, on a percentage basis, it might not be able to compensate for the short calls. This curve slopes down to the right because, as the price of the common goes up, the 10 rising bonds cannot gain fast enough to make up for losses coming from the two short calls.

One could experiment with adding extra bonds to bring up the right side. However, this is bound to bring down the left side at the same time. An alternative plan for responding to a rising stock price might be to roll the calls up to a higher strike if the underlying goes above a predetermined price.

Look at this investment! It yields up to 58 percent if the stock remains around its current price, and it is profitable across a broad range of prices. The overall expected return (as seen in the lower left area of the figure) is 30 percent, plus or minus 18 percent. Contrast this with just owning the bonds, where the expected return is 27 percent plus or minus 41 percent. Evidently, the main impact of selling calls on *this* investment is to bring the variance down quite a bit.

Wendy's International (WEN)

Now let's look at an example using a convertible preferred stock—the Wendy's $2.50 convertible preferreds. Details on the preferred, as well as the common, are given in Table 5.2.

With a little trial and error, I found that 220 shares in this preferred conveniently put the number of equivalent shares just over 400, so that we could consider selling four covered calls. (Note that *equivalent shares* means the number of common shares you would have after converting, and is computed by taking the number of preferred shares times the conversion ratio.)

I selected the at-the-money Jan03 30 calls to sell. The performance graph of the combined position is shown in Figure 5.7.

As in the previous example, this investment would be profitable across a broad range of common stock prices. While the stock is currently in a long-term uptrend, if the downside risk is bothersome, you could consider buying some puts to compensate. This would raise the left side but lower the right side and the center of the performance lines. Figure 5.8 shows the performance of a possible position where two long at-the-money puts have been added. With the two puts, the performance line was tilted—up on the left side, down on the right.

Both of these examples were done using a securities margin of 100 percent, fully paying for the convertible. Investors interested in turbocharging these trades are welcome to experiment with buying the convertibles on margin.

TABLE 5.2 Wendy's

Convertible Preferred	Common Stock
Issue $2.50	Price 30.20
Price 59.00	Volatility 28%
Conversion Ratio 1.893	52 Week High 31.45
Current Yield 4.2%	52 Week Low 20.00
Div Dates 3-15, 6-15, 9-15,12-15	Dividend 0.06/Q

Projected % Change in Preferred vs. the Common when the Common Is 30.20 and the Preferred Is 59.00				
Common	+50%	+25%	−25%	−50%
Preferred	+30%	+16%	−22%	−45%

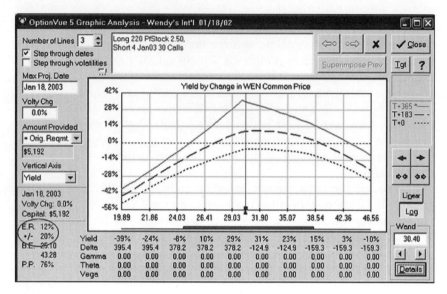

FIGURE 5.7   Combined Position—Wendy's

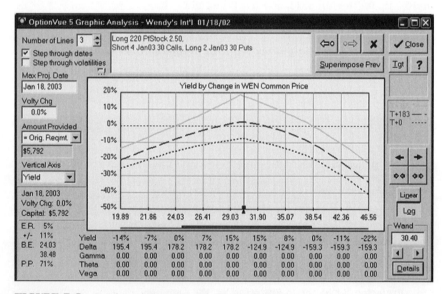

FIGURE 5.8   Combined Position with Two Long Puts

Possible Pitfalls

It is important to be aware of the potential pitfalls of this investment approach. The following section is a quote from an article entitled "Covered Call Writing with Convertible Securities," by Donald T. Mesler, published in the May 1982 issue of the *AAII Journal.*

> *Anyone actively engaged in an option writing program quickly realizes that there is a great deal more to the strategy than is evidenced by the profit profile describing the outcome at expiration.*
>
> *For example, if the stock drops sharply, should it be sold, hedged with another option at a lower exercise price, or held unhedged? Various rollover rules have been developed which define the strategy for replacing options when stock prices are dynamic. All investors should understand the alternatives and chart a plan of action in advance.*
>
> *Convertibles complicate these issues further because they are only a proxy for stock, not a direct substitute. For example, if the underlying stock advances and the option is assigned, the owner of the convertible does not, in fact, have stock to deliver. Stock must be purchased in the open market for delivery or conversion instructions must be issued. By this action the convertible will be exchanged for stock which can then be used to meet the option assignment.*
>
> *When converting, however, any premium over conversion value for the convertible is lost. In the case of a bond, accrued interest is also sacrificed. Therefore, it is frequently a superior strategy to buy stock on the open market to satisfy an option assignment. The convertible is liquidated in a separate transaction.*
>
> *Convertible positions also require more intense surveillance. For example, call provisions may necessitate conversion earlier than planned. Further, in merger/takeover situations, convertible holders often receive special offers which must be evaluated carefully. Nevertheless, with proper selection and careful monitoring, these factors seldom have a negative impact on the option writing program. They are a small price to pay for the higher expected returns which the convertible offers.*

Convertible securities are for more conservative investors. In terms of risk, they fall somewhere between the risk levels of common stock and high-grade corporate bonds. The upward curvature of their performance conveys an inherent edge. And selling a few covered calls, and/or possibly buying a few puts, can mitigate what little downside risk they have.

A good source of information is the Value Line Convertibles Survey, available on a trial and subscription basis from www.valueline.com. As it is important for the investor to understand convertible securities in more detail than covered here, I recommend that the reader enter into a service like this and learn more before investing.

When searching for investment candidates, a favorable stock/convertible price relationship is important. You need a convertible whose price is significantly enhanced by its conversion value. Such a convertible moves when the common moves, and this is important if you're going to use options positions with the convertible. I look for a conversion premium of 25 percent or less—meaning that the security's conversion value comprises 75 percent or more of the value of the convertible.

There are more than 200 stocks that have both actively traded convertibles and listed options. Portfolios can easily be constructed to satisfy individual requirements for quality, diversification, and risk.

INVESTING IN A ROUGH MARKET

What can you do when the market looks like it's in a complete meltdown? Investors are dumping their shares, buyers are too scared to step in, and long-term holders sit in dejected silence. Is there an appropriate option strategy if you think this might be the bottom?

While some prefer to stay out until a bottom has been clearly formed, others, like myself, are incorrigible bottom fishers. I know myself, and what I know is that I just can't stand to be out of a rising market. So if I don't try to pick the bottom, I'll just end up paying more for stocks on their way up.

"Okay, then. Just buy now and hold for long term—what's the problem?" you might say. Well, what if these stocks go to half price again from here? I'll be in anguish.

Can options help? Yes they can. At the same time that I buy stock, I can also buy puts. This gives me all the upside potential of owning the stock, while the puts serve as an insurance policy in case the stock keeps dropping.

Interestingly, buying calls creates the very same performance curve as buying stock and buying puts, but uses a lot less money. An appropriate number of calls can be bought that provides the same upside potential as owning the stock, but for a fraction of the cost. Thus, more of your capital can remain in cash.

Investing this way creates a built-in stop. For example, if the calls cost 15 percent of what buying the stock would have cost, then buying the calls is equivalent to buying the stock and setting a 15 percent downside stop. Using calls also gives you two extra advantages. The big advantage is that if the stock dips 15 percent or more and then comes back, you're still in it. (With stock, you would have been stopped out and then missed the recovery.) The other advantage is that your idle cash gets to earn interest in the meantime.

One caveat: If the stock ends up at the same price come expiration, the option will have lost all its time value. If this was an at-the-money or out-of-the-money option, it lost all its value. In contrast, if you had bought stock, you'd have broken even.

When buying calls, the question naturally arises, "What duration and what strike price should I select?" This is an important question, because it can make the difference in the calls costing anywhere from 10 to 50 percent of the equivalent quantity of stock. The duration depends on how long you expect the recovery might take. If you think it might take six months, then get six-month options or perhaps a little longer. Remember, if your first calls end up worthless because the market drops another 20 to 50 percent, you can be thankful you didn't have shares, then buy calls again. As for strike price, I would recommend buying the at-the-money calls.

Why not use LEAPS? You can, but LEAPS cost more, and therefore you have more capital at risk. If you use LEAPS, you would probably want to set a stop-loss point.

When the market has fallen sharply, buying a few calls is a great way to put your toe in the water immediately, rather than waiting for a clear bottom to form. Rather than setting a stop on the calls, you can just figure that the calls might become a complete loss. But who knows? They might get you in on the first leg of a new uptrend. Often the first gains as a market comes off a bottom can be some of the largest percentage gains. Buying calls gives you the feeling of being "in," and yet having your losses limited automatically.

Using the Covered Combo in Volatile Markets

In tumultuous markets you would think there would be abundant options trading opportunities. Turns out, it's not that simple. In such an environment, options are very expensive. That would suggest finding a way of selling them, but what is a good, safe way to sell them? Covered writing is okay, but it leaves you holding the bag in a swift decline. And naked writing is pretty dangerous in a volatile environment.

Question: Would you enjoy picking up some good stocks just below current price levels? If so, the answer may very well be the covered combo.

The covered combo strategy consists of a covered write (long stock and short call) plus a short put. In order to receive some good premium and downside protection, an at-the-money or just-out-of-the-money call is typically selected to form the covered write.

The put is typically selected at a strike below the current stock price, at a price where you would be happy to buy more shares of this stock. Technically, this short put is a naked option. However, it's not a dangerous option. If the stock falls below the put's strike price you may be assigned, thus buying more shares. You simply need to be prepared to do this.

Since the covered combo has you selling options, this strategy takes full advantage of currently inflated option prices.

In a volatile market, literally hundreds of stocks can be ripe for covered combos. A key is to pick a stock you'd like to own, or perhaps one you own already. Then you figure out how many shares to buy (if any) and which calls and puts to sell.

Say, for example, we liked Microsoft (MSFT), once trading at 96. Microsoft's historical volatility chart shows IV (implied volatility) at extremely high levels currently (see Figure 5.9). This means its options are expensive.

The following covered combo might be considered:

Buy 500 shares of Microsoft stock	at 96
Sell 5 calls Jul 100	at 10.5
Sell 5 puts Jul 90	at 7

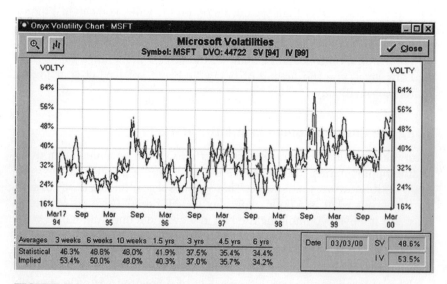

FIGURE 5.9 Historical Volatility of Microsoft

Let's analyze this trade. With the stock at 96, the proposed out-of-the-money call sale would give us 10.5 points of downside protection. In other words, the stock could drop to 85.5 before we incurred a loss. These expensive options give us a lot of downside protection!

Then add to that the credit received from selling the puts. Regardless of where the stock price goes, the extra 7 points received from selling the puts can be considered as helping us buy the original 500 shares of stock for 7 points less. Considering the proceeds from the puts and the calls together, we're effectively buying the stock for approximately 78.5. That's 17.5 points below current market value!

If the stock falls below 90, our then in-the-money puts would probably be assigned, and we'd be buying an additional 500 shares of stock at 90. So the first 500 shares cost us 78.5 each. The second 500 (if the stock drops below 90) cost us 90 each. That means we got 1,000 shares at an average price of 84.25. Not bad, when you consider that the current price of Microsoft is 96. Magic!

So what's the catch? The catch is that if the stock falls further, we're losing $1,000 per point on our 1,000-share stock position. But presumably this was an acceptable risk for us as willing stock investors. If, instead, the stock soars, we make $10,580 and no more, as our upside gains are capped by the short calls. Figure 5.10 illustrates the Microsoft covered combo.

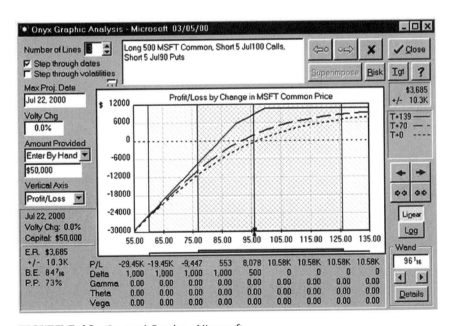

FIGURE 5.10 Covered Combo—Microsoft

Notice that the shaded areas, representing the first and second standard deviation price moves, extend to an extremely wide price range, reflecting the high-volatility environment. The OptionVue 5 software used this high volatility in its projection of possible future stock price behavior. Even when we let the program assume this continued high volatility (which is unlikely to continue through July expiration, 139 days hence), this investment looks very good.

Interestingly, the graph does not show what happens in all circumstances. It is conservative. It only shows what happens if the stock goes straight from its current price to other prices represented along the horizontal axis. If the stock drops to 90 and you get assigned an extra 500 shares, and then the stock goes back up, your outcome is better than the graph depicts—much better.

Buying Deep In-the-Money Options

Buying deep in-the-money (ITM) options is a good way of carrying out directional trading in a high-volatility environment.

Although markets are unpredictable, one thing is certain: High volatility won't last forever. Sooner or later, volatility has to come back down. As it does, the at-the-monies (ATMs) and out-of-the-monies (OTMs) are going to be hurt, while the deep ITMs will be relatively unaffected, since they have very little time value.

One reason I like using deep ITM options is that as the market trends, it naturally experiences one- or two-day setbacks, and these setbacks affect my deep ITM calls very little on a percentage basis. I am more comfortable seeing my position through, and because they have very little time premium, I am not nervous about time decay.

On a risk/reward scale, purchasing deep ITM options falls between the higher-leverage/higher-risk purchase of ATM or OTM options, and the more sedate buying of vertical debit spreads. Buying vertical debit spreads and buying deep ITM options are both good strategies for insulating yourself from the effects of falling volatilities. However, the purchase of deep ITM options is more straightforward, as it does not involve as many transactions.

Buying LEAPS can accomplish a similar thing. However, buying deep ITM (usually nearby) listed options is a little higher on the risk/reward scale because they move point-for-point with their underlying. Also note that LEAPS possess a much greater vega risk (exposure to a fall in volatility).

Some traders might object that deep ITM options have a wider bid/asked spread, causing the trader to experience higher transaction costs. I have not found this to be a problem, especially if you can direct trades to the best market. If you cannot direct your trades, placing an order between the bid and the asked is often successful.

Some investors also object, psychologically, to paying a higher price than about 6 per option, preferring options priced between 2 and 5. This is not rational. A friend once refused to buy a stock priced above 100. I explained to her that the price itself makes no difference; it's the financial ratios that count.

Holding deep ITM calls (or puts) is like buying (or shorting) the underlying stock, in a sense, as deep ITM options move point-for-point with their underlying. However, buying deep ITM options costs less than the stock, allowing you to either leverage up or retain cash for other investments.

For example, let's consider Dell stock and options. At one time, Dell was trading at 26.5 and seemed to be in the early stages of an uptrend. To go long, you could buy 1,000 shares of stock for $26,500. Or you could consider buying calls. The nearbys (with three weeks to go) were priced as follows:

Strike	Bid	Asked	Time Premium
30	0.40	0.50	0.45
27.5	1.20	1.30	1.25
25	2.50	2.60	2.55
22.5	4.40	4.60	0.50
20	6.50	6.70	0.10

As you can see, the deep ITM calls have a time premium of only 0.10. That means the passing of time and a possible volatility drop could only take 0.10 away from you in the next three weeks! The equivalent of 1,000 shares of stock can be had by buying just 10 of these options for $6,700. In effect, it's like buying cheap, $6 warrants. If Dell simply rises three points, the warrant will go to $9.

Contrast that with the experience of those who buy the ATM or OTM options. First, with their delta of 50 each (as the stock moves one point, the option moves about half a point), getting a 1,000-share equivalent stake would require buying 20 of the ATM options. This position would cost $5,200. Say the stock moves up a bit, then pulls back over the next couple of days, returning to its starting price. Now your option is worth a bit less than what you paid, making you wish you'd waited until now to buy it. Then the stock advances a couple of points. Nice, but your options are worth about 3 at this point—up only slightly because of one week's time decay. Rather frustrating.

The ITM option buyer, however, is satisfied to see his option up two points at the end, and never having seen it fall below his purchase price in the meantime. So when you're looking at going long (or short), consider using deep ITM calls (or puts).

Using Index Options to Protect a Stock Portfolio

"The worst bear market since 1974–1975," the *Wall Street Journal* said of the Nasdaq in the year 2000. Those of us who endured it may never forget it.

The good news is that hedging with options is a terrific way to fight back. The simplest ways of hedging a stock portfolio are buying puts or selling calls. Of the two, buying puts is preferable, because if a wave of selling carries the market deep, puts work harder for you the farther the sell-off goes. This happens automatically because as the puts get driven into the money, their delta increases. In contrast, short calls would be going out of the money at that time, their delta dropping, and their protection growing weaker.

You can either buy puts on each of your individual stock holdings, or buy an appropriate number of index puts. I prefer the latter because it's much simpler to get in and out of puts at various stages of a bear market. Ideally, you should pick an index that is indicative of your portfolio and has a liquid options market. For instance, the QQQ (Nasdaq 100) matches up well with a portfolio of tech stocks and its options are heavily traded.

To figure an appropriate number of index options to buy, start with the dollar value of your stock portfolio, divide by the price of the index, and apply a "fudge factor" for beta. For example, if you have reason to believe your stocks are 30% more volatile than the QQQ, multiply by 1.30. The result is the number of equivalent deltas of the index your portfolio represents.

Let's say you have a $150,000 portfolio of high-tech stocks. Divide by the price of the QQQ (currently 40) and multiply by a beta fudge factor of, say, 1.30, and you have approximately 4,900 QQQ deltas. In other words, it's as though you have approximately 4,900 shares of the QQQ.

To hedge this fully, you would need to buy enough puts (and/or sell enough calls) to bring your net delta down to zero. Using at-the-money puts, with a typical delta of 50 each, this would require 98 puts (4,900 divided by 50).

To partially hedge, you could buy fewer than 98 put contracts. To over-hedge (something I like to do when I feel *sure* the market is going down), you could buy more than 98 contracts.

To illustrate how effectively options can be used to cushion the pain of a bear market, I would like to relate my experiences of late 2000.

From September 1 through mid-November, I allowed my stock portfolio to go unhedged, because I was not convinced that we were in a bear market. (In retrospect, I can see all the head-and-shoulder formations clearly now.) As a result, my portfolio was decimated. However, in mid-November I decided to fight back. I sold off several losing stocks to raise cash and I bought puts as the market went into another swoon. Several up- and downswings later, and with some lucky timing, my portfolio was soon back to its September 1 value.

I say this not to brag (goodness knows there were many who suffered in the sell-off), but to illustrate what a powerful weapon options are. Rather than just selling all my stocks and sitting out, nervous about missing out on the next big rally, I was able to keep most of my favorites and offset their declines with put gains.

Since options are so expensive in a downtrending market, it is important to buy and sell them in rhythm with the market. I'm not sure how one obtains a feel for the rhythm of the market, except through experience. But I will say that the market is way more predictable during a sell-off. For example, following a sharp break and a 50 percent rebound, it's a pretty safe bet to go short. You could stay short until the market either returns to the previous low, or has a climactic sell-off day. If you can catch the Nasdaq in a climactic sell-off day, that's a beautiful opportunity to sell the puts and let your stocks go back up unhedged (maybe even buy a few calls for a 24-hour play), as there most certainly will be a smart rebound. When the rebound is finished, you can think about shopping for puts again. And so it goes.

I would not just buy puts and let them sit. This might work for some, but I prefer to time the market. I browse through a lot of stock charts every day. If I see a lot of stocks ready for another break, then I figure the market is about to break. That's when I buy puts. Then I sell my puts in three to six days when it looks like the current sell-off has run its course. I'll say more about timing the market, especially during a downturn, in Chapter 8.

CHAPTER 6

Theoretical and Practical Matters

In this chapter we will discuss how options pricing models, volatility models, and other essential tools of the trade are best applied in practice. We'll see how the different kinds of options pricing models work, and what models were meant to be used with what kinds of options. We'll also discuss the best ways of estimating volatility—the all-important and most difficult-to-obtain input to any options pricing model. I'll talk about the methods and rationale for using slightly different volatilities to compute the fair values of each option on a given underlying. We'll also have a further discussion of the greeks, and other practical matters.

Rather than delving deeply into mathematics, I will hold the discussion to a practical level and use laymen's terms. Don't skip this chapter! It contains several important concepts. Options are math-intensive animals. While computer programs exist that can do the math for you, it behooves the options trader to know something about what is going on "under the hood," and not just blindly follow the recommendations of an options analysis program.

OPTIONS PRICING MODELS

An options pricing model is the foundation of an options trader's work. Not only do fair option values help the trader decide which options to buy or sell, and for what price, the options pricing model is also essential for simulating the future performance of contemplated positions.

We'll look at the most popular models in use today, discuss their underlying principles, and give you some important information on how they're meant to be applied.

In nature, random processes tend to distribute themselves in the shape of Gauss's famous bell-shaped curve, where more probable events cluster around the center of the curve and less likely events populate the sides. This so-called *normal* probability distribution seems to apply pretty well in the financial markets as well. We find that the future price of a stock or commodity is predicted fairly well by a bell curve centered over today's price. However, an adjustment is needed to account for the fact that price movements are not linear. An example will serve to illustrate the problem. Suppose a stock goes up 5 points, then 5 more points, then 5 more points. Was each successive 5-point increase equally likely? No. The final 5-point increase was an easier achievement than the one preceding it, and that one was easier than the one preceding it. This is because each successive 5-point increase is a smaller *percentage* increase.

Stated another way, in terms of probability, a stock can double just as easily as it can go to half its price. For a stock at 100, this means it can go up 100 points or down 50 points with equal probability. The normal probability distribution does not express this. We must call upon a mathematical function called a logarithm to solve the problem for us. It turns out, when you take the logarithm of various stock prices, then apply the normal distribution, the results fit reality quite well (not perfectly, but pretty close; more on this later). In other words, make the horizontal axis beneath the bell curve be the logarithm of stock prices, and voilà! You have a curve that works. This kind of distribution is called a *lognormal* distribution.

The assumption that stocks and other financial instruments follow a lognormal probability distribution is a principle underlying all of the most popular options pricing models.

Numerical Methods

The first options pricing models used *numerical methods*. A numerical method is an approach where a process is repeated many times and the results tabulated. For example, to prove that the odds of a coin coming up heads is 50 percent, a numerical method would be to flip a coin many times and tally the results. The more iterations, the greater the accuracy.

In options pricing, one numerical method, called the Monte Carlo simulation, involves randomly generating future prices for the underlying in a way that simulates a lognormal distribution, and where the projected time frame is the option's expiration date. For each of these potential prices, we compute and store the intrinsic value of the option (at expiration). We then accumulate these into an average. A sufficiently accurate option fair value will be obtained after a sufficiently large number of samples have been taken and tallied.

Another numerical approach is called the binomial model. This approach is based on the idea that, from a given point in time, a stock price may go to two different new price levels with equal probability. From each of those prices, the stock price may go to different new prices, and so on, eventually branching out into a large number of possible prices. To show how this works to simulate the normal probability distribution, I'll ask the reader to remember from math class a triangular arrangement of pegs (see Figure 6.1.)

If you recall, balls dropped into the top would hit the pegs, trickle down, and collect in columns at the bottom. Under ideal conditions, the distribution of balls would approximate a normal distribution, especially when a large number of balls are used in a large layout.

The binomial model uses the same principle, except that we fiddle with the probabilities of the left and right branching—making it slightly more likely that the stock price will go higher than lower. This is to simulate a *log*normal distribution. Other factors affecting an option's fair value, such as the potential for early exercise and the way a stock's price drops at

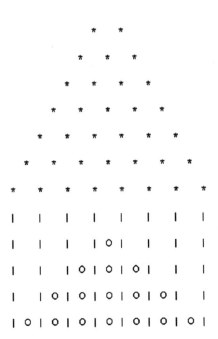

FIGURE 6.1 Triangular Arrangement of Pegs

ex-dividend dates, can also be taken into account during the process. Consequently, the binomial model is extremely accurate at high resolutions. It also works faster than a Monte Carlo simulation.

The principle drawback of numerical methods is that they require a large number of iterations, causing them to be computer intensive. In the early days, this was a big problem. I remember it taking 10 seconds or more to compute the fair value of an option in 1982, using one of the very first personal computers and the binomial pricing model. That means it must have taken a minute or more to compute an option's fair value back in 1973 when listed options first began to trade!

A minute doesn't sound too bad if all you need is the fair value of one option, but when there are thousands of options, it becomes impossible to recompute their values fast enough in response to changing conditions during the trading day. That's why the Black-Scholes model was such a godsend.

The Black-Scholes Model

Mathematician Fischer Black and economist Myron Scholes, both teaching at the University of Chicago in 1973, developed the first closed-form solution to the options-pricing problem. A closed-form solution is simply an equation—a formula. For the first time, an option's fair value could be computed in a single pass; no iterations. While not a simple formula, the Black-Scholes formula made it much easier to compute the fair value of an option, transforming options pricing in the very same year that the options exchange opened in Chicago. Thus it played a big part in allowing the derivatives market to flourish.

I promised not to delve into mathematics. Nevertheless, I think you should see what the Black-Scholes formula looks like:

$$C = SN(X1) - Ke^{-RT}N(X2)$$

where C = the fair value of a call option
S = the current price of the stock
K = the strike price of the option
R = the short-term rate of interest
T = the duration of the option

$$X1 = \frac{Ln\left(\frac{S}{K}\right) + \left(R + .5V^2\right)T}{VvT}$$

$$X2 = X1 - VvT$$

  $N(X)$ = the value of the cumulative normal density function
  V^2 = the variance rate of return on the stock
  V = the square root of the variance (i.e., volatility)
  Ln = the natural logarithm function
  e = the exponential function

Several assumptions underlie the Black-Scholes formula:

- The markets for options, bonds, and stocks are frictionless.
- The risk-free rate is constant over the life of the option and equal to R per unit of time.
- All investors agree that stock prices follow a stochastic process (ref. Section A-4a of *Option Pricing*, by Jarrow and Rudd[1]).
- The underlying security pays no dividends.

I wanted you to see that the Black-Scholes formula is not as complicated as you might have thought, especially for a formula that was so incredibly important, and timely, to the financial markets.

Since the pure Black-Scholes model does not take into account stock dividends, it needs to be modified when valuing options on dividend-paying stocks. Adjusting the Black-Scholes model for dividends is accomplished by subtracting from S in the formula the present value of dividends incurred during the life of the option.

The Black-Scholes model applies to European-style options, not to American-style options. However, during the years subsequent to 1973, adaptations were developed. Most notably, the Roll model is an early-exercise adjusted model for American-style call options that is based on the fact that, for call options, early-exercise is never economically feasible other than right before a dividend. So the Roll model takes the maximum of fair values computed at each ex-dividend date using the Black-Scholes model.

Puts were a bigger problem, however. It can be economically feasible to exercise a sufficiently deep in-the-money option *at any time*. The problem of valuing American-style puts was so challenging that there was no closed-form solution until my own work in 1984. The Yates model starts with a dividend-adjusted Black-Scholes calculation, and adds extra value because of the early-exercise privilege. I call this extra value the early-exercise premium. You see, the value of a European-style put goes below parity when the option is more than a certain amount in-the-money (see Figure 6.2). For instance, a 10-point in-the-money put option might be fairly valued at 9. This happens because an equivalent strategy

---

[1]Robert Jarrow and Andrew Rudd, *Option Pricing* (Homewood: Dow Jones Irwin, 1983), Section 8-2.

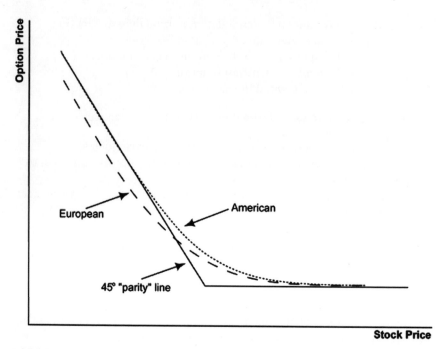

FIGURE 6.2   Values of European- and American-style Put Options

to owning a deep in-the-money put is shorting the stock, and professional traders find it more economical to short the stock than to buy a put that is valued at parity. Discounting the option brings it into equilibrium. Only then is it equally attractive. Besides market forces, the Black-Scholes formula itself will show you that the fair value of a deep in-the-money put is less than its intrinsic value.

The effect of the Yates adjustment is equivalent to bending the European-style put valuation curve upward at the left (the in-the-money segment) just enough to lift it above the parity line. Most of the bending occurs in the near-the-money area of the curve, with proportionately less bending as you go farther in or out of the money. The result is an appropriate valuation curve for American-style puts. Coefficients of the model were optimized to produce minimal error as compared with the binomial model at a high resolution, using a wide variety of historical data. Thus the Yates model was fashioned by an engineer driven by necessity, rather than by a theoretician. It was a pragmatic solution—not unlike when a farmer faces a challenge and decides it's time to weld together some parts and create a new tool to make his life easier.

Practical Uses

Quick and easy option fair value calculators are available on many financial web sites. Unfortunately, almost all of them indiscriminately use an unadjusted Black-Scholes model. There is no distinguishing of American versus European options, or accounting for dividends. Let the user beware!

The correct options pricing model to use for options on futures is the Black model, developed by the same Fischer Black who helped develop the Black-Scholes model. The Black model is similar to the Black-Scholes model, only simpler. The difference is an important one, yet sometimes I see the Black-Scholes model being mistakenly used for options on futures.

Besides these problems, there is usually an even bigger difficulty with most fair value calculators. One of the inputs is bound to be volatility, and usually the person has no idea what to fill in there. The slightest difference in volatility can make a difference in the option value, so you'd better use a good number. If you're guessing at volatility, who cares what model you're using? You might as well just try and guess the fair value as well!

COMING UP WITH THE RIGHT VOLATILITY

Volatility is a measure of the standard deviation of price changes. It is the square root of variance. So one way of coming up with a volatility is to apply standard variance formulas from elementary statistics to a recent history of prices. We call volatility measured this way *statistical volatility* (SV).

The simplest of these formulas uses only daily closing prices. Other, more powerful formulas make use of other valuable information contained in the daily open, high, and low prices. One difficulty is determining how many days of recent history to include. Usually an arbitrary time period is selected, as the rationale for deciding on a long or a short time period is conflicting. While using more data should lead to a better estimate, unfortunately, it is a better estimate for that time period only and it may not reflect the present volatility as well as an estimate based only on the more recent data.

So we often choose to use a volatility measured from the underlying's recent price movements. Of course, ideally, what we really need to feed into the option fair value calculator is future volatility—how volatile the underlying will be during the remaining life of the option. However, no one can know this, so the best we can do is refer to recent volatility measurements and estimate the future volatility.

The other way of measuring volatility uses the options themselves.

Each option, by virtue of its very price, is making a statement about how volatile its underlying is. Volatility measured this way is called implied volatility. The higher the option's price (all else being equal), the higher the implied volatility (IV). To understand how IV is computed, you can think of IV as the options pricing model being worked backward to determine volatility, normally one of the key *inputs* to the formula.

In truth, pricing models cannot be worked backward. IV has to be derived by working the pricing model forward repeatedly through trial and error, experimenting intelligently with different volatilities until the theoretical option price converges with the actual market price.

Using the implied volatility measured from a particular option to compute the fair value of the same option would be meaningless, as it would always return a fair value equal to the current price. So in practice, we average together the IVs from many, if not all, of the options of a particular asset, often giving more weight to the options of greater trading volume. We also keep a brief, recent daily history of these average IVs and average those into one grand average IV.

Now, we can feed this grand average IV into the option fair value calculator. Or would some kind of proportionate mix of SV and IV be appropriate? You see, coming up with a good volatility number to use for an option's fair value calculation is a challenge! I believe IV is better to use than SV because IV embodies the collective expectation of all market participants as to the future volatility of this asset. To use IV is to hitch a ride on the shirt tails of all the others who have (presumably) struggled to come up with an appropriate volatility to use.

But let us say, after weighing the various methods, we have finally chosen our number. Unfortunately, there is a problem with applying a single number, whether it be SV or the grand average IV, to all the options of a particular asset. With many assets, the options are systematically valued at different volatility levels, not only as you move up and down the strikes (volatility skew), but also as you move across the various expiration months (intermonth volatility differences). Since this can make significant differences in options values, let's take a closer look at how the options pricing model can be adjusted to reflect this.

VOLATILITY SKEW

With many assets, the options of various strikes are priced using steadily increasing or decreasing volatilities as you move from strike to strike. In most index call options, for example, volatilities decrease as you move from the in-the-money (ITM) strikes toward the out-of-the-money (OTM) strikes. In many commodity call options, the reverse is true: Volatilities increase in the calls as you go farther out-of-the-money.

The fact that volatility skew is systematic means that we can try to deal with it in our models. Fortunately, one finds that when the IVs of all the options of a particular month and type (e.g., the March calls) are plotted, they form either a straight line or a smooth curve, as demonstrated in Figure 6.3. In this graph, the vertical axis represents IV and the horizontal axis represents how far in- or out-of-the-money each option is in terms of a convenient formula:

$$\frac{\text{Ln}\left(\dfrac{K}{S}\right)}{\text{Sqrt}(t)}$$

where S stands for the price of the underlying, K stands for the strike price, Ln is the natural logarithm function, and Sqrt(t) means the square root of time until expiration. Mapping IVs into this formula for the horizontal axis allows us to plot current IV readings in a framework for easy viewing and comparison of multiple skew curves.

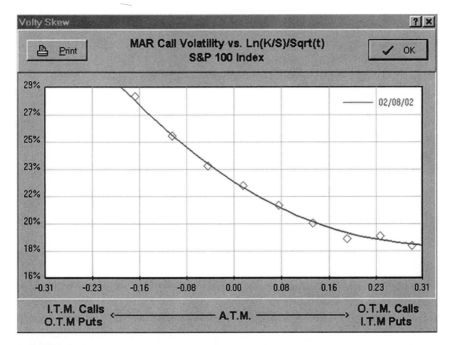

FIGURE 6.3 Plotting IVs of One Month and Type

Such a curve (or even a straight line, if that's what it is) is easily modeled using a parabolic formula. You may recall from high school math class that the formula for a parabola is

$$y = ax^2 + bx + c$$

In this application, y would be volatility and x would be the degree to which each option is in- or out-of-the-money. An algorithm can determine the constants a, b, and c that cause the curve to fit the data points most closely.

Once this curve is fitted, we can use the curve to give us an appropriate volatility number for any of the March OEX calls, not only at the current OEX price, but also at other projected OEX price levels.

The curve also provides us with a context in which to judge the fairness of current option prices. For example, in the figure, notice that the second data point from the right lies above the line, while the third data point from the right lies beneath the line. Since each of these data points represents an option, this is saying that the one option is currently overvalued, while the other option is undervalued.

By fitting a different curve to each group of options (of the same month and type), this approach deals with the intermonth volatility differences and models the skew at the same time.

WHAT CAUSES VOLATILITY SKEW?

There are at least two good reasons for the existence of volatility skew. The first is CEV (constant elasticity of volatility). When we discussed CEV in Chapter 3, we noted that CEV is the name for the observed tendency of volatility to change when the price of the underlying changes. For example, with most stocks and stock indexes, as prices increase, volatility declines; when prices decline, volatility increases. This negative correlation would be indicated with a negative CEV factor.

CEV largely explains why index call options trade at lower IVs as you go farther out-of-the-money. The options market is anticipating that if the market moves higher, volatility will decrease, working against the increase in out-of-the-money call option values. Thus it values those calls cheaper now. Likewise, puts, trading at higher IVs as you go out-of-the-money, are already priced to anticipate higher volatility levels if the market were to fall.

CEV is an important factor in other markets as well. For example, in commodities, where volatility spikes happen more often when the price of the commodity goes up, the correlation is positive and the CEV factor is positive. This causes OTM call options to be valued at progressively higher IVs.

Note that CEV is systematic only in broad, general terms. Not all price changes are accompanied by a volatility change, and even when they are, the relative magnitudes of the resulting volatility changes can vary. In practice, however, we find that it is appropriate to model CEV as an integral part of our options analysis. Also, we find that a linear CEV model is sufficient. In other words, we can assume that volatility changes proportionately with price, at least for small to moderate price changes.

Leptokurtosis

Another source of volatility skew is leptokurtosis. This may sound like the name of a disease. However, it is a term for how the behavior of real prices seems to deviate from the lognormal distribution. Studies have shown that stock prices, as well as the prices of many other financial instruments, follow a lognormal distribution with some degree of leptokurtosis[2].

One feature of leptokurtosis is that extreme price moves happen more frequently than they should. Therefore, out at the extreme ends (the "tails") of the bell curve, the line is lifted and extends farther out. The other feature is that the center of the curve is higher, indicating a greater propensity for prices to remain where they are. To balance out these increased probabilities, the leptokurtic curve is lower midway out on either side, just beyond the left and right "shoulders" of the curve. (See Figure 6.4.)

The options markets are more or less aware of leptokurtosis and

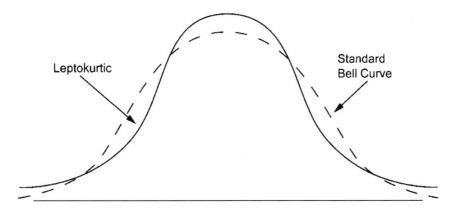

FIGURE 6.4 Leptokurtic Curve

---

[2]Eugene Fama, "The Behavior of Stock Market Prices," *Journal of Business* 38, 1 (January 1965), pp. 34–105.

value options accordingly. This accounts for much of the volatility skew that we see.

One wonders why more options pricing models based on leptokurtosis haven't been developed and put into use. Perhaps it is because of difficulties modeling the leptokurtic distribution, or perhaps it is because traders had already become so accustomed to using the first options pricing models—those based on a lognormal distribution. In any case, a standard options pricing model, together with a good volatility skew model, turns out to be an excellent practical solution. Note that an options pricing model based on leptokurtosis would not do away with the need to model volatility skew. Other causes of the skew, including CEV and other deviations from the lognormal distribution, such as a real or perceived price floor or ceiling, would still need to be taken into account.

Irregular Empirical Distributions

As we have said, stocks and other asset types exhibit price changes according to an imperfect lognormal distribution. Besides leptokurtosis, I expect that many stocks and other assets have individual systematic deviations from the lognormal distribution. Someday I intend to develop the capability of computing and displaying an asset's empirical distribution— its historical distribution based on the past several years' price changes. With such a tool we may find, for example, that a particular stock has a propensity for sudden, radical price drops (along with, perhaps, gradual increases). The empirical distribution for this stock would be lopsided. It would have a fat tail on the left. The options market might remember this and build an appropriate premium into the put prices. On the other hand, it might not. If not, this would present an opportunity, assuming the stock's pattern of crashing from time to time continues. If a sufficient number of stocks can be found that have lumpy or oddly shaped empirical distributions, it might be possible to set up a trading system that systematically takes advantage of these using various options strategies.

Intermonth Volatility Differences

One often sees nearby options trading at higher levels of implied volatility than the farther out options. What causes this?

Remember that one of the underlying assumptions of the Black-Scholes model is that markets are smooth and continuous. In real life, markets can, and often do, jump. Sometimes, in response to surprising news or a sudden order imbalance, the price of a stock can jump several points from one trade to the next, allowing investors no opportunity to make a decision or trade at any intermediate price levels. Indeed, this kind of jump often happens from the close of trading one day to the opening of trading the next, because significant company news is often released during off hours.

The effect of potential price jumps is to bolster the values of all options. However, nearby options are bolstered more because a price jump would affect them most. The farther out options have more time in which to smooth out the effects of price jumps.

BALANCING FACTORS

In options, a lot of things balance out. The markets are more efficient than they may seem at times. Apparent discrepancies or IV differentials are usually there for good reason. For example, the volatility skew in index call options would seem to work in favor of call buyers looking for a rally. However, the CEV effect will lower implied volatilities across the board as the index advances, with the result that a call option might end up trading at very nearly the same implied volatility after the rally. The same might be true of buying index puts in expectation of a sell-off, except in reverse: Volatility skew would hurt but CEV would help.

When the market is expecting a big change in the price of a stock, with either direction just as probable, the nearby options will usually trade at higher implied volatility levels than the farther out options. This would, on the surface, attract traders to put on calendar spreads—buying the farther out options and selling the nearbys. However, big price action in the underlying would hurt calendar spreads. So making the nearby options more expensive is the market's way of laying odds that calendar spreads won't be profitable—again, balancing things out.

As a final example, covered writing and naked put selling are equivalent strategies in the sense that their performance diagrams are the same shape—meaning their risk/reward characteristics are the same. Comparing the two strategies, put selling is better from the standpoints of fewer transactions and the fact that your collateral gets to earn interest. However, covered writers get to sell the slightly more expensive call options (stock call options are more expensive than stock put options, for reasons given in the next section). Also, covered writers receive stock dividends. All factors considered, the two strategies are nearly identical.

PUT/CALL PARITY

With a potential news announcement that could cause a stock to jump in price, one might think that the stock's calls would reflect the excitement with extra premium, but not the puts. As it turns out, the puts will be more expensive as well.

This happens not only because the news might somehow turn out to be disappointing, but also because of a strategy used by professionals called a conversion. A conversion consists of buying the stock, selling a call, and buying a put. The call and the put are of the same strike price and expiration date. You can think of a conversion as a covered write plus a protective put purchase. Or you can think of it as long stock plus short synthetic stock.

A conversion is theoretically a risk-free position. Its performance graph is a flat horizontal line. That is because no matter where the price of the stock goes, the outcome is the same, as the three elements of the conversion perfectly offset each other. Since the outcome is certain, the only way to make a profit with a conversion is if you can put it on for a bargain.

If a call is expensive and its corresponding put (same strike price and expiration) is cheap, traders will buy conversions using that call and that put. Their trading will cause downward pressure on the calls and upward pressure on the puts, until both are driven to *parity*, at which point it is no longer worthwhile to buy any more conversions.

A similar thing happens if a put is temporarily more expensive than its corresponding call. Traders will do reverse conversions—shorting stock, buying calls, and selling puts—again driving call and put prices back into parity. Thus, calls and puts of the same strike price and expiration always trade at close to the same IV.

Again, when I speak of calls being more expensive than puts, or vice versa, I mean in terms of IV levels. IV is *the* definitive parameter for judging cheapness or dearness of options. Next to price, IV is the most important parameter to have in view when looking at the array of options on a particular asset. IVs are usually fairly uniform across the array or, if there is a skew, IVs usually vary in smooth, regular intervals. Any anomaly should jump right out—it would be a mispriced option.

In terms of absolute price levels, it is natural for a perfectly at-the-money (ATM) call to be more expensive than the corresponding put when the underlying is a stock or index. This is because stocks, costing hard cash and the opportunity to earn interest on it, are discounted to the present. That means stock prices (and stock indexes as well) are on a long, gradual upward slope at the rate of general interest rates. This might seem difficult to believe, because such movement is masked by the noise of daily price fluctuations, but it's true. It has to be so in order to compensate for the lost opportunity to earn interest.

On the other hand, a perfectly ATM call should be the same price as its corresponding put when the underlying is a futures contract. This is because the futures contract does not cost cash. Yes, you have to put up collateral, but that collateral can be cash in a money market fund or some other security. For this reason the Black model—the correct options pricing model to use for options on futures—is simpler than the Black-Scholes model, yet essentially the same in other respects.

THE GREEKS REVISITED

Your automobile has one gauge that tells you its velocity. An airplane has several gauges—one for ground speed and others to show how the airplane is moving in space. As we saw in Chapter 1, in options, there are four gauges. They have Greek names, so we call them the greeks. Paul Forchione, in his book *Trading Options Visually*, discusses the greeks so well, I couldn't top him. So this section is reprinted with his permission:

> *Understanding the relative impact of the greeks on positions you hold is indispensable. Here are a few general observations.*
>
> *The delta of an at-the-money option is about 50. Out-of-the-money options have smaller deltas and they decrease the farther out-of-the-money you go. In-the-money options have greater deltas and they increase the farther in-the-money you go. Call deltas are positive and put deltas are negative.*
>
> *When you sell options, theta is positive and gamma is negative. This means you make money through time decay, but price movement is undesirable. So profits you're trying to earn through option time decay when you sell puts and calls may never be realized if the commodity moves quickly in price. Also, rallies in price of the underlying asset will cause your overall position to become increasingly delta short and to lose money. Conversely, declines in underlying asset price will cause your position to become increasingly delta long and to lose money.*
>
> *When you buy options, theta is negative and gamma is positive. This means you lose money through time decay but price movement is desirable. So profits you're attempting to earn through volatile moves of the underlying asset may never be realized if time decay causes losses. Also, rallies in price result in your position becoming increasingly delta long and declines result in your position becoming increasingly delta short.*
>
> *Theta and gamma increase as you get close to expiration (they especially accelerate 30 days prior to expiration) and they're greatest for at-the-money options. This means the stakes grow if you're short at-the-money or close-to-the-money options near expiration be-*

cause either the put or call can easily become in-the-money and move point for point with the underlying. You can't adjust quickly enough to accommodate for such a situation.

When you sell options, vega is negative. This means if implied volatility increases, your position will lose money, and if it decreases your position will make money. When you buy options, vega is positive, so increases in implied volatility are profitable and decreases are unprofitable.

Vega is greatest for options far from expiration. Vega becomes less of a factor while theta and gamma become more significant as options approach expiration.

For me, trading is the ongoing pursuit of profits while mathematically managing risk. I think of trading in terms of sets of numbers that continually evolve.

At any point in time, every options position can be reduced to a set of four numbers: delta, gamma, theta, and vega. These numbers are referred to as "the greeks" of a position. An options pricing program will calculate these greeks regardless of how many long and short strike prices are involved in the position. Together, as a set of numbers, these greek parameters become a "snapshot-in-time" which shows the expected impact upon the overall position of various changes that may occur.

For example, delta tells you how long or short your position is. Gamma tells you how quickly your delta will change as the underlying moves. Theta is the dollar gain of your position in one day from time decay (negative if you are losing money). And vega is the amount your position will profit or lose if implied volatility changes.

I look at these four numbers as a unique, comprehensive description of my position at that moment in time. These numbers are dynamically interrelated. They will change as time goes by and as market circumstances change (the underlying rallies or declines and/or option implied volatility increases or decreases).

For that reason, throughout the day I review my delta, gamma, theta and vega exposure and continually make decisions about reallocating my risk among the four greeks. My decisions are based on an assessment of how I see the current market environment unfolding as well as on my personal risk profile. I stand ready to modify my positions if and when I judge they're vulnerable to my market assessment.

There are times I want to be "delta neutral" because I don't want to run the risk of losing money if I'm wrong about market direction. There are also times I want to intentionally bias my delta one way or the other.

Viewing the profit/loss curve of my options positions and adjusting my positions so the curve reflects my expectation of future volatility and price movement is what trading is all about. The slope, or curvature, of my profit/loss curve tells me the degree of risk I'm taking with respect to movement in the underlying asset, and what differentiates one volatility trader from another is the degree of curvature each is comfortable with.

Even if you and I share the same market opinion, trading decisions you make frequently will be different than mine because your tolerance for risk is different. You may be more willing to be significantly delta long or short. Or you may be less inclined to take vega risk or more willing to accept unfavorable, negative theta. There are several ways for our decisions to diverge. It's not that one approach is right and another is wrong. It's a matter of understanding where you're taking risk at that exact moment and consciously deciding if you want to make any changes in your exposure. You may decide to make no changes now, but you must be open to modifying your position later that day or tomorrow if there are changes in the market or in your comfort level.

I'm often asked "What's the best bullish (or bearish) trade in a particular commodity?" My response is always the same: There is no "best" directional trade because what's best for you is probably different than what's best for me, even if we're both bullish.

Why? Your risk profile is different than mine. You may be willing to lose money through negative time decay if you're setting your sights on large potential profits. I, on the other hand, may have more modest profit expectations and don't want to incur significant negative time decay. As a result, the bullish trade I do (e.g., credit put spread) will be different than the one you do (e.g., bull call spread or long call).[3]

TRUE DELTA AND GAMMA

Standard pricing models produce delta and the other greeks as a by-product. All too often, these models compute delta and gamma assuming a constant volatility. However, we know that volatility changes with changes in the price of the underlying. Even when pro-

---

[3]Paul Forchione, *Trading Options Visually* (Smithtown, NY: Trade Wins, 1998), pp. 123–124, 128–129.

jecting a very small change in the price of the underlying, volatility may change a small but important amount. When delta and gamma are computed by taking this into account, projecting a small change in volatility (based on the skew model and CEV) to accompany a projected small change in the price of the underlying, the result is *true* delta and gamma—more accurately representing the true behavior of the option.

The difference this makes is sometimes very significant. Take far OTM put options on the Standard & Poor's (S&P 500) futures, for example. One put, at the time of this writing, has a delta of 9.32 using the standard model but a delta of 6.63 using the true delta model. While this may not seem like much of difference in absolute terms, the trader who takes a large position in these puts will see a very wrong net delta using the standard model and, perhaps without being aware of it, construct an imbalanced hedge.

UNDERSTANDING THE LIMITATIONS OF YOUR MODEL

Dirty Harry once said, "A man's got to understand his limitations." While Harry was probably referring to the greedy, unrestrained mind of a criminal, I'm going to say that options traders have got to understand the limitations of the models they are using.

We once heard from a customer who lost money on a trade that his software had "picked" for him. Options trading software is just a model. All models, while valuable, have their limitations. Traders who have gained a mastery over their software understand not only how valuable the models are, but also where the sources of risk, or uncertainty, lie.

Here is what options analysis software *can* do with precision: With a price projection for the underlying and a projection for volatility levels (or at least an assumption that current levels will continue), the program *can accurately project the future fair values of options involved in your position.* The marketplace follows these models very well. In other words, the options marketplace is not going to abandon conventional pricing models any time soon and run amok. If you enter what turns out to be an accurate prediction of the price of the underlying, as well as an accurate volatility projection, then the option price(s) the program says will be there at the future date will be extremely close. That much options analysis software can do.

There are three things an options analysis program *cannot* predict, which the user must provide.

1. **Price movement of underlying.** Options analysis software makes no attempt to predict the future price direction of an underlying asset. That is why a graphic analysis has price as the horizontal axis—so you can see what happens to your position across a broad range of underlying asset prices.

2. **Volatility changes—overall, intermonth, and interstrike (skew) changes.** In times of greater volatility, options are more expensive. When it's quiet, options are cheap. A change in volatility can have a big impact on your options position. Yet, to my knowledge, there is no model that can predict the timing or magnitude of the next volatility change. And when a change comes, it may affect the options of a certain month more than another, or affect options unevenly across strikes (a change in skew).

   Software can be programmed to track recent volatility and, unless you override these numbers, it typically applies them to the future. In other words, it assumes that the current volatility situation will continue. If you have reason to believe otherwise, you can usually indicate an expected change in volatility in the program's model. Current volatility skews, intermonth volatility differences, and CEV can also be tracked by a sufficiently advanced program and assumed to continue into the future.

   Isn't there *some* predictability to volatility? Haven't we read repeatedly how you can profit by selling options when volatility is high and buying options when volatility is low? Yes, it is true that when volatility goes to an extreme, it is bound to return to normal levels. However, when and how fast it returns to normal is anybody's guess.

   When an option expires, its final value is determined only by the price of the underlying. However, from the time an option is born until the final minute of its life, volatility is an unpredictable wind that blows more or less premium into it.

3. **Intermonth spread changes in agricultural futures contracts.** When modeling futures options prices, an options analysis program must first predict how each future's price will behave relative to the one futures contract selected to be the independent variable. Then option fair values are computed based on those modeled futures prices.

   In agricultural futures, each contract can, and often does, trade as an independent commodity. That is because in agriculturals, timing of delivery is everything. Corn for March delivery is not the same as corn for July delivery. Each contract trades on its own supply/demand curve. Two contracts can even represent two completely different crops. For instance, "August Soybeans" and "November Soybeans" represent two different crops.

In options analysis software, agricultural futures are often modeled using a constant basis model. The constant basis model simply says that current intercontract price differentials will continue. In this context, if you project that one of the contracts will go up a dollar, the software assumes the other contracts will go up one dollar as well. A more sophisticated model presumes that the contracts will move proportionately as they have in the past. But even that is not going to be very accurate in a lot of scenarios.

The intermonth spread changes in agriculturals are difficult to model accurately and will always be a source of unpredictability and risk for the options trader who takes a position in two or more different contract months.

In conclusion, just as with many of the machines and instruments we use, our knowledge of their limitations is the key to maximum and reliable benefit (and not getting hurt!). Every time you drive a car, you know that you could get hurt. And every time you use options software to trade an option you could lose money. Just the same, options trading software helps in so many ways—visualizing strategies, finding opportunities, avoiding mistakes, recording trades—that to trade options without software would be like flying an airliner without instruments.

DEALING WITH ANOMALIES AND PRICING DIFFICULTIES

New options traders get excited when they find a badly mispriced option. Unfortunately, 99 times out of 100 it is nothing but a bad quote. Fortunately, bad quotes are rare these days in stock and index options. However, bad quotes are common in futures options. For some reason, futures options quotes are not disseminated very well intraday. Depending on the market, bid and asked prices can be worthless or nonexistent. A last trade price can be way off sometimes. Volumes are the previous day's volumes, not today's cumulative volumes as they are in stock and index options. In short, you're trading from a partial black hole. Even if you're receiving real-time streaming quotes from a reputable vendor, the option price you see on your screen may not reflect the actual price on the trading floor.

However, users of options trading software have a significant advantage because they can deal with these holes in futures options prices. You may be able to figure out where prices really are—not with absolute certainty, but with a certain degree of confidence—and thereby be able to place good orders.

The starting point for checking the saneness of an individual option price is to check its IV in comparison with the IVs of options around it. If an individual option's IV deviates from the pattern of other option IVs, you probably have a bad price.

Consider the set of prices for May Coffee call options which existed at one time in the past. Can you spot the anomaly in Table 6.1?

Right, the 160 calls cannot possibly be trading at 1.70. They might have traded at that price once (perhaps earlier that day), but I guarantee you will not be able to go in and sell any of them at 1.70. How do I know that? For one thing, their price is out of line. The 160s ought to be priced somewhere between the 150s (1.40) and the 170s (0.50). More importantly, their IV is out of line. If you extrapolate the apparent curvature (skew) of the other option IVs, you will see that the 160s ought to be trading at approximately 49.5 percent.

Let's say you need to trade these 160 calls. How can you figure out where they're actually trading, so you can place a reasonable order?

Using an options analysis program, you can step the option price until you find the IV that should be right for this option (in this case, 49.5 percent). In this example, you would have found that an option price of 0.85 is correct.

Therefore, 0.85 is the probable mid-price for the bid and asked that actually exists on the floor. You can take it from there, adding (if buying) or subtracting (if selling) an appropriate amount of slippage, depending on your urgency to make the trade and your experience with this market's liquidity.

When an individual option stands out like this, it's easy to deal with. Now let's take a look at a more difficult example.

One February day, the orange juice market opened with a gap to the upside on news of a cold wave crossing the United States. Option volatilities, which had been sleeping at around 24 percent, were bound to jump. I had been holding a straddle for several days. I was ready to place an order to sell my straddle, but at what price? (I wanted to place a limit order, not a market order.)

TABLE 6.1 May Coffee Call Options

Strike	Option Price	IV
170	0.50	N.A.
160	1.70	59.5%
150	1.40	46.5%
140	2.50	43.6%
130	4.90	42.7%
120	9.00	41.9%

During the first hour of trading, options prices trickled into my system at the rate of about one every five minutes. (The options which had not yet updated still showed yesterday's settlement prices.)

I could see from the options prices that were coming in that the market was generally valuing these options at a new volatility level of about 38 percent. The options I needed to trade had not updated yet. However, based on the 38 percent figure, I was able to use the above procedure and obtain likely prices for my options. I placed my order and was filled.

Later in the day, after all the options prices had updated, I could see that my trades occurred at decent prices. In other words, I had correctly assessed the prices of my options.

In conclusion, you can deal with missing prices and pricing anomalies in the futures options arena. The key is IV. By paying attention to general IV levels and skew curvatures, you can assess the appropriateness of any individual option's price. When a price is obviously wrong, you can use the trick of stepping price until IV is in line to figure out what the actual price probably is.

CHAPTER 7

Tips for Beginners

Many people ask how they should prepare themselves to trade. That's a good sign. It's right to prepare yourself before jumping in. Here are some of the steps I consider important, not only for beginners, but also for experienced traders at all levels.

Read. Read another book about options. Read a good book about trading. For a list of some of the best, see the bibliography at the end of this section. When you read about the experiences of seasoned traders, you benefit from their mistakes without having to pay for it by losing your own money! Bypassing years in the school of hard knocks, you can arrive at successful trading years earlier. By the way, even after you're an experienced trader, you should still read a trading book once in a while!

Attend a seminar. You can learn valuable information from instructors who have traded successfully for years. Just as importantly, you can meet other people who have workable methods and swap valuable ideas with them.

Do some paper trading. Decide on a period of time in which you will restrict yourself to mock trades (no real money involved). After you decide on a period of time, double it. There is no reason to be in a hurry. There will always be trading opportunities. Odds are you will be glad you weren't using real money during this training time!

Some doubt the value of paper trading. However, if handled properly, it can be good practice and an excellent representation of how you might actually perform. Obviously, you have to be honest with yourself. A specific decision to trade must be accompanied by an immediate entry in a log. Once a trade is entered, you're stuck with it. No fair using the delete key! Enter the current date and time with every trade. As for price, to be conservative you should enter the "asked" on purchases, the "bid" on sales.

One of the problems people have with paper trading is maintaining their motivation. Here's an idea: You might tell yourself that unless you achieve a certain profit objective during the trial period, you're not going to allow yourself to get started with real money. Instead, you're going to have to go around again and do another trial period. This creates an incentive to do well in the trial period.

Select and use good trading tools from the start. Get into the groove with good software and favorite Internet sites, so that you build confidence to make sound trading decisions based on discipline. This will enable you to have a system and be in the game for the long run.

Using an options pricing model will help you intelligently select the best option or option strategy to trade. Using graphic analyses will help you visualize the way positions should perform. Referring to historical volatility charts will give you a perspective on the current volatility environment. In short, having these "instruments" in front of you will help you trade more intelligently. Trade without them and you'll be stumbling in the dark.

A good portfolio manager, specifically designed for options, will make it easy to keep track of your paper trading and get you into the habit of good recordkeeping. A good portfolio manager should also provide you with the ability to create another good habit—setting an objective and a stop for every position you enter. The program should be able to alert you when any of your positions hits its objective or stop, so you can take action.

When you start trading, start small. Trade in lots of just two to five contracts at first. Again, there is no reason to be in a hurry. We hear horror stories of beginners who get greedy and place large initial orders. After two or three mistakes, they're out of trading capital and out of the game!

If you place just a small part of your capital at risk at any one time, in any one position, you'll give yourself the space to make a few mistakes and still have capital to continue trading and apply what you've learned. You'll also be able to survive a streak of just plain bad luck. The markets are fairly random, and your decision-making system, whatever it may be, can sometimes fail several times in a row. You have to be able to survive a string of losses.

When should you exit a trade? That's simple. You exit a trade when the prospects don't look good anymore. Whether you're showing a gain or loss at the time is irrelevant. What matters is whether the position is likely to make money going forward.

A key question that always seems to clear the mind is to ask yourself if you would enter the trade anew at this point. In other words, if you had no position, would you place a trade to open the position now? If so, hold on to the trade, assured that it's a good one. If not, you might want to consider closing the trade very soon.

Some traders, myself included, have difficulty closing a successful trade at a good time. We hold on past the peak. Let's say it's a simple long stock position. The stock has shot up, filling you with glee. You brag about it to friends. Now it's time for a reality check. Would you buy the stock now? No? Likely, not many other fools would buy at the new, high price either! When you sense that happiness welling up and you feel like bragging, it's time to seriously consider selling. Almost every time I've bragged about a stock, or an option position, that was the peak.

Select the right kind of broker. For trading options, I definitely recommend trading with a firm that specializes in options. At this time there are only a handful of online brokerages specializing in options. Without naming them here, you can recognize them by the fact that their advertising and literature clearly welcome options traders. Having your account at one of these brokerages gives you a better chance of having your orders executed properly and your account records, including margin requirements, handled properly. Trading is challenging enough without having to deal with a broker who does not understand options.

How do I open an account? Most online brokerages make it easy to open an account. You just click the "Open an Account" link in their web site, and begin filling in the required information and click-signing agreements. Then they usually require a signature or two on real paper, so there will be instructions on how to print the necessary forms and where to sign. You will send these papers in with your check or other instructions on how to fund your account.

How much capital should I start off with? I recommend starting off with at least $10,000, and closer to $50,000, if possible. At $10,000 you're going to be under pressure to make your first few trades winners, so that you start building your account. Try to keep your trades small at first—I mean *really* small (e.g., $1,000 in each trade)—and keep at least half of the account in cash at all times. If your account does go south at first, resist the tendency to get careless and take more risks with the remainder. The market brings new opportunities every week, sometimes exceptional ones, and if you still have some cash, you're there to participate and fight back.

What are the margin requirements like? When buying options, the margin requirements are zero; you just have to pay for the options in full. Requirements are very reasonable in equity and index options when shorting covered options (that is, when the options you're selling are not naked). Margin requirements for selling naked options on low-priced stocks or indexes are reasonable (although you won't be able to do it with just $10,000). Requirements for selling naked options on high-priced stocks or indexes are quite high. Some brokerages charge even higher than the exchange minimum requirements for naked options (it's their prerogative to do so). If you plan on selling naked options, you should ask the brokerage about their margin requirements up front.

Should I use only limit orders? Market orders and limit orders both have their place, depending on your urgency to trade. I use both kinds. When the market is calm and I feel like there is time to fool around and try to save a few bucks, I use a limit order and go in somewhere between the bid and the asked. More often I use a limit order at the asking price (if buying) or the bid price (if selling).

However, there are times when it's best to use a market order. For instance, when I decide its time to get out of a trade, I want out! I have rarely received a bad fill using a market order in stock options and index options. It's the futures options markets that can be dicey, especially in New York. I would not recommend using market orders in the New York futures markets.

Feel comfortable with your trading. If you find a strategy boring, do something more exciting. If you find a strategy too anxiety producing, switch to something calmer. If you find that you are trading positions that are too large, start trading smaller positions. If you find the risk of naked writing intolerable, don't do it. *You must discover your own risk tolerance level and an approach that is interesting to you.* Sometimes this can take years.

Expect to pay some dues at first. To arrive at a trading approach that is comfortable for you will take some trial and error. Don't be surprised if your trading account goes downhill during this time. Again, paper trading prior to real trading is a good idea. Still, when you begin real trading, it is very common for some things to go wrong at first.

Act only on your own analysis. Once you have formulated your own approach, it's okay to listen to the opinions of others, but do your own research and make decisions independently. Do not listen to the news. If you do listen to the news, take everything with a grain of salt. Newscasters do not know whether the market will go up or down, and at the end of the day they do not know why it moved the way it did. No one does.

The market already knows what you know. Resist the temptation to believe that you have an edge because of some event that is coming or has just happened. For example, "Interest rates are going to be reduced tomorrow, so the stock market should go up." The fact is, everyone probably already knows this and the market has already discounted it. Or, "Company XYZ just announced better-than-expected earnings, and the stock should go up in the next few days as the word gets around." If you think you are among the first to find out about this company's numbers and most other people don't know yet, you are just fooling yourself. Believe me, unless you are privy to inside information, you (and I) are probably among the *last* to receive the news.

The markets quickly digest news. Only surprises move the markets, and even then only for brief periods. It takes a pretty big event, such as the terrorist attacks on September 11, 2001, to move the markets for several days. Otherwise, surprising news only takes a few minutes to a few hours to be digested. After that, the market goes back to its own moods and undulations. For that reason, surprise news that moves the market in a direction that helps a short-term position you have on at the time can often be used as an exit opportunity.

The market has a mind of its own. I once listened as two investors with different viewpoints debated economic fundamentals. One, with a bullish view, pointed out that interest rates have been reduced to very low levels, and historically that has always precipitated a bull market. The other, with bearish leanings, countered that consumer debt had climbed to record levels and would eventually cause consumer spending to slam into a brick wall. The bull then argued that an aging population was continuing to pour dollars into retirement plans at a relentless pace, and that most of this ends up invested in stocks. Then the bear called attention to the plunging Japanese stock market and the tenuous situation of the Japanese banks. On and on they argued, each one countering the other, back and forth. Fundamentalists can argue endlessly. Meanwhile, the market moves on, oblivious to both.

Why did the market go down today? It went down because, on balance, several thousand more people needed to sell today than needed to buy—for lots of different reasons. Add to that a few thousand others who were waiting to sell but hoping for higher prices but, when they saw the market dropping, caved in and sold today. Subtract from that several thousands of willing buyers whose price points were hit today. Mix in a few dozen surprise news releases that caused some investors to make on-the-spot buy or sell decisions. Finally, toss in the actions of tens of thousands of short-term speculators. In the final analysis, when you hear the newscaster give his or her reason why the market went down today, you can just laugh.

The markets have short, medium, and long-term trends. These can be traded. From time to time the markets swing to incredible price or volatility extremes and then return to sanity. Those are opportunities as well. Some believe that certain patterns, such as head-and-shoulders tops or double bottoms, are reliable to trade. I tend to agree. The reason these patterns exist is because of the well-known herding tendencies of investors. And speculative traders who use technical analysis probably reinforce the patterns. Watch the markets and let them speak to you. In the end, the markets themselves are the ultimate authority.

Approach the market as something to prepare for. If you do this, instead of rushing in willy-nilly, you'll have much better success. Novice traders should seriously consider all these principles if they are to become sound, consistent traders.

Here are some other excellent materials on options:

The CBOE Prospectus from the Chicago Board Options Exchange
Options as a Strategic Investment, 4th Edition, by Lawrence McMillan
Trading Options Visually, by Paul Forchione
The New Option Secret, by David Caplan
The Commodity Options Market, by Kermit C. Zieg Jr.

A large number of free educational articles and trading tips are available at http://www.optionvue.com and http://www.optionvueresearch.com. Also, you may want to visit http://www.invest-store.com/optionvue for a large selection of trading books and other resources.

THE PSYCHOLOGICAL BATTLE

People were not made to trade. They were made with emotions. Emotions are wonderful in life; I'm so happy I'm an emotional being! However, emotions play havoc with trading.

The ideal trader is one who decides on a system and carries it out precisely. The ideal trader does not get discouraged after a loss or a string of losses. He feels no remorse over an opportunity barely missed. He does not become elated or smug after a gain or a string of gains. During a swift market move, when others may be panicking, he feels nothing. He just continues to follow his system. Day by day he follows his regular routine, analyzing the markets with the same interest, even after a period when his system has not been working.

But who is really like this? I'm not. I don't know many who are. We can strive to be perfect traders, but emotions will always be there. Sometimes you just have to acknowledge them and work with them. For example, during countertrend moves (e.g., a short-term rally during a bear market), I sometimes begin to feel the emotions welling up in me that must also be there in other market participants (i.e., optimism). When that happens, I try to recognize what is happening and think contrarily. For example, after the market has moved up for several days, I'll begin feeling optimistic. At that point, I stop myself and think, "I'm feeling optimistic about stocks. I'll bet others are feeling this way too. That means the end of this run might be near."

Here are some other thoughts that might help in controlling your emotions as you trade. When in a position that you're uncomfortable with (e.g., when the market is making a run against you), it may help to ask yourself, "If I weren't in this position already, would I be entering it now?" If the answer is yes, hold tight. If the answer is no, then get out. In other words, transport yourself into an imaginary situation where you're sitting with cash, just calmly watching the market. Would you, in that situation, be jumping into the position you're already in?

Another thing I find helpful is deciding ahead of time what I'm going to do. Off hours, when I look at the charts, I may get a feel for what I think the market is going to do (I'm a short-term directional trader these days). I'll decide right then on a plan. Then I'll also imagine other tacks the market might take, and I'll decide what to do if any of those scenarios play out. Sometimes I write down my plans, sometimes not, but at least I have them firmly in mind. Having my responses preplanned allows me to trade mechanically instead of emotionally. This is especially helpful when your system is somewhat arbitrary (that is, depending on human judgment), as mine is. Not only does this help me trade mechanically, it also helps me do away with useless remorse over trades that went bad or over having closed a position too soon. I remind myself that I was only following the plans that were made earlier in calm forethought.

We do the best we can as traders. That's all we can do.

Options trader and writer Kenneth Trester also wrote a section on the psychological battlefield in his book *The Complete Option Player.* I thought these words, reprinted with his permission, were especially well put.

As you prepare to enter the options game, your greatest obstacle to success probably will be the psychological battlefield that you must survive. To be a winner, most novice option traders think that all they need is a little luck—a few big winners right off the bat and they'll be on Easy Street. It's just a matter of being at the right place at the right time, or so they think. Of course, they couldn't be more wrong.

Proper money management is just as important as using the right strategy, probably more so. Most people fail to realize that. For example, if they just buy options (even if they are theoretically undervalued), they could have a long losing streak and, if they're not careful, lose their entire investment capital. Most people aren't careful. Typically, after a few losses traders become hesitant—they take profits away so they can't hit any home runs, and they run up their commissions by over-trading. Their goose was cooked before they began, because they were emotionally unprepared to trade options.

Your foremost opponent when you trade options is not the exchange and its members, nor the other traders. It's your emotions, and if you can't control them, you're going to be licked. Don't get down about it though; most money managers have the same problem.

The best way to keep your emotions out of your investment decisions is to have a well-defined game plan. Write it down and stick to it.

Decide how much money you are willing to risk in options during the next twelve months, and don't blow it all in the first few months. This is really important—plan to spread your option trades over the entire year. Can you risk that much money? Is the money you could lose more important to you than the money you could make? Would a loss affect your life-style? If you answer "yes," you shouldn't be trading at all. You also should trade as if options are chips on a poker table—if you're afraid to lose, you will.

Plan to diversify, both over time and position. If you spread your purchases over one year, for example, and buy both puts and calls on several stocks, you won't be wiped out if the stock market is dull for months on end (it can happen). Also, you'll have a better chance of being around when things pick up and options pay off. Always invest the same dollar amount in each position. If you do, you'll eliminate the risk of having small investments in the winners and big investments in the losers.[1]

TRADING MISTAKES AND WHAT I LEARNED

My number-one trading mistake, and one that has hurt me many times over the years, is trading too much size—investing too much of my account in any one investment. I'm a gunslinger by nature, I guess.

I enjoy a little gambling in Las Vegas whenever I can go. Interestingly, my money management is very good in Las Vegas. I can control my losses and am usually able to stop gaming whenever my daily allotment of trading capital is gone. Perhaps the reason I'm effective in that environment is

---

[1]Kenneth Trester, *The Complete Option Player* (Sarasota, FL: Bookworld Press, 1997).

because of the realization that with the next throw of the dice or deal of the cards, my odds of winning are just under 50 percent (knowingly over-simplified to make a point), so I know there is no sense in risking a large amount. Also, the outcome of my bet is known very soon, and just a few moments later there is another play. There is something about the frequency of plays that keeps me satisfied with small bet sizes.

In options however, I sometimes fool myself into believing that a trade has a higher probability of success than it really does. This happens more often in directional trading, where the odds of success are next to impossible to quantify. This leaves me to my imagination, which is not a very reliable predictor as it turns out. I realize that I need a more mechanical, systemized approach. And I know that I need to get better at money management.

Sometimes you can run into problems with the mechanics of placing and executing trades—for instance, ordering calls instead of puts, and vice versa, or ordering to sell instead of buy. But I've been able to minimize these occurrences by staying focused and being careful. Where I've been hurt worse is in the execution and reporting of market orders. One time, I bought index puts using a market order when I sensed the market was falling. But since it was a situation of "fast market conditions," the floor did not feel obliged to return a fill report to me anytime during the remainder of the day. The market continued to fall, just as I thought it would, and, had my position been confirmed, I would have been able to sell them for a big profit near the end of the day. But with confirmation not forthcoming until an hour after the close, I was forced to hold them overnight. The next morning the market opened up strongly and all I could do was sell my puts for about even money.

That was a long time ago, however. With modern electronic trading, I suppose it is possible that nothing like that will ever happen again. Nevertheless, it's important to pay attention to when an exchange declares "fast market conditions." In a fast market, the professionals are not held to their usual restraints. If you send a market order into a fast market, the market makers have license to, and sometimes will, have their way with you. I found this out the hard way one time when I placed a market order to close a spread in orange juice. The spread was worth about 2 points, net, and was actually trading for about 2 points. However, they made me pay 4 points to cover! I took it to arbitration but, with the buddy system they have out there in New York, it was no use. That one mistake took a big bite out of my account. I will never again place a market order in fast market conditions, especially in futures options.

Finally, I learned a long time ago to cut losses early. As a new trader, I sometimes allowed a loss to grow bigger. Without giving specific examples right now, I know there were times when I stayed with a losing position day after day, week after week, grinding it out. Now I understand that if the market is telling me that I'm wrong, I might as well admit it and get out of the position right away. It gives me an immediate sense of relief (that I'm not fighting the market anymore) and frees me up to begin thinking about what I want to do next.

SOME THOUGHTS ON HOW TRADING FITS IN WITH REAL LIFE

I have found that trading must be compartmentalized. That is because it is so out of touch with reality. When trading, you make decisions involving thousands of dollars. In everyday life, you decide whether to eat out or eat leftovers and save $20. That is as it should be. You have to live like a real person. To deal with the disparity, I find it helpful to think of my trading account as not containing real money, but "trading money," if you will. It won't become real money until I call up the broker and ask him to send me a check. Some may object that not considering my account "real money" might cause me not to care sufficiently about it. But don't worry—I'm serious enough about trading not to fritter away my capital!

Another way the trader needs to compartmentalize is in how much he thinks about, and talks about, his trading. I believe it's helpful to prepare for the next day's trading soon after the markets close. That way I'm all finished; there is nothing more to think about. I may even have a large position on overnight and still sleep like a baby. While the markets are closed there are no decisions to be made and nothing to worry about. (God help us if they ever go to 24-hour trading!)

I have also found that it's best not to discuss trading with anyone in the family, or among friends, unless they are genuinely interested in trading and can handle the kind of dollars you are dealing with. Otherwise, they will flat out not be able to relate. I know of someone who regularly talks about how much he made or lost that day in his trading. This is so obviously an ego trip for the person, I wonder how he cannot realize what he is doing and stop it.

It's okay to say in general terms how your trading is going, if someone asks. But I would not talk in specifics with family members or friends. It only causes trouble. Talk about a big loss and it upsets them. Tell them about a big gain and it will also upset them, because it gets them more excited than they need to be as they try to fit what you've said into the framework of their normal, everyday life. For example, if you tell your teenage child you made $20,000 that week, they might expect you to buy them a car. If you tell them the following week that you lost $20,000, they'll think you're a complete idiot for not taking the $20,000 out when you had the chance and buying them that car. They'll remember for a long time how you "lost their car." They can't compartmentalize like you can, so you have to do it for them. Don't talk about your gains and losses.

Even when talking with other traders, it's best not to brag. People have a tendency to brag about gains but not admit to losses. I've even seen myself do this! But that's not being honest. In the end, all that matters is if and when you can withdraw some capital and bring it home. As I said, that is when it becomes real money.

Finally, I would like to reflect on the moral aspect of trading. I would assert that there are many activities more worthwhile than making money at the expense of others losing it. For instance, things like reading a book, writing a song, spending time with family or friends, and so on. When it comes right down to it, there is very little redeeming value to trading. I'm not saying that it's bad; only that it's pretty close to neutral. The only good thing that can be said is that you're contributing liquidity to the markets. As a trader, you're speculating, investing, or hedging, and all participants play an important role in greasing the wheels of capitalism. I would say that the main reason I trade is the challenge of beating the odds. I like winning at a somewhat complicated game that I understand better than many. For me, there is joy in winning.

Another aspect of this involves one's heart. If you believe in God, as I do, you have to pay attention to what He says. Jesus said you cannot love both God and money. Now, I don't know about you, but I intend to love God, not money. So I have had to ask myself if my interest in trading stems from a love of money. Honestly, I don't believe it does. I'm interested in trading because of the challenge of beating the system in some way and overcoming barriers within myself. I like having money, but I don't love it. And it's probably best if one's motivation to trade stems from reasons other than the love of money. What about you? Hopefully you would agree that before rushing into trading (or anytime after you've begun), it would be good to ask yourself why you want to trade, and be aware of your true motivation.

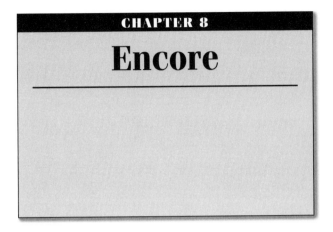

CHAPTER 8

Encore

DIRECTIONAL TRADING USING PATTERN RECOGNITION

One interesting way to trade is swing trading using pattern recognition. And I have a favorite pattern—it's what I call a *breakdown*. It happens when a stock experiences a sharp sell-off, recovers somewhat, and then rolls over and begins to drop again. I will buy puts at that juncture for a 1- to 10-day play. I've made some good money this way in the past couple of years, especially during the Nasdaq bubble burst of 2000. Figures 8.1 through 8.4 contain charts that illustrate successful patterns.

Now, for all the breakdowns that work, there are as many that don't. Figures 8.5 and 8.6 show some examples of breakdowns that failed to follow through.

Fortunately, a stop level is easily selected, to limit your risk. I use a stop equal to the stock's recent high price, as marked in the figures. Using nearby puts, I usually find that, on average, half of my investment is lost if the stop gets hit. On the other hand, trades that work return anywhere from one and a half to four times my investment.

I like using the nearby puts for maximum leverage, even when the option has only two days of life left. While this may sound restrictive (and it is, from a time standpoint), I can't resist the leverage. In the final two days before expiration, at-the-money options can usually be bought for just 0.50 to 1.00. I have hit many home runs buying these low-priced options. Obviously you don't put a lot of money into these kinds of wagers, as there is a good chance of losing it all.

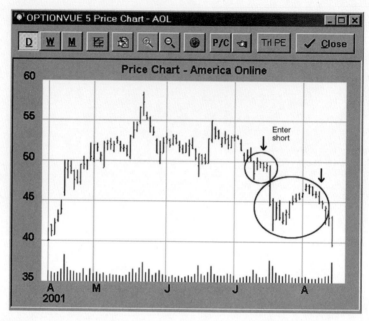

FIGURE 8.1   AOL (Two Good Breakdowns)

FIGURE 8.2   Genesis Microchip (Two Good Breakdowns)

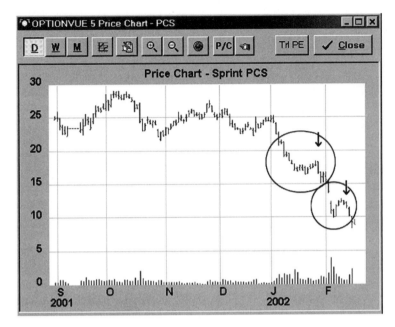

FIGURE 8.3 Sprint PCS (Two Good Breakdowns)

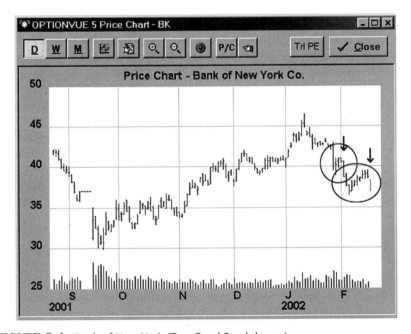

FIGURE 8.4 Bank of New York (Two Good Breakdowns)

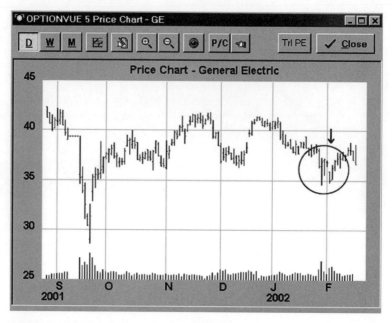

FIGURE 8.5   General Electric (Failed Breakdown)

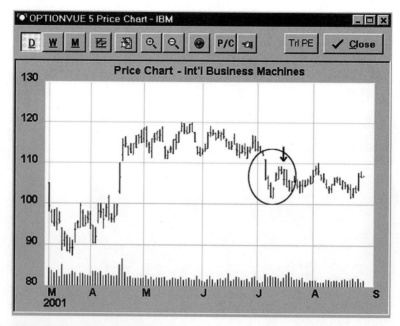

FIGURE 8.6   IBM (Failed Breakdown)

Note that the breakdowns I like to play are very much like coming off the right shoulder of a head-and-shoulders formation, except the left shoulder doesn't have to be there. Other patterns may be traded as well, including all the technical analysts' favorites—cup and handle, triangle breakouts, head and shoulders, and so on.

The reason I like breakdowns is that sell-offs seem to happen more swiftly and reliably than up moves. Thus, down moves are usually cleaner plays. A good sell-off goes for three or more days, sometimes culminating with a climactic selling day on high volume, which is often the best day to exit.

In contrast, uptrending markets tend to be choppy, with frequent retracements and consolidations that can last for days. Thus, swing trading an up market is a challenge. How many times has the options trader looked back on a beautiful 30-day rally, during which several of his favorite stocks doubled, and asked himself, "How did I manage to lose money?" It was because the trader tried to play the 1- to 5-day moves and the market did not behave predictably on that level.

Therefore, up markets might better be played using longer-term (i.e., 30-day) positions. And the best option strategy for longer-term positions would be spreads, because spreads have smoother performance and better profit potential in that time frame. Or you can buy deep in-the-money calls, LEAPS or just the stock itself.

Recognizing a Good Breakdown

Here's how to recognize a good breakdown. The first sharp sell-off (the one you're not in on) tips you off that something may be seriously wrong with the company. All the better if there is no news to account for it, or if the news that accompanied the fall is of the "first shoe" variety. Thus you have more possible "shoe drops" to look forward to. Following that, the stock often spends several days recovering some of its lost ground or perhaps just moving sideways. Then it begins to sell off again. That's your entry point.

The best option strategy for a sell-off, without question, is straight put buying—not only because the move is often so swift and clean, but also because increasing volatility usually accompanies the sell-off, pumping up all option values, including your puts.

Exit timing is arbitrary. I'm sorry; I have no firm rule for exiting. I simply watch the chart and when it seems to me like the move could be spent, I exit. I do it largely by feel. Sometimes, as I said, there is a selling climax—one big down day with big volume. If there is, I'll be sure and get out sometime that day.

Another approach, for those who prefer to be more systematic, is to use a trailing stop from inception of the position. If the stock moves your way at first and you're seeing a gain, you'll want to protect that gain and not allow it to turn into a loss. (Sometimes these sell-offs end abruptly in a quick rebound!) And if the stock moves the wrong way from inception, it's usually best to admit that the breakdown was false and get out quickly. After that, sometimes the stock moves sideways and upwards for a few days, then breaks down again—this time for real. You can always jump aboard again at that point.

Some of the most reliable breakdowns are ones where the stock experienced a significant rally over the past several months. I think the reason these might be better stems from human behavior with respect to profit taking. Investors, experiencing the good fortune of seeing their stock go up, begin to think about selling. As the stock advances further, they feel more like taking their profits. However, rather than selling when they feel like selling, they tend to play a game of "let's see if it can go up just a bit more." As long as it keeps advancing, they keep holding on. Inevitably, the stock experiences a downturn, which triggers some investors to go ahead and sell. This cascades into more selling, and in a few days just about everyone who had their finger on the sell-trigger goes ahead and sells. During this time, a sense of fear (of losing back any further profits) tends to dominate.

Figure 8.7 gives an example of a high quality breakdown. Nike fell for five straight days after breaking its trend-line off a right shoulder formation, making this a real home-run trade for put buyers.

One factor contributing to the success of this approach, I believe, is the potentially large number of investors also noticing the breakdown. Many traders use trend-lines and moving averages. Therefore many other traders will notice the breakdown and possibly place trades that will exacerbate the move. You just want to be in your position before the bulk of the crowd, if possible.

Overall Market Breakdowns

The breakdown pattern works with indexes as well as it does on individual stocks, perhaps even more reliably. The Nasdaq bubble burst in the spring of 2001 is a classic example. In Figure 8.8, we're going to focus especially on the brief period of time between March 7 and April 14, 2000.

The sharp drop beginning on March 7 was the first hint that the bubble had been pricked. High-flying tech stocks with market capitalization in the billions but little to no revenues or profits were hit hardest. The subsequent rally was very noticeably an FTQ (flight-to-quality) rally, with stocks like Cisco, EMC, and Dell leading the way. Dot-coms and biotechs did not

FIGURE 8.7 Breakdown—Nike

FIGURE 8.8 Breakdown—Nasdaq

participate. While the Nasdaq 100 hit a new high in this rally, the Russell 2000 did not, tipping us off to underlying weakness.

When the market came off this top (the "head" of the head-and-shoulders formation), it was a good opportunity to go short. Momentum quickly built and the market plunged for six days, climaxing in a 400-point Dow sell-off and recovery in the same day. The market then paused and rallied for a few days, after which the next wave of selling started. This was the drop off the right "shoulder"—one of the most powerful and reliable times ever to place a directional trade.

Both of these sell-offs—the one off the head and the one off the right shoulder—culminated in a degree of panic selling, as evidenced by a big volatility spike, making it easy to sense when to exit. Puts easily increased tenfold during each sell-off, helped by expanding volatility. While just about all tech stocks fell, the high-flying dot-com and biotech stocks fell the most spectacularly during these times.

The retracements (rallies) may be played as well. However, going long using straight call buying might not be the strategy to use. Options are very expensive at that stage—hurting your leverage and presenting you with volatility risk—because as the market advances, the implied volatility levels of all options come down, making it seem like you're fighting an uphill battle. It might be better to use bull call spreads, lean toward buying deep in-the-money calls, or simply buy the underlying stocks. If you do buy straight calls, treat them like hot potatoes; be ready to sell them near the end of a good, strong up day.

Conclusion

Once a market bubble has begun to burst, it goes to completion with great force. I think the reason this happens is because the herd behavior of investors rises up and overpowers all other market forces. Investors, seeing their profits start to go away, all head for the exits at once. Such a time presents, to my knowledge, the best of all trading opportunities.

As for trading individual stocks, certainly the breakdown strategy works better when the overall market is in a downtrend. And I'd be willing to concede that perhaps the reason I've been able to make money at this the past two years was because I had the wind at my back. But that's okay. If we go into a long-term bull market and my breakdown pattern stops working, I'll put it away and use other strategies. When the bear market comes back, I'll bring it out and start using it again.

Meanwhile, I plan on continuing to refine this approach. I have already built into my software the ability to scan for stocks exhibiting a breakdown pattern, and I am currently exploring whether stocks that have recently experienced a significant run-up make for more reliable breakdown trades.

TIMING THE MARKET USING THE VIX

Another interesting way to trade is to use volatility index (VIX) reversals to time the market. Having recently devoted some time to the study of VIX reversals, I can tell you that they are more than interesting. They are downright exciting. After setting up a system for myself and doing some back-testing, I now give more weight to what the VIX is telling me than to price pattern recognition.

The VIX indicates how expensive OEX options are. OEX options were once the most heavily traded index options in the world. While this is no longer the case, they are still very popular. Thus the VIX serves as a good indication of how expensive stock and stock index options are, in general.

The VIX has been termed "the fear index" because it expresses a consensus view about expected future stock market volatility. While that is true, I prefer to think of the VIX as a hedger's expense index. The VIX rises when the market is falling, reflecting investors' willingness to pay more for puts to protect their stock portfolios. On the other side of the trade, market makers require higher put prices as they take on more and more short put positions. As providers of stock market "insurance," if you will, market makers raise their "premiums" as the market falls.

Once the market turns up and investors begin to feel more comfortable with their stocks, they stop buying insurance and the VIX drops. This drop is almost always very swift. After having climbed for several days, when the VIX suddenly reverses and starts dropping, this often marks a short-term, if not an intermediate-term, bottom in the market.

We can begin to understand how to recognize VIX reversal patterns by looking at some examples from a three-month period during the summer of 2001. Four clear examples of VIX top reversals are marked in Figure 8.9. (We'll examine VIX bottom reversals later. For now, let's just focus on VIX top reversals.)

The two most important factors in gauging a good quality VIX reversal are that the reversal be preceded by a buildup lasting several days, and that the VIX be above average relative to recent history. You will notice that all four of the marked reversals were preceded by a ramping-up period lasting several days, and culminated with the VIX peaking at above-average levels. That is why I marked only these four reversals. Other reversals occurred during this time. For instance, one occurred late in June and another on the seventh trading day in August. These were notable, but not of the highest quality.

I would also call your attention to the fact that the VIX gapped up on the open on every one of the four best VIX reversal days. That very often characterizes the top day.

After noting a rising for several days, reaching a relative extreme, I look for a 3 percent retracement off the high. I have found that a 3 percent retracement is just about optimal for triggering a signal. In other words, I look for the VIX to make a high, and then pull back 3 percent from there. (That's 3 percent, not 3 points. For instance, if the VIX peaks at 36, I'll be looking for $36 \times .97 = 34.92$.) The high need not have been set today; it may have been set on the previous day.

Figure 8.10 shows a chart of the S&P 500 index (SPX) during the same period. All four of the most notable VIX reversals coincided with short-term market bottoms, although after the fourth VIX reversal, the market waffled for three days and then went up for one day, so in that case the rally was not as crisp as we would have liked.

The VIX peaks when the market hits bottom, and the VIX bottoms when the market hits a short-term top. Thus you could say that the VIX is a coincident indicator, because the VIX hits its top, and the market its bottom, on the same day. Although the VIX is not a leading indicator, it is valuable because of the way it moves to short-term relative extremes and then reverses. A chart of the VIX speaks to us in ways that the price chart cannot. When the market is dropping day after day, and you're in the midst of it, trying to figure out exactly when to cover your short position, it can be pretty hard to tell just by looking at the price chart. But take a look at the VIX chart, and you can get a good idea.

To illustrate how strongly the VIX can signal a bottom, let's take a look at what the market and the VIX looked like on the morning of July 24, 2002—at the culmination of a dramatic sell-off. The charts in Figures 8.11 and 8.12 were taken at 9:30 A.M. CST that day—one hour into the trading day. In other words, the final bar in this pair of charts represents just one hour of trading.

After climbing for days, the VIX gapped open into the upper 50s and was starting to come down. The market itself had opened lower and was coming back. The VIX was giving us a high quality signal, and the stage was set for a powerful rally. Indeed, the Dow finished up 489 points that very day, and advanced another 500 points during the next 3 trading days.

A VIX top reversal is not only a signal to go long, but also a signal to close out any short positions I may be holding at the time. I know of

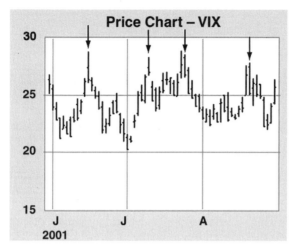

FIGURE 8.9 VIX Top Reversals

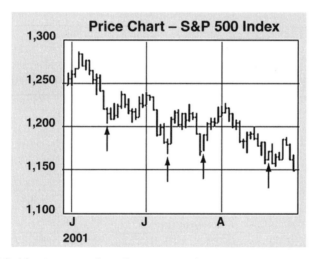

FIGURE 8.10 Corresponding Short-term Market Bottoms on S&P 500

no better signal for exiting a short position than a VIX reversal signal to go long.

While others who espouse VIX reversal trading recommend taking a position at the close of the VIX reversal day, I prefer entering *during* the day. Many times the VIX reversal day is characterized by the market dropping sharply and then recovering sharply before the close. I enjoy getting in on that day's action.

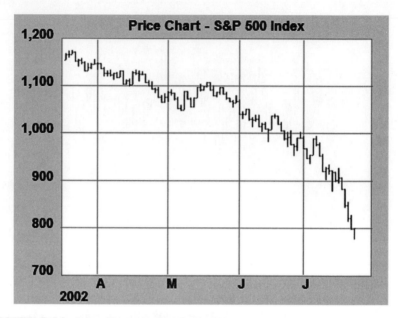

FIGURE 8.11   Price Chart—Market Dropping

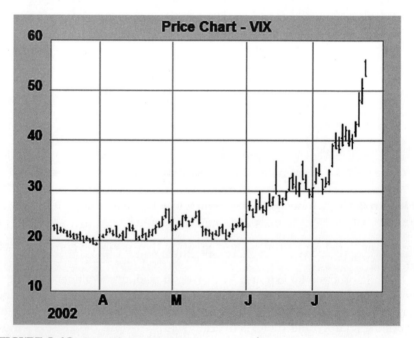

FIGURE 8.12   Price Chart—VIX Rising

VIX Bottom Reversals

Just as VIX top reversals signal market bottoms, VIX bottom reversals often signal market tops. However, VIX bottom reversals can be more difficult to recognize. That's because as the VIX settles down into lower levels, it tends to trade in a narrow range. While VIX top reversals practically jump right off the page, VIX bottom reversals are more subtle, and can be difficult to recognize until after they are past. So you have to tune in more sensitively to VIX bottoms. However, if you're too sensitive, a fake signal can get you into a short position too early. Interestingly, however, in my back-testing even short positions entered too early worked out eventually, if you had the courage to stay through the market moving the wrong way for a few days.

Again, you would want to see the VIX trend downward for several days and go beneath recent average levels. After setting a low (either today or yesterday), you would look for the VIX to make a 3 percent rebound off that low. While VIX tops are often characterized by a gap opening, I don't usually expect to see that with VIX bottoms.

As VIX bottoms are more subtle and difficult to recognize, that leads to what seems to be a weakness in the system—that it can give too many signals to go short, causing you to get short too early sometimes. In my simulations and back-testing, I came across a period in early 2002, for instance, where my system gave four short entry signals before giving a long entry signal (see Figures 8.13 and 8.14). If I was following this system, I would have gotten short on the first signal and held it all the way through. Since it's best to hold a short position all the way to the next long signal, this position would have been held for more than a month and would have been profitable at the end.

However, the first and second signals were not optimal, as they were too early. So, naturally, I thought of tightening the model to try to eliminate the early short signals while keeping the good short signals. However, I found that tightening up the entry parameters did not help, since eliminating the early signals also eliminated the good signals.

I have tried working on a variety of early exit rules for stopping losses on short positions. Surprisingly, any change only made the results worse overall. It turns out that it is always best to see the position through, as the market always turned down and the short position eventually became profitable.

Note that I was back-testing only a 1.5-year period ending in September 2002—a bear market. The model and the parameters might need adjusting when we go into a bull market. In general, I don't expect VIX reversal trading to work as well in a bull market because of the false short signals that may come up. But those short signals shouldn't be ignored because, even in

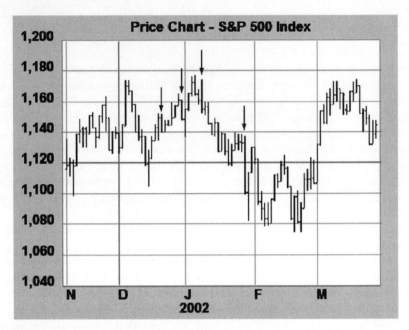

FIGURE 8.13 Four Short Entry Signals

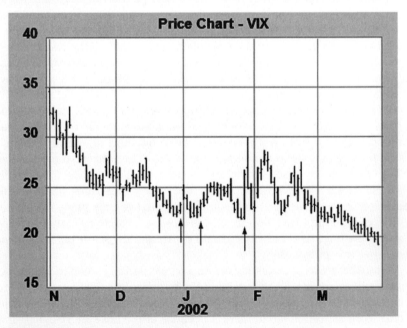

FIGURE 8.14 VIX Bottom Reversal—Four Short Entry Signals

a bull market, there are brief, nasty little sell-offs. And you can make a lot of money if you can time those pullbacks.

Exit Rules for Long Positions

The exit rules for long positions are not what one might expect. In an up-trending or sideways market, hold for four days. Sell at the close of the fourth trading day after opening the position. I realize this may seem odd. But of all the exit rules I tried, this one gave me the best results. In the 1.5-year test period I was using (March 2001 to September 2002), the four-day rule worked remarkably well. (That doesn't mean it may not need adjusting at some point).

If the market is downtrending, rallies last only about a day. So you need to get out at the close of the next trading day. These rallies are well worth playing, because they are sharp and powerful. However, remember that with a rally comes declining volatility, and you'll need to play it using ITM call options, or simply buying stock or futures. The OTM and ATM call options may disappoint. For larger accounts, the other way of playing this would be selling naked puts. A short put position would benefit from both the rising market and the declining volatility, a double bonus.

If the market is downtrending, and you've gone long, the market needs to start going your way soon. If the market is down the next day, any time after the first hour of trading, you should exit the long trade immediately. Not only that, but if your brief long trade interrupted a short position, you should resume the short position immediately.

Finally, I found that while long signals take precedence over being short, short signals should be ignored while you are long.

Everything Is Relative

Many VIX watchers pay attention to absolute levels. For instance, they may say that the VIX at 22 percent or less indicates it's time to go short, and the VIX at 50 percent or higher signals a time to go long. Instead, I prefer to pay attention to patterns, and to the current VIX level in relation to recent levels. While the VIX has peaked in the 50s three times in the past six years, there is nothing that says the VIX couldn't spike higher next time—perhaps even as high as it did in October 1987 (120 percent). Or perhaps intermediate-term bottoms will be signaled by the VIX only going into the 40s for the next few years. You never know.

The Bigger Picture

Let's step back and take a look at the VIX over a longer time frame. Refer to Figures 8.15 and 8.16. There are some important observations to be made here. In the past six years there have been six significant VIX peaks, all corresponding to short-term market bottoms. Three of those times, the VIX poked above 40 for just one day, and that was the bottom day for the market. The other three times, the VIX went above 40 and stayed above 40 for many days. Then it spiked into the upper 50s one day, and that marked the culmination of the market's sell-off (note that the late 2001 spike had several days in the 40s, even though you can't see it in this weekly chart). Credit goes to Jim Graham on our staff for this study, the results of which were published July 12, 2002, in our company's regular e-mail broadcast and are now posted on our web site.

It is appropriate to pay attention to these patterns, and to assume that they may repeat. For instance, if I saw the VIX stay in the 40s for many days, then move swiftly higher, and one day open up a gap to nearly 60 percent, I would go long with an extra large trade. Why? Because every time we've seen that pattern in the past several years, it signaled a grand bottom. (A "grand bottom" is what I like to call an intermediate-term bottom.) I would use an extra large position in this case, because I would expect an extra high probability of success.

Of course, a trader must be careful. Minimum and maximum levels exhibited in the past might not hold in the future. While the VIX is mean reverting, there is no law that says the VIX could not penetrate to some new high or low level never seen before. So the trader needs to be careful not to assume that the VIX is bound by some kind of floor and ceiling levels.

Coming off a grand bottom, it is important to hold your long position until the market has advanced at least 12 percent. The last three grand bottoms have seen the market advance very quickly at least that much:

April 4, 2001	15%
September 21, 2001	13%
July 24, 2002	17%

Any short signal that the VIX may give during the first few days following a grand bottom should be ignored, as the rally following a grand bottom is very powerful and must be allowed time to play out.

What Instruments to Trade?

VIX timing signals may be traded using options, index futures, trust shares (such as the Standard & Poor's Depositary Receipts, or SPY "spyders"),

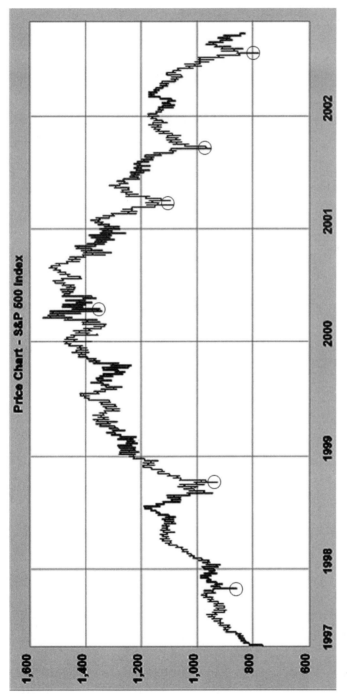

FIGURE 8.15 Market Fluctuation over Six Years

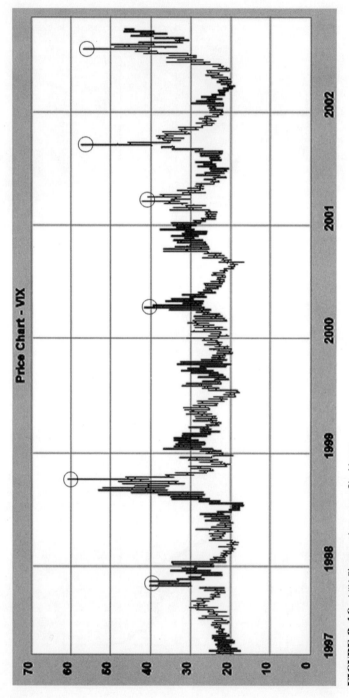

FIGURE 8.16 VIX Fluctuation over Six Years

or shares of individual stocks. When using options, special care must be taken to counter the effects of time decay and volatility changes. To go short, purchasing puts works well when the market goes down quickly, because the accompanying increase in volatility pumps up their value and time decay does not work against you very much. However, as we have seen, a short position sometimes needs to be held for longer than just a few days. In this situation, buying ITM puts with very little time value is an effective approach.

However, when going long, buying calls can be a problem because, as the market climbs, the accompanying volatility decrease will work against your calls. One way to counter this is to buy ITM calls with very little time value. Well-capitalized investors may consider selling naked puts instead (note that high margin requirements are usually associated with selling naked index options). Nevertheless, shorting puts would be the ideal approach, because it benefits from both the expected price movement and the drop in volatility. Finally, one could perhaps sell puts *and* buy calls, constructing a synthetic. However, it's not clear that using a synthetic would have any advantage over simply buying futures or shares of the SPY.

Summary

VIX reversal trading is attractive for its high success rate—shown by my studies to be 75 percent+ and by Connors and Che to be 65 percent+. It also has a high $win/$loss ratio. That is, the magnitude of the average gain is greater than the magnitude of the average loss. And, unlike other timing methods that may work for a while and then stop working, VIX reversal trading should always work. Of course, no trading approach is easy. You'll still have positions go against you. But the VIX sure does an excellent job of calling the bottoms, especially the big ones—to the day.

WHY A VIX SPIKE STOPS A MARKET SELL-OFF

Since a VIX spike (often with a gap opening) always seems to happen at the culmination of a sell-off, I have often wondered if there could be a cause-and-effect relationship. That is, rather than just signaling the bottom, could the extremely expensive options actually have a braking effect on the market's fall?

After giving it some thought, I believe that expensive options might actually play a role in stopping a sell-off. Let me explain my hypothesis.

As the downward market snowballs, many who were loosely holding their stocks give way and add to the selling. Many portfolio managers, needing to lighten up but preferring not to sell their stocks, buy puts instead. As the market falls, demand for puts grows day by day. Market makers absorb this demand by taking on short put positions. As they do, they open short futures positions (in the S&P 500) to hedge. The selling of futures contracts translates into selling of shares through arbitrage.* Thus, the portfolio managers' put buying transfers selling pressure to the market indirectly, contributing to the market's fall. As put buying approaches a crescendo, the market makers begin to approach a saturation point in terms of their positions, and start moving put prices up in jumps. (By the way, the call prices have to go up as well because of put/call parity, but calls are not relevant in this scenario.)

At some point, portfolio managers decide they can no longer pay the prices being asked for puts, or that they have bought enough puts. They may also feel that the market has fallen so far that it shouldn't fall much further, and decide to self-insure any remaining risk, at least until the market has recovered somewhat. Thus they take themselves off the teeter-totter, if you will.

At this point we need to step back and get a glimpse of the grand picture. There has been massive selling. Some of this selling has been *direct* selling—people selling stocks, and institutions selling stocks or stock index futures (e.g., the S&P 500 futures) to hedge. But another segment has been selling *indirectly* through buying puts. When this segment stops buying puts, as I imagine happens when the price of puts gets too high for them, that's when the teeter-totter swings the other direction. Bargain hunters and the background buyers who are always there begin to gain the upper hand, and the market begins to move up.

---

*Note that buying and selling in S&P 500 futures transfers into buying and selling of stocks by means of program trading. Most large investment firms have arbitrage departments assigned to watch the S&P 500 futures and to trade the futures against actual stocks. When the futures are depressed to a certain point from selling, arbitrageurs will buy the futures and simultaneously sell hundreds of stocks in a "program trade," thus lifting the futures and pushing down stocks (effectively ending the opportunity). Likewise, when the futures are inflated to a certain point from buying, arbitrageurs will sell the futures and simultaneously buy stocks, thus pushing down the futures and lifting stocks.

Thus the buying and selling of the futures is effectively, although indirectly, the buying and selling of stocks. This transfer mechanism is very powerful and efficient.

Once the tide begins to flow the other way, the momentum feeds on itself. As the market moves higher, market makers need to buy in some of their short futures positions because their short put positions are shrinking and no longer require as many futures contracts for hedging. This futures buying represents upward pressure on the market, sending it higher. At the same time, some portfolio managers, feeling relieved and perhaps optimistic, *for sure* don't buy any more puts, and may even feel the need to close some of their put positions while they can still get something for them. This put selling indirectly transfers buying pressure onto the market, again contributing to the rally. Meanwhile, many direct sellers, sensing that the market may have hit bottom, turn around and become direct buyers. And up it goes.

Thus the flow of money into puts during a sell-off, and the consequent inflation of put prices, seems to act like an air bag for the market, ultimately stopping its crash and contributing to the market's rebound.

Again, I'm not *certain* this is what happens, but I believe it is likely. I have been discussing this hypothesis with key members of the investment community to get their feedback and see if they also believe this is what happens. Any readers who have an opinion are welcome to send me an e-mail as well. Figure 8.17 illustrates the whole process.

Point A **Direction: Market Is Falling, VIX Rising**	
Retail	Uncertain owners sell, accelerating drop.
Institutional (Portfolio Mgrs.)	Some selling shares, some selling S&P futures; many, unwilling to sell shares, buy puts to protect holdings.
Market Makers	Take other side—short put positions; balance by shorting S&P futures.

Point B **Direction: Market Falls Further, VIX Jumps**	
Retail	Uncertain owners still selling.
Institutional (Portfolio Mgrs.)	More put buying.
Market Makers	Less willing to take other side as short put positions mount; increase prices at which they are willing to trade.

Point C **Direction: Market Reaches Bottom, VIX Tops Out**	
Retail	Most uncertain owners have already sold.
Institutional (Portfolio Mgrs.)	Not willing to pay higher put prices, self-insure.
Market Makers	Positions stabilize as put buying slows. Perhaps some professional options traders come in, willing to sell high put premiums.

Point D **Direction: Market Begins to Turn Up, VIX Dropping**	
Retail	Bargain hunters begin to gain upper hand.
Institutional (Portfolio Mgrs.)	Bargain hunters—for sure, sense no need to buy puts. Begin selling back puts while they have some value.
Market Makers	Short put positions shrinking in value. Buying in short S&P futures positions to cover.

Point E **Direction: Market Moves Higher, VIX Drops**	
Retail	Buying accelerates out of fear of missing bargain prices.
Institutional (Portfolio Mgrs.)	Continued buying.
Market Makers	Continued buying to cover short S&P futures.

FIGURE 8.17 Anatomy of a Selling Climax

The VIX

The VIX, or volatility index, measures implied volatility in index options from real-time OEX index option bid/asked prices. Produced by the CBOE since 1993, this index is calculated by taking a weighted average of the implied volatilities from eight OEX calls and puts. The options selected are the closest to the money and the closest to having 30-day duration. Using an appropriate weighting scheme, the VIX represents the implied volatility of a hypothetical 30-day, ATM option. That is, after multiplying by a constant.

When the CBOE developed the VIX, they used the consulting services of Professor Robert E. Whaley of the Fuqua School of Business at Duke University. Noting that all options, except options in their final week, have more calendar days than trading days remaining, Professor Whaley reasoned, in his paper "The Investor Fear Gauge," published February 4, 2000, that since stock return volatility over the weekend is approximately the same as it is for other trading days, the implied volatility measured using standard options pricing models needs to be multiplied by the square root of the number of calendar days divided by the square root of the number of trading days.

For an option with exactly one calendar week remaining, this would be the square root of 7 divided by the square root of 5, or 1.18. Options of other durations would presumably have different adjustment factors. But since the VIX represents a hypothetical 30-day option, one would presume that, with 22 trading days within the usual 30 calendar days, the adjustment factor would be the square root of 30 divided by the square root of 22, or 1.167. By comparing some IV numbers from the OEX matrix at various snapshots in the past with the VIX at those times, I found this to be roughly correct.

Thus the VIX is 1.167 times higher than the implied volatility of a hypothetical 30-day OEX option. One could question the need for this adjustment, as it tends to isolate the VIX, making it incomparable to other volatility numbers. It is also useless as a number to be plugged into a standard options pricing model. That is, unless you have some kind of trading-days-based options pricing model—something I've never seen nor heard of anyone using.

Interest rates and costs of carry, important elements in any options pricing model, continue through the weekend. I believe that's why standard options pricing models are calendar-day based. The VIX would have to be adjusted back down before it could be plugged into a standard, calendar-day-based options model.

Thankfully, the constant adjustment factor does nothing to hurt the VIX's usefulness in comparison with itself. That is, viewing a historical chart of the VIX is good for gaining a general indication of volatility levels in the past.

Finally, note that the VIX is not the only indicator of its kind. There is also a VXN to reflect implied volatilities in the NDX (Nasdaq 100) options, and a QQV to reflect implied volatilities in the QQQ (Nasdaq 100 Holders) options. There may be others.

Starting the Business (on a Shoestring)

About the time that I was writing my first options software on my first PC, I was also increasingly discontented with my position with IBM. I enjoyed most of my years at IBM. And while my education at Purdue laid a foundation, it was at IBM that I learned what engineering is all about. I worked with a lot of good people and helped to develop some exciting products. However, the division I was in had run into a stagnant period and was not pursuing anything new and exciting. The company execs were having trouble figuring out what business opportunities to pursue next. When you're an animal the size of a dinosaur, you look for big meals and in the process pass over many smaller meals. The problem is, many apparently small business opportunities grow into large opportunities over time—and it's impossible to know ahead of time which ones will turn out big. So, in my humble opinion, you have to invest in several areas at a time. I believe IBM could have been, and probably should have been, what Cisco, Oracle, and Sun became.

Anyway, I was assigned to a job coordinating test procedures and pushing paper. I don't think I did any development work—the work I truly love—for almost a year. That's when I started exploring job opportunities outside the company and landed a job with Tandem Computers—with a 26 percent pay increase!

Tandem was a new technology company, and its high-flying stock was one of the darlings on the Nasdaq. Based in Cupertino, California, their product was fault-tolerant, expandable minicomputers for business applications that needed to be up and running all the time. They hired me to help finish the development of a new smart terminal that worked with their system. The Tandem work environment, with flexible hours and the engineers coming to work in shorts and sandals, was radically different than I was used to. But it didn't take me long to adapt! And I'll never forget the company party (called a "beer bash") that started every Friday at about 4:00 P.M.!

During those early days at Tandem, I continued developing my personal trading software after hours. I worked all day at Tandem and then worked on my hobby until midnight. Once the software was ready, I put it to work trading spreads. That's when it occurred to me to convert my software into a general purpose options analysis program and see if I could sell a few copies to individual traders.

So I spent a few months preparing the software and named it Option-Vue at the suggestion of a friend. Actually, there were two editions at first—OptionVue A, geared for covered writing or single option positions, and OptionVue B, mainly geared for spreads. I prepared separate versions of each program for the IBM PC and the Tandy TRS-80 models II and III. I priced them at $129 each.

Then I hired an ad agency to help me prepare print ads and press releases. I thought of a business name (Star Value Software) and had a logo designed. I also spent a lot of time developing literature and cover letters for various target audiences. I was constantly improving upon these. These were new business activities to me, but I learned fast and enjoyed these tasks very much.

In March 1983, I suddenly found myself out of a job. Tandem was trimming its work force and my number came up. I think they were happy with my work, but the moonlighting probably bothered them. Plus my endeavors had expanded to the point where they occupied some of my thoughts during work hours. I also think my direct supervisor secretly had my welfare in mind when he set me free to pursue what he could see was my heart's desire, although he could not come right out and say so. Being fired came as a real shock. But then, some pain always goes with being pushed out of the nest, right?

Yet something strange and wonderful happened to me then. It was the first time I had ever faced a situation in my career where I was free to pursue my heart's desire, yet the transition was anything but safe. If I was going to pursue this new business idea full-time, I was going to have to trust the Lord for income. My wife and I were just starting out and we did not have a nest egg. All we had was our home equity to borrow against, plus a couple of credit cards we could draw upon (reluctantly), and a motorcycle I could sell (very reluctantly). The business was only selling about 10 copies of the software per month at that point, and that level of income did not even cover the business expenses.

Yet, with my wife's encouragement, the decision was made almost immediately to pursue the new business full-time. There was a warm summer rain that day in Texas, and I remember going out for a run and deliberately stomping in every puddle along the way.

Starting a new business is not easy, but I had boundless energy for it. I worked day and night. I must have poured in 80 hours a week during the first year. Karen and I were making babies too, so Karen was busy with the kids and could not help much except to answer the phone whenever I needed to run errands. I used a spare bedroom in the house as my office for the first year or so, and then a custom-built office inside the garage for about another year. While I worked in the house I had no employees.

I explored selling my software through distributors and retailers at first, but they were not interested in such a specialized program. For that reason we have always sold direct to the customer and directly supported our customers.

At one point early in the process, when our software was geared to the simpler needs of individual traders, I received a phone call from a Philadelphia exchange market maker named Steve Wasserstrom. He asked me if my software could perform some functions that he would need to support his professional trading. I had to admit that it could not. However, the next day I called him back and asked if he could describe for me in more detail what was needed. I also asked him whether there was the potential for selling very many copies if I developed the kind of program he was asking for and priced it reasonably. He assured me that I'd probably sell at least a dozen copies in Philadelphia alone, and there were four other exchanges where I could sell the software as well.

Necessity is the mother of invention, and with our existing software not selling enough to make ends meet, I decided to go for it. In just two months (again, 80-hour weeks) I had the software ready. I named it ProVue, and gave it a price tag of $425.

Steve Wasserstrom bought his copy. Then I prepared a flier to mail to all of the options market makers in the United States. I painstakingly typed in all the 2,000-plus names into my TRS-80 III and printed mailing labels. Then, with my three-year-old son helping, my family spent three days stuffing and sealing. I think the postage was more than $500. My expectations were to sell at least 20 copies as a result of the mailing, maybe even hundreds. I was not prepared for what actually happened.

We sold one. That's it; one copy.

I was devastated. While I didn't realize it at the time, this was when I began learning about the importance of name recognition. People don't just pop for some new product unless they've heard of your company before. However, at the time, I did not realize that this was the problem. Rather, I felt that no one wanted my product. So I turned my attention to another pursuit for a while.

I had already made a utility program for transferring files back and forth between my TRS-80 III and my IBM PC for my own use. I submitted this program to Radio Shack's third-party developer program, and from there it was passed along to a Dallas firm who agreed to publish it and pay royalties on sales. The name of this software was Let's Talk, and it appeared on the shelves of every Radio Shack across the country for a short time. Unfortunately, Let's Talk never sold very many copies, and I probably only realized about $1,000 in royalties.

Meanwhile, several more ProVue sales trickled in from Philadelphia, so I turned my attention back to options analysis software. I kept improving the software, developed some customer contacts in New York, and went to a couple of trade shows. I kept improving my literature and sales approach, and even read a couple of books on sales techniques.

Despite my efforts, it was always a struggle to make ends meet in those days. During those first couple of years, income barely exceeded business expenses, and what was left over barely met my family's needs. Often a copy of the program sold just in time to meet a payment deadline. I do not begrudge those years, however. Karen and I grew closer to the Lord as we depended on Him so intimately for our daily bread. In those days, half of our sales came in the mail, and we used to *run* to the mail box after the mailman came.

Somehow, we were never late on a mortgage payment and we never went hungry. The credit cards got run up to the max though, and I remember many times making a quick run to the bank with even the smallest of deposits. My only complaint during that period was that, because of our debt situation, we were not able to give to the church and other worthy causes the way we would have liked.

But everything was about to change in 1985. That's about when the *Investor's Daily* newspaper started. I started placing ads there, and boom— we were suddenly doing all the business we could handle. I was taking calls all day, eating supper, and filling orders until midnight. There was no time for development work. In a short time I moved out of the house, set up an office, and hired my first employee—and soon after that, another employee. I trained these people to do the clerical and sales work. That freed me to return to the development work, a constant need for any software company, and the work I love to do.

In the beginning, I was using a development system from IBM, writing code in BASIC—a simple but adequate language. Then, sometime in 1983, I read about a new development system from Logitech based on a language called Modula 2. I bought a book on Modula 2 and soaked it up during a one-week vacation. I loved the language. It contained advanced capabilities I needed for my work. So I bought the Logitech system and put it to work immediately. It was time for a new generation of options software anyway, so I rewrote all the BASIC code in Modula 2 and proceeded to take the software up a couple of notches. It was time for our second generation of software.

With most of our customer interest coming through responses to the *Investor's Daily* ad, we were hearing from individual traders much more than professional traders. These people were asking for powerful features like those of our more powerful ProVue software, but not exactly. We needed a program that more closely met the needs of the individual trader. So, in response to this demand, I created OptionVue Plus. Now we had OptionVue Plus for the individual trader, and an updated version of ProVue for the professional trader. OptionVue Plus sold for $695 and ProVue for $895. Both programs worked with Dow Jones for automatic price updates.

Along with the higher price tag, we introduced the concept of selling an inexpensive trial version of the software that worked for 30 days, thinking that customers would feel more comfortable buying the software after they had a chance to use it for a while. It's the same approach we still use today. We sold almost 2,000 copies of OptionVue Plus during the five-year life of the product.

In 1987, Karen and I moved our family, and the company, from Austin, Texas, to a Chicago suburb called Vernon Hills. We preferred the northern climate and wanted to be closer to her folks. With the move, we renamed the company OptionVue Systems International and incorporated it for the first time. (Actually, we named it Options Software International for a short time, but this conflicted with the name of an existing company and we were forced to choose a different name.)

In September 1989 we introduced OptionVue IV—our third generation of options analysis software, and a considerable advancement in capabilities over OptionVue Plus. I'm not sure why we named it with a four, except that I vaguely recall there being other software packages on the market that were called "three" or "four," and we wanted to use a name that sounded sophisticated.

DOS was the operating system on the early PCs, so naturally the early generations of our software were designed to run in a DOS environment. We lingered far too long in the DOS realm, however. Windows was out for nearly three years before we decided it was time to write a new, Windows-based program. The reason for the delay was that we felt it was very important to keep coming out with improvements in the program, both to satisfy prospective buyers and to please our existing customers. We knew that once we began rewriting the software for Windows (and it *was* a *complete* rewrite), our users would see no upgrades for two years or more as we spent time going sideways.

In order to develop the new Windows version, we had to select a new development system. There were many available, but we narrowed it down to just two possibilities: the Microsoft C++ Development System and Borland's new Delphi System. We worked with both of these systems for several weeks and then made our choice. We felt that Delphi was better because it used a language (Pascal) that was similar to what we were used to (Modula 2) and it was more robust. Just about every statement that we wrote in Delphi was both more powerful and able to carry out our intentions more reliably. The Microsoft system was quirky and temperamental. Thanks to Delphi, we were able to develop the Windows version of Option-Vue much faster. And it's a good thing.

OptionVue Systems nearly died before we could get the new Windows version developed. Yet somehow our sales reps were able to keep generating just enough interest in the DOS version to keep us alive. I had an engineer helping me with development through this effort. Scott Frank, a young man from Texas, moved up to the "great white north" to join us. Scott and I must have put in 50-hour weeks together for the two and a half years it took to develop OptionVue 5, our company's fourth and current generation of options analysis software.

It turns out that instead of going sideways, OptionVue 5 was a significant advancement over OptionVue IV. Just about every area of the software was redesigned to be more streamlined and powerful. OptionVue 5 was introduced in December 1997 and has since been upgraded through more than 40 new releases containing hundreds of feature enhancements. It is still our company's main product.

Over the years, we have added a market quote service (DataVue), an online service for scanning the market for trading opportunities (OpScan), new interfaces with outside data vendors, educational materials in many formats, and a full-scale options-oriented web site. Just recently, we launched a new offshoot company called OptionVue Research that provides online options analysis tools, daily trading advice, and money management services.

There is a lot more I could write about the company's achievements, especially in recent years as the staff has grown and the pace of change has quickened. But rather than go into all these details, I'd like to share about some of the people I've had the pleasure of meeting and working with.

I've met a lot of interesting people over the years. For instance, when OptionVue was just starting out, Karen and I traveled to New York to display our software at a trade show. All we had was a table on which to spread out our literature. At the next table, also at one of their company's first trade shows ever, were Steve Achelis and his wife. They were handing out brochures about Steve's new MetaStock program. We shook hands and traded copies of our software. Over the years, Steve and I have collaborated on many projects and have always held each other in high regard. MetaStock grew to become one of the most popular technical analysis programs ever. (Note that Steve sold his company a few years ago and is no longer working there.)

One person who had a big influence on OptionVue's products, and contributed to our success, was Geert Strubbe of Belgium. He has faithfully represented our products throughout Europe for more than 10 years, teaching people how to trade options using the OptionVue software.

More recently, we've started a relationship with Paul Wise in Australia. He also teaches people how to trade options and represents our products there.

Another Paul who played a role in our company's history is Paul Forchione. Paul worked at OptionVue for a brief period as a sales rep, before going to work with David Caplan at Opportunities In Options and then striking out on his own. Paul teaches traders how to use our software to manage delta-neutral positions, especially in bond options.

I've enjoyed friendly relationships with many of the educators in the options business. For instance, the folks at the Options Industry Council and the Options Institute, like Jim Bittman, Marty Kerney, and others. Also independents like Larry McMillan, Larry Connors, Ken Trester, Bernie Schaefer, Rance Masheck, Jon Najarian, George Fontanills, John Sarkett, and Sheldon Natenberg, as well as principals David Krell and Gary Katz at the ISE. I also have fond memories of Jim Yates (deceased), David Caplan (no longer in the business), and Marc Clemons, who used to write for our newsletter and help us put on options trading seminars. All of these people, and others not mentioned, have contributed to my success in untold ways, with ideas, encouragement, referrals, and collaboration on business endeavors. I'm eternally grateful.

I've even enjoyed friendly relationships with most of our competitors, while they lasted. Note that we never had thoughts of eliminating any competition, but simply remained focused on pouring excellence into our own products and services. I'd like to believe that we simply outdistanced them.

Over the years, the company has experienced more ups and downs than I have mentioned. Thankfully, we have continued to grow and maintain a strong capital position, but our trust is not in the balance sheet. It is in the Lord, who sustained us during the difficult times, and does to this day. I don't worry about the future or whether the business will continue to be successful. We're in His hands.

BUSINESS PHILOSOPHY

Engineering

I like developing software because I enjoy building logical systems that are useful and intuitive to operate. A well-designed system extends the human capabilities beyond one's natural abilities—sometimes *far* beyond. In short, I like putting computers to work—doing something useful.

To me, satisfaction increases as the power of the system increases. And the power of the system increases as various high-performance, problem-free systems are combined and brought to bear on a common problem or need. For example, a program to seek out and list the most potentially profitable options trades would make use of algorithms to calculate margin requirements, options fair values, slippage and commissions estimates, and many other factors. The algorithms to perform these subfunctions are powerful systems in their own right. So the strength of the system "pyramids" as you build it up, level upon level.

I like providing practical solutions to real-life needs. In the financial realm, traders need more than theory—they need tools that will help them make money. That's why we've always geared the company's products and services to the needs of real traders.

Customers

Customer satisfaction is my greatest reward. There is nothing I enjoy more than hearing a customer say something like, "Wow, this is just what I was hoping to find, and so much more!" Feedback like that is what keeps me going.

Having started the business on a shoestring, my appreciation for the customer runs deep. That remains so even now that the business is larger and I have less direct contact with customers. Yet our business is still small. I think some customers imagine us to be larger than we really are. While we're growing, we have just one office and a trim budget, so every customer is important to us financially.

I like to think of our relationship with the customer as a partnership. We provide (and keep improving) the software, data, and services they need to support their trading. In return, customers provide us with the funds to support our operations. We also welcome feedback. We pay a great deal of attention to customer suggestions, and they are vital to our future, even though a sizable and ever-present backlog keeps us from getting to some of their ideas right away. The way I see it, when a customer points out a problem or makes a suggestion, he is not only doing himself a favor, but also helping us make our products better. He is also benefiting all our other customers in the process. It's a win-win-win situation! That is the nature of a partnership.

We enjoy providing a personal level of support and service. That is why we still have live people answering the phones. And that is why we still give the customer a phone call, even if they have ordered from our web site. When someone orders the trial package from us, a support rep is assigned to work with the customer and help them get up to speed with the software and our services. After the final purchase, the same rep is available to help them with any further needs and subscription renewals.

Employees

There is a line in the movie *Das Boot* (a German U-boat movie) that I'll never forget. It comes at the end of a long ordeal when one of the crewmen was able to repair the batteries and get them working again. The captain said, "You've got to have good men." It's absolutely true. You've got to have good people. Not only when your company faces challenges, but at *all* times, it's essential to have a higher caliber of people working with you.

The people at OptionVue Systems are a higher caliber. They work hard. They work smart. They are courteous to each other as well as to our customers. Every one of them has skills that go beyond my own. I appreciate their dedication and am proud of what we have accomplished together. I look forward to many more years of working together.

Glossary

all or none (AON) order   A type of order that specifies the order can only be activated if the full order will be filled. A term used more in securities markets than futures markets.

American depositary receipts (ADRs)   Certificates issued by a U.S. bank that represent foreign securities the bank holds in the country of origin. They are traded like domestic common stock in the United States, and options are available on many of them.

American-style option   A call or put option contract that can be exercised at any time before the expiration of the contract.

arbitrage   The simultaneous buying and selling of the same security at two different prices on two different markets, resulting in profits without risk.

ask, asked price   Price at which the trader making the price is willing to sell an option or security.

assignment   Notification by the Options Clearing Corporation (OCC) to a clearing member and the writer of an option that an owner of the option has exercised the option and that the terms of settlement must be met. Assignments are made on a random basis by the OCC. The writer of a call option is obligated to sell the underlying asset at the strike price of the call option; the writer of a put option is obligated to buy the underlying at the strike price of the put option.

at-the-money (ATM)   An at-the-money option is one whose strike price is equal to (or, in practice, very close to) the current price of the underlying.

back month   A back month contract is any exchange-traded derivatives contract for a future period beyond the front month contract. Also known as far month.

backspread   A strategy that involves buying and selling a different amount of two different option contracts of the same type, in the same expiration month. *See also* long backspread, short backspread.

bar chart   A chart used to plot price movements, with each day's vertical bar indicating the price range.

bear, bearish   A bear is someone with a pessimistic view on a market or particular asset, who believes that the price will fall. Such views are often described as bearish.

bear call spread   A vertical credit spread using calls only. This is a net credit transaction established by selling a call and buying another call at a higher strike price, in the same expiration. It is a directional trade where the maximum loss equals the difference between the strike prices less the credit received, and the maximum profit equals the credit received. Requires margin.

bear put spread   A vertical debit spread using puts only. A net debit transaction established by selling a put and buying another put at a higher strike price, in the same expiration. It is a directional trade where the maximum loss equals the debit paid, and the maximum profit equals the difference between the strike prices less the debit. No margin is required.

beta   A prediction of what percentage a security will move in relation to an index. If a security has a beta of 1, then the position will tend to move in line with the index. A beta of 0.5 suggests that a 1 percent move in the index will cause the security price to move by 0.5 percent.

   Note: Beta can be misleading since it is based on past performance, which is not necessarily a reliable guide to the future.

bell curve   *See* normal distribution.

bid   The price that the trader making the price is willing to pay to buy an option or security.

bid-ask spread   The difference between the bid and ask prices of a security. The wider (i.e., larger) the spread is, the less liquid the market and the greater the slippage.

binomial pricing model   An options pricing model that assumes the price of the underlying can either rise or fall by a certain amount at each predetermined interval until expiration. *See also* Cox-Ross-Rubenstein.

Black-Scholes pricing model   An options pricing model used to compute the value of European-style options, invented by Fischer Black and Myron Scholes. The primary inputs are the underlying price, the strike price, the risk-free interest rate, time to expiration, and the standard deviation of the stock return.

box   A position created by combining a long call and a short put at one strike price, and a short call and a long put at another strike price, all with the same expiration.

breakeven price   The price(s) of the underlying at which a position breaks even (i.e., is neither profitable nor unprofitable) at a specific point in time.

broker   The middleman who passes orders from investors to floor dealers, screen traders, or market makers for execution.

bull, bullish A bull is someone with an optimistic view on a market or particular asset, who believes that the price will rise. Such views are often described as bullish.

bull call spread A vertical debit spread using calls only. This is a net debit transaction established by buying a call and selling another call at a higher strike price, in the same expiration. It is a directional trade where the maximum loss equals the debit paid, and the maximum profit equals the difference between the strike prices, less the debit. No margin is required.

bull put spread A vertical credit spread using puts only. This is a net credit transaction established by buying a put and selling another put at a higher strike price, in the same expiration. It is a directional trade where the maximum loss equals the difference between the strike prices, less the credit, and the maximum profit equals the credit received. Requires margin.

butterfly A spread strategy involving three contracts of the same type at three different strike prices. A long (short) butterfly involves buying (selling) the lowest strike price, selling (buying) double the quantity at the central strike price, and buying (selling) the highest strike price. All options are in the same expiration month.

buy write *See* covered call.

calendar spread Also called a time spread, a calendar spread involves the simultaneous purchase and sale of options of the same type, but with different expiration dates. Horizontal debit spreads, horizontal credit spreads, diagonal debit spreads, and diagonal credit spreads are all examples of calendar spreads.

call option An option contract that conveys the right to buy a standard quantity of a specified asset at a fixed price per unit (the strike price) for a limited length of time (until expiration).

call ratio backspread A long backspread using calls only.

canceled order A buy or sell order that is canceled before it has been executed. In most cases, a limit order can be canceled at any time as long as it has not been executed. (A market order may be canceled if the order is placed after market hours and is then canceled before the market opens the following day). A request for cancel can be made anytime before execution.

CEV (constant elasticity of volatility) The observed tendency of volatility to change when the price of the underlying changes. For example, with most stocks and stock indexes, as prices increase, volatility declines; when prices decline, volatility increases. This negative correlation would be indicated with a negative CEV factor.

circuit breakers A system of trading halts and price limits on equities and derivative markets, designed to provide a cooling-off period during large, intraday market movements. *See also* trading halt.

clearing house   Ensures the financial integrity of the futures and options contracts traded on the exchanges for which it clears. It acts as the buyer to every clearing member seller, and the seller to every clearing member buyer. In this way, it guarantees performance of all trades it accepts. A clearing organization is also charged with the proper conduct of delivery procedures and the adequate financing of the entire operation. Examples are the Options Clearing Corporation (OCC) and the Board of Trade Clearing Corporation (BOTCC).

clearing member   A member firm of the clearing house. While every clearing member must also be a member of the exchange, not all members of the exchange are members of the clearing organization. Trades of nonmembers must be eventually settled through a clearing member.

closing price (range)   The price (or price range) recorded during the final moments of a day's trading activity that is officially designated as the "close."

closing transaction   Selling a previously purchased position (or buying back a previously sold position), effectively canceling out the position.

collar   A trade that establishes both a maximum profit (the ceiling) and minimum loss (the floor) when holding the underlying asset. An example would be owning 100 shares of a stock, while simultaneously selling a call, and buying a put. The premium received from the sale of the call offsets the premium due from the purchase of the put. Strike prices are often chosen at levels at which the premiums net out to zero.

collateral   *See* margin.

combination   A position involving puts and calls held together, either long or short, with different strike prices and expirations, especially when the position is not readily identifiable as one of the main option strategies.

commission   The charge paid to a broker for transacting the purchase or the sale of stock, options, or any other security. *See also* round turn.

commodity   A raw material or primary product used in manufacturing or industrial processing or consumed in its natural form.

condor   A strategy that includes an out-of-the-money call spread plus an out-of-the-money put spread. Thus the strategy involves four contracts, in the same expiration, at four different strike prices. Usually, both spreads are sold, creating credit spreads.

contract   The legal agreement between the buyer and seller of a transaction, as defined by an exchange. This is also the term describing a trading unit of a future or option.

contract size   The number of units of an underlying specified in a contract. In stock options the standard contract size is 100 shares of stock. In futures options the contract size is one futures contract. In cash-based index options the contract size is typically $100, $250, or $500.

conversion   A strategy that includes a long position in the underlying combined with a short synthetic.

convertible security   A security that can be converted into common stock at the option of the security holder. Examples are convertible bonds and convertible preferred stock.

cost of carry   The cost of holding an asset for a period of time. It is the combination of all charges, including interest, insurance, and storage, minus any earnings that may proceed from the holding (i.e., dividends). Note that if the asset must be paid for in cash or requires a cash deposit that does not get to earn interest, then the opportunity cost of lost interest earnings must be added to the cost of carry (this is often the most important component). Positive carry means that the earnings exceed the holding costs; negative carry means that the holding costs exceed the earnings.

covered   An option strategy is said to be covered when all short options are completely offset with a position in the underlying or a long option in options on the same asset. The loss potential with such a strategy is therefore limited.

covered call   A strategy involving a long position in the underlying plus a short call.

covered combo   A strategy involving a long position in the underlying, plus a short call and a short put.

Cox-Ross-Rubinstein pricing model   A binomial options-pricing model invented by John Cox, Stephen Ross, and Mark Rubinstein.

credit   The amount received for placing a trade, resulting in a net inflow of cash into the investor's account.

cross hedging   The practice of using opposing positions (long or short) in different, yet related, assets to reduce the overall risk. For instance, holding a long crude oil position plus a short heating oil position tends to neutralize the trader's exposure to movement in the overall energy group. (The investor's goal in this case may be to play crude oil to move up relative to heating oil.)

cycle   *See* expiration cycle.

day order   An order to purchase or sell a security, usually at a specified price, that is good for just the trading session in which it is given. A day order is automatically canceled at the close of the market if it is not filled.

debit   The amount the investor pays for placing a trade, resulting in a net outflow of cash from his account

delivery   The tender and receipt of a commodity or financial instrument in settlement of a futures contract.

delivery date   The date by which a financial instrument or commodity (or other instruments such as warehouse receipts or shipping certificates) must be delivered to fulfill the terms of a futures contract.

delta   One of the "greeks," delta measures the rate of change in an option's theoretical value for a one-unit change in the underlying. Calls have positive deltas and puts have negative deltas.

delta-neutral   A strategy in which the deltas of the options held (plus any position in the underlying) offset one another, with the result that the position has little to no exposure to near-term price movements (of the underlying).

derivative   A financial instrument, traded on or off an exchange, whose price is derived from the value of one or more underlying securities, indexes, debt securities, commodities, other derivative securities, or any agreed pricing index or arrangement. While derivatives involve the trading of rights or obligations based on the underlying, they do not directly transfer property.

diagonal credit spread   A type of calendar spread where an option is purchased at one strike price and expiration, and another option of the same type is sold at a more in-the-money strike price and a different expiration. It is usually a net credit transaction. It is called diagonal because the options have different strike prices and different expiration dates.

diagonal debit spread   A type of calendar spread where an option is purchased at one strike price and expiration, and another option of the same type is sold at a more out-of-the-money strike price and a different expiration. It is usually a net debit transaction. It is called diagonal because the options have different strike prices and different expiration dates.

directional trade   A trade designed to take advantage of an expected price movement.

early exercise   A feature of American-style options, allowing the owner to exercise an option at any time prior to its expiration date.

equity   This term has three separate but widely used definitions related to finance:

- The residual dollar value of a trading account, assuming the liquidation of all open positions at the current market price.
- The net worth of a company—the amount by which assets exceed liabilities.
- A term synonymous with common stock.

equity option   An option on shares of an individual common stock. Also known as a stock option.

European-style option   An option that can only be exercised on the expiration date of the contract.

exchange traded   The generic term used to describe securities, futures, options, and other instruments that are traded on an organized exchange.

exercise   The act by which the holder of an option takes up his rights to buy or sell the underlying at the strike price. For instance, a call option holder's demand that the number of units of the underlying specified in the contract be delivered to him at the specified price; or a put option holder's demand that the number of units of the underlying asset specified be bought from him at the specified price.

exercise price   *See* strike price.

expected return   The return expected on an investment or position, considering all possible outcomes and the probability of each outcome.

expiration, expiration date, expiration month   The date by which an option contract must be exercised or it becomes void and the holder of the option ceases to have any rights under the contract. In the United States, all stock and index option contracts expire on the Saturday following the third Friday of the specified month.

expiration cycle   Traditionally, there were three cycles of expiration dates used in options trading:

January Cycle (1):	January/April/July/October
February Cycle (2):	February/May/August/November
March Cycle (3):	March/June/September/December

Each stock was assigned one of these three traditional cycles. Today, equity options expire on a hybrid cycle which involves a total of four or five option series: the two nearest-term calendar months and the next two or three months from its traditional cycle.

fair value   *See* theoretical value, theoretical price.

far month, far term   *See* back month.

fill   When an order has been completely executed, it is described as filled.

fill or kill (FOK) order   A type of order where the trader stipulates that a trade be filled immediately and entirely, if possible, or else canceled. This is like the all-or-none (AON) order in that the entire order must be filled at once. However, the FOK order has a time constraint while the AON order does not.

floor broker   An exchange member who is paid a fee for executing orders for clearing members or their customers.

floor trader   An exchange member who generally trades only for his own account or an account controlled by him. Also known as a local.

follow-up action   The trades an investor makes subsequent to implementing a strategy. Through adjustments, the investor transforms one strategy into a different one in response to price changes in the underlying or other factors, in order to better position the strategy going forward.

front month   The first month of all available contracts listed on an exchange. This is usually the most actively traded contract, but volume gradually shifts from this to the second month contract as the front month nears expiration. Also known as near month.

fundamental analysis The study of basic underlying factors to forecast future prices, including economic and industry analysis. For commodities, it includes factors affecting supply and demand. For stocks, it includes examining the company's financials and operations, especially sales, earnings, growth potential, assets, debt, products, and competition.

future The term used to designate all contracts covering the sale of financial instruments or physical commodities for future delivery on an exchange.

futures contract A standardized, transferable legal agreement to make or take delivery of a specific amount of a commodity of a certain grade or type at a predetermined date in the future. The price is determined at the time the agreement is made. Futures contracts are traded on organized futures exchanges, and delivery and physical possession take place on the contract date unless the contract has been closed out by an offsetting transaction. Futures are also available on various financial products and indexes.

futures option An option on a futures contract.

gamma A measure of the amount by which delta changes with a one-point increase in the price of the underlying. Gamma is positive for all options. If a call option has a delta of 45 and a gamma of 10, then the option's expected delta will be 55 if the underlying goes up one point. If we consider delta to be the velocity of an option, then gamma is the acceleration.

good 'til canceled (GTC) order An order that is effective until it is either filled by the broker or canceled by the investor. This order is automatically canceled at the option's expiration.

greeks The Greek letters used to describe various measures of the sensitivity of the value of an option with respect to different factors. They include delta, gamma, theta, vega, and rho.

hedging Taking a position opposite to a position held to minimize the risk of financial loss from an adverse price change.

historic volatility *See* statistical volatility.

holder The purchaser of an option. Also known as the option buyer.

horizontal credit spread A type of calendar spread. It is a credit transaction in which the investor buys an option in a nearer expiration month and sells an option of the same type in a farther expiration month with the same strike price.

horizontal debit spread A type of calendar spread. It is a debit transaction in which the investor sells an option in a nearer expiration month and buys an option of the same type in a farther expiration month with the same strike price.

immediate-or-cancel (IOC) order An option order that gives the trading floor an opportunity to partially or totally fill an order, with any unfilled balance immediately canceled.

illiquid   An illiquid market has a low volume of transactions and/or a small number of participants. In an illiquid market, a security or an option is usually priced with a wide bid/asked gap, resulting in the trader paying more in transaction costs.

implied volatility (IV)   The volatility that the underlying would need to have for the pricing model to produce the same theoretical option price as the actual option price. The term *implied volatility* comes from the fact that options imply the volatility of their underlying, just by their price. A computer model starts with the actual market price of an option, and measures IV by working the option fair value model backward, solving for volatility (normally an input) as if it were the unknown.

   In actuality, the fair value model cannot be worked backward. However, options analysis software can compute IV by working forward repeatedly through a series of intelligent guesses until the volatility is found that makes the fair value equal to the actual market price of the option.

index   A compilation of several stock prices into a single number (e.g., the S&P 500).

index option   An option contract with an index as the underlying asset. These are usually cash-settled.

initial margin   The proportion of a security's market value an investor must pay when buying securities on margin, or the total amount of margin required when a futures or short option position is opened. The Securities Exchange Act of 1934 gives the board of governors of the Federal Reserve the responsibility to set initial margin requirements: initial margin requirements for futures contracts are set by the futures exchanges. Individual brokerage firms are free to set higher requirements.

in-the-money (ITM)   The term used when the strike price of an option is less than the price of the underlying for a call option, or greater than the price of the underlying for a put option. In other words, the option has an intrinsic value greater than zero.

intrinsic value   The amount of any favorable difference between the strike price of an option and the current price of the underlying (i.e., the amount by which it is in-the-money). The intrinsic value of an out-of-the-money option is zero.

joint clearing members   Firms that clear on more than one exchange.

last trading day   The last business day prior to the option's expiration when the option may be traded. For equity options, this is generally the third Friday of the expiration month.

LEAPS   Long-term Equity Anticipation Securities are calls and puts with expirations as long as two to five years. Currently, equity LEAPS have two series in existence at a time, always with January expirations, and only about 10 percent of equities have LEAPS. Some indexes also have LEAPS.

leg   A term describing one component of a spread position. For example, a calendar spread has two legs; a butterfly spread has three.

legging   A risky method of implementing or closing out a spread strategy one leg at a time. Instead of utilizing a spread order to insure that both the written and the purchased option orders are filled simultaneously, an investor gambles that a better deal can be obtained overall by entering two or more separate orders.

leverage   A means of increasing potential return without increasing investment, such as using borrowed funds to buy stocks on margin. Option contracts are leveraged, because they allow you to control a greater amount of the underlying asset with fewer dollars, providing the possibility of higher returns on your investment.

limit order   An order placed with a brokerage to buy or sell a predetermined number of contracts (or shares of stock) at or better than the specified price. Limit orders can be placed as day or GTC orders (day is the default). Limit orders may cost slightly higher commissions than market orders but are often better to use, especially with options, because the price you'll pay is strictly limited.

liquid   A liquid market has a high volume of transactions and many participants. In a liquid market, a security or an option is usually priced with a narrow bid/asked gap, resulting in the trader being able to trade greater quantities while paying less in transaction costs.

listed options   Options that are traded on an exchange.

long   You are long if you have bought more than you have sold in any particular market, commodity, instrument, or contract. Also known as having a long position, you have purchased an asset with the intention of selling it at a higher price sometime in the future. Thus when you are long you expect the asset to increase in price.

long backspread   This strategy involves selling one option near the money and buying two (or more) options of the same type farther out-of-the-money, with the same expiration. Requires margin.

long option   Buying an option. *See also* long.

long straddle   *See* straddle.

long strangle   *See* strangle.

long synthetic   *See* synthetic.

long underlying   Buying the underlying (i.e., stock). *See also* long.

maintenance margin   The amount that must be maintained on deposit at all times in a margin account to cover a position. If the equity in an account drops to or below this level due to adverse price movement, the broker issues a margin call, requiring the investor to either deposit more funds or securities, or close positions to reduce the requirements.

margin   The legally required amount of cash or securities deposited with a brokerage to insure that an investor can meet all potential obligations. Margin (or collateral) is required on futures contracts and investments with open-ended loss potential, such as writing naked options. *See also* initial margin; maintenance margin.

mark to market   The revaluation of a position using current market prices, usually for the recalculation of margin requirements or for accounting or tax purposes.

market maker   A trader or institution that plays a leading role in a market by being prepared to quote a two-way price (bid and ask) on request—or constantly, in the case of some screen-based markets—during normal market hours.

market order   An order to buy or sell a security immediately at the best available current price; sometimes referred to as an unrestricted order. A market order is the only type of order that has guaranteed execution. It should be used with caution in placing option trades, because you can end up paying more than you anticipated (when buying) or selling for less than you anticipated (when selling).

market-if-touched (MIT) order   An order that is placed with a price, below market if buying or above market if selling, that automatically becomes a market order if the specified price is reached.

market-not-held order   A type of market order in which the investor gives discretion to the broker regarding the price and/or time that a trade is executed. It is called "not held" because the broker is not held to the usual requirement of filling the order as quickly as possible.

market-on-close (MOC) order   A type of day order in which the investor specifies that the order be delayed until right before the market closes, at which time it becomes an active market order. Thus the order is executed at or near the closing price of the day on which the order is entered.

maximum price fluctuation   The maximum amount a contract price is allowed to change, up or down, during one trading session, as fixed by exchange rules.

minimum price fluctuation   *See* tick.

naked   A position where options are sold short and are not matched with either a covering position in the underlying or a long position in another option of the same type expiring at the same time or later than the options sold.

near term, near month   *See* front month.

normal distribution   A statistical distribution based on a random process where observations are evenly distributed around the mean; also called the bell curve.

not-held order   *See* market-not-held order.

offer   *See* ask.

offset Closing an outstanding long or short position by making an opposite transaction.

one-cancels-the-other (OCO) order A type of order that treats two or more option orders as a package, whereby the execution of any one of the orders causes all the other orders to be reduced by the same amount. Can be placed as a day or GTC order.

open interest The cumulative total of all option contracts of a particular series sold but not yet repurchased or exercised.

open order An order that has been placed with the broker and is still active or "working." It remains open until it is either filled or canceled.

opening transaction The creation of, or addition to, a trading position.

option A contract that conveys the right to buy or sell a specified quantity of an asset at a specific price within a specified period of time. *See also* call option, put option.

option chain A list of all the options available for a given underlying asset.

out-of-the-money (OTM) An out-of-the-money option is one whose strike price is unfavorable compared to the current price of the underlying. For a call option, this is when the strike price is greater than the price of the underlying. For a put option, this is when the strike price is less than the price of the underlying. An out-of-the-money option has no intrinsic value, only time value.

over the counter (OTC) market A decentralized market (as opposed to an exchange), where geographically dispersed dealers are linked together by telephones and computer screens.

position The number of contracts bought or sold for which no offsetting transaction has been entered into. An opening transaction to buy places the investor in a long position. An opening transaction to sell places the investor in a short position.

premium The price of an option contract.

protective put A strategy that involves buying a put option in conjunction with a long position on the underlying, in order to hedge.

put option An option contract that conveys the right to sell a standard quantity of a specified asset at a fixed price per unit (the strike price) for a limited length of time (until expiration).

put/call ratio A ratio is used by many traders as a leading indicator, computed by dividing the total put volume by the total call volume.

put/call parity The relationship between the price of a put and the price of a call with the same strike price and expiration date, where the two options are at the same level of implied volatility. If the two options have different implied volatilities, it creates an arbitrage opportunity for professional traders to buy the lower implied volatility option and sell the higher implied volatility option, driving the two options back into parity.

put ratio backspread   A long backspread using puts. *See* long backspread.

realized gain (loss)   The difference between the original cost of a position and the proceeds received when it is closed. A positive difference is a gain and a negative difference is a loss.

reversal   A short position in the underlying combined with a long synthetic. Also known as a reverse conversion.

rho   An indication of an option's sensitivity to changes in interest rates. Rho measures the change in an option's theoretical value with respect to a unit change in the risk-free interest rate.

risk-free rate   The prevailing rate of interest for securities issued by the government of the country of the currency concerned (i.e., U.S. Treasury securities).

rolling   A trading action in which the trader simultaneously closes an open position and creates a new position. As the front month expiration date approaches, traders who want to maintain their positions often roll them over into the next contract month.

round turn   When an option contract is bought and then sold (or sold and then bought). The second trade closes the position, completing the round turn. Futures brokerage commissions are usually quoted on this basis.

short   You are short if you have sold more than you have bought in any particular market, commodity, instrument, or contract. Also known as having a short position, you have sold an asset with the intention of buying it at a lower price sometime in the future. Thus, when you are short you expect the asset to fall in price.

short backspread   A strategy that involves buying one option nearer the money and selling two (or more) options of the same type, farther out-of-the-money, with the same expiration. Requires margin.

short option   Selling an option. *See also* short.

short selling   A trade where the investor (through a broker) borrows a security and sells it with the expectation the price will fall. When it is repurchased later, the security is returned to the party who initially loaned it. If repurchased at a lower price, the short seller profits. Requires margin.

short straddle   *See* straddle.

short strangle   *See* strangle.

short synthetic   *See* synthetic.

short underlying   Selling an asset short. *See also* short selling.

slippage   The portion of transaction costs associated with the bid/ask spread, arising from the fact that you usually buy at the ask price and sell at the bid price, and ask price is usually higher than bid price.

spread   A strategy involving positions in two or more different options on the same underlying, in which the investor is long in one or more options and short in one or more other options, usually of the same type (calls or puts). The investor usually enters into a spread with the expectation of benefiting from a favorable change in the price relationship between the two (or more) options.

spread order   An order for the simultaneous purchase and sale of two (or more) options of the same type. If placed with a limit, the two options must be filled for a specified price difference, or better.

standard deviation   From statistics, the square root of the sum of the squares of the deviations of each member of a population (in financial terms, a group of prices) from their mean. In a normal distribution, one standard deviation encompasses 68 percent of all possible outcomes.

statistical volatility (SV)   A measure of the actual price fluctuations of an asset over a specific period of time on a percentage basis. It can be measured using any recent sample period, but regardless of the length of the sample period, SV is always normalized to represent a one-year, single standard deviation price move of the underlying.

stock option   *See* equity option.

stop order   A "stop" or "stop-limit" order is an order to sell when the asset price falls to a particular point, or to buy when the asset price rises to a particular point. Sent to the exchange floor, these orders remain inactive until there is a trade at the specified stop price on the exchange where the order was sent. At this time a stop order becomes an active market order, and a stop-limit order becomes an active limit order. Stop and stop-limit orders are often used to limit an investor's losses, but they can also be used to open a new position. It can be a good idea to use stop orders if you will be unable to watch your positions for an extended period.

straddle   A strategy involving the simultaneous purchase (or sale) of call and put options with the same strike price and expiration date. In a short straddle, both the calls and puts are sold short, for a credit. In a long straddle, both the calls and puts are bought long, for a debit.

strangle   A strategy involving the simultaneous purchase (or sale) of call and put options with different strike prices but the same expiration date. Strangles are usually constructed using out-of-the-money options. In a short strangle, both the calls and puts are sold short, for a credit. In a long strangle, both the calls and puts are bought long, for a debit.

strategy   An option strategy is any one of a variety of option investments. It includes using options individually or in combination with the underlying and/or other options to create positions that possess desired risk/reward characteristics.

strike price   The price at which the owner of a call option contract can buy the underlying asset, or the price at which the owner of a put option contract can sell the underlying asset. This is a fixed price per unit and is specified in the option contract. Also known as striking price or exercise price.

synthetic   A strategy that uses options to mimic the underlying asset. A long synthetic uses a long call combined with a short put to mimic a long position in the underlying. A short synthetic uses a short call and a long put to mimic a short position in the underlying. In both cases, the call and put have the same strike price and expiration date.

technical analysis   Any number of methods where future price movements are predicted based on historical data such as prices, trading volume, open interest, numbers of advancing issues and declining issues, short selling volume, and so on. Many traders use this type of analysis to make trading decisions, especially short-term trading decisions.

theoretical value, theoretical price   The mathematically calculated value of an option. It is determined by using a pricing model and inputting (1) the strike price of the option, (2) the current price of the underlying, (3) the amount of time until expiration, (4) the volatility of the underlying, (5) the current interest rate, (6) dividend flow information (if stock or index option), and (7) the style of the option (American or European). Also known as fair value.

theta   An indication of an option's sensitivity to the passing of time. Theta measures the theoretical change in an option's value over the next 24 hours. Long option positions have negative theta. Short option positions have positive theta.

tick   The smallest unit price change allowed in trading a specific security, future, or option.

time decay   A term used to describe how the value of an option declines over time. Time decay is quantified by theta.

time spread   Another name for a calendar spread. *See* calendar spread.

time premium   The amount by which the value of an option exceeds its intrinsic value. It reflects the statistical possibility that an option will have intrinsic value at expiration rather than finishing worthless. If an option is out-of-the-money then its entire value consists of time premium. Also known as time value.

trading halt   A temporary suspension of trading in a particular issue due to an order imbalance, or in anticipation of a major news announcement. An industrywide trading halt can occur if the Dow Jones Industrial Average falls below parameters set by the New York Stock Exchange.

trading floor   The physical place on an exchange where trading occurs. Not all exchanges have trading floors. Some rely entirely on computerized trading systems that enable dealers to place bids and offers and trade from many locations.

trading pit   A specific location on the trading floor of an exchange designated for the trading of a specific asset or options.

trailing stop   A trailing stop is a stop order that is adjusted by the investor periodically as the price of the security continues to move favorably.

transaction costs   All charges associated with trading, including brokerage commissions, slippage, and fees for exercise and/or assignment. *See also* slippage.

true delta, true gamma   More accurate than standard delta and gamma, true delta and true gamma are computed using a method that takes into account a projected change in volatility along with the usual projected change in underlying price.

type   Refers to the type of option, as either a call or a put.

uncovered   *See* naked.

underlying   The asset specified in an option contract that is transferred when the option contract is exercised, unless the option is cash-settled. With cash-settled options, only cash changes hands at exercise, based on the current price of the underlying relative to the strike price of the option.

unrealized gain (loss)   The difference between the original cost of an open position and its current market price. A negative difference indicates a loss; a positive difference indicates a gain. Once the position is closed, it becomes a realized gain or loss.

vega   The measure of an option's sensitivity to changes in volatility. It is the amount of gain or loss you should theoretically experience if implied volatility goes up one percentage point.

vertical credit spread   A strategy that involves the simultaneous purchase and sale for a net credit of two options of the same type with different strike prices but the same expiration date. *See also* bull put spread, bear call spread.

vertical debit spread   A strategy that involves the simultaneous purchase and sale for a net debit of two options of the same type with different strike prices but the same expiration date. *See also* bull call spread, bear put spread.

volatility   Volatility measures the amount by which an asset has fluctuated, or is expected to fluctuate, in a given period of time. Assets with greater volatility exhibit wider price swings, and their options are more expensive than those of less volatile assets. (Volatility is not equivalent to beta.)

volatility trade   A trade designed to profit from an expected change in volatility.

volume   The quantity traded in any market or security. It can be measured in dollars or in the number of units traded (i.e., number of contracts for options, or number of shares for stocks).

warrant   A long-term call option often provided with a new issue of a security, as an enticement. For instance, corporate bonds may be sold with warrants to buy common stock of that corporation. Warrants are generally detachable.

wash sale   When an investor repurchases the same or substantially similar asset within 30 days of the sale date and reports the original sale as a tax loss. The Internal Revenue Service prohibits wash sales since no real change in ownership takes place.

write   To sell an option in an opening transaction. While this position remains open, the writer is obligated to fulfill the terms of that option contract if the option is assigned.

writer   A trader who sells an option is called the writer, whether the option is covered or uncovered.

Yates model   A refined version of the Black-Scholes pricing model that takes into account dividends and the possibility of early exercise.

Index

About the CD-ROM

Introduction:

The files on the enclosed CD-ROM are OptionVue 5 Trading Education Software, containing 40 supplemental articles which complement the book, a brief overview of the software product, and hyperlinks to the OptionVue website. One of these links will be set up and maintained exclusively for readers of *High Performance Options Trading*.

Freeware needed for CD viewing (QuickTime and Adobe Acrobat Reader) are included for user convenience.

Minimum System Requirements:

Processor:	Pentium II or better
RAM:	64 MB
Hard Drive:	64 MB of RAM
Monitor:	1024×768 monitor resolution or higher
Operating System:	Windows 98/Me/NT/2000/XP
Software:	QuickTime 4.0 or higher
	Adobe Acrobat Reader or Higher
Internet Connection:	Dial-Up (56K bps) or Direct (ISDN, Cable Modem, DSL, T1) connection to the Internet

Using the Files:

Insert the enclosed CD into your CD-ROM drive. CD will auto-start. If not, click on "Start" and choose "Run." Select "Browse," choose D Drive. Double click on OptionVue 5. Click OK.

Once running, the CD has interactive menus to direct the user.

User Assistance:

If you have a damaged CD-ROM, please contact Wiley Product Technical Support at:

Phone: 800-762-2974
URL: www.wiley.com/techsupport

If you need assistance with using the files on the CD-ROM, or if you have any questions regarding the OptionVue 5 source code or software, please contact info@optionvue.com.

To place additional orders or to request information about other Wiley products, please call (800) 225-5945.

For information about the CD-ROM see the
About the CD-ROM section on page 221.

WILEY

John Wiley & Sons, Inc.